THE CRAFTSMAN

THE CRAFTSMAN

Richard Sennett

ALLEN LANE
an imprint of
PENGUIN BOOKS

ALLEN LANE

Published by the Penguin Group
Penguin Books Ltd, 80 Strand, London WC2R 0RL, England
Penguin Group (USA) Inc., 375 Hudson Street, New York, New York 10014, USA
Penguin Group (Canada), 90 Eglinton Avenue East, Suite 700, Toronto, Ontario, Canada M4P 2Y3
(a division of Pearson Penguin Canada Inc.)
Penguin Ireland, 25 St Stephen's Green, Dublin 2, Ireland (a division of Penguin Books Ltd)
Penguin Group (Australia), 250 Camberwell Road, Camberwell, Victoria 3124, Australia
(a division of Pearson Australia Group Pty Ltd)
Penguin Books India Pvt Ltd, 11 Community Centre, Panchsheel Park, New Delhi – 110 017, India
Penguin Group (NZ), 67 Apollo Drive, Rosedale, North Shore 0632, New Zealand
(a division of Pearson New Zealand Ltd)
Penguin Books (South Africa) (Pty) Ltd, 24 Sturdee Avenue, Rosebank, Johannesburg 2196,
South Africa

Penguin Books Ltd, Registered Offices: 80 Strand, London WC2R 0RL, England

penguin.com

First published in the United States of America by Yale University Press 2008
First published in Great Britain by Allen Lane 2008
1

Printed in England by Clays Ltd, St Ives plc

A CIP catalogue record for this book is available from the British Library

978-0-713-99873-3

Mixed Sources
Product group from well-managed
forests and other controlled sources
www.fsc.org Cert no. SA-COC-1592
© 1996 Forest Stewardship Council
FSC

Penguin Books is committed to a sustainable future
for our business, our readers and our planet.
The book in your hands is made from paper
certified by the Forest Stewardship Council.

For Alan and Lindsay

travail, opium unique

Contents

PART THREE: Craftsmanship

Acknowledgments

I owe a peculiar debt to the philosopher Richard Foley. At a point when I was stuck in my work, he asked me, "What is your guiding intuition?" I replied on the spur of the moment, "Making is thinking." Foley looked unconvinced. In the effort to persuade him, I thank my friends Joseph Rykwert, Craig Calhoun, Niall Hobhouse, and the late Clifford Geertz for advice and my editors Stuart Proffitt and John Kulka for comments on the manuscript.

In this project I learned from my students. In New York I particularly thank Monika Krause, Erin O'Connor, Alton Phillips, and Aaron Panofsky; in London, Cassim Shepard and Matthew Gill. My research assistant, Elizabeth Rusbridger, proved a marvel, as has Laura Jones Dooley, the manuscript editor of this book.

Many of the cases studies of craftsmanship concern musical practices. I've drawn on my early experience as a working musician for these, as well as more recently on discussions about musical craft with three friends, Alan Rusbridger, Ian Bostridge, and Richard Goode.

Finally, Saskia Sassen, Hilary Koob-Sassen, and Rut Blees-Luxembourg made me the best gift a family can give a writer: they left me alone to think, smoke, and type.

Prologue: Man as His Own Maker

Pandora's Casket
Hannah Arendt and Robert Oppenheimer

Just after the Cuban Missile Crisis, the days in 1962 when the world was on the brink of atomic war, I ran into my teacher Hannah Arendt on the street. The missile crisis had shaken her, like everyone else, but it had also confirmed her deepest conviction. In *The Human Condition*, she had argued a few years previously that the engineer, or any maker of material things, is not master of his own house; politics, standing above the physical labor, has to provide the guidance. She had come to this conviction by the time the Los Alamos project created the first atomic bombs in 1945. Now, during the missile crisis, Americans too young for the Second World War had also felt real fear. It was freezing cold on the New York street, but Arendt was oblivious. She wanted me to draw the right lesson: people who make things usually don't understand what they are doing.

Arendt's fear of self-destructive material invention traces back in Western culture to the Greek myth of Pandora. A goddess of invention, Pandora was "sent to earth by Zeus as punishment for Prometheus's transgression."[1] Hesiod described Pandora in *Works and Days* as the "bitter gift of all the gods" who, when she opened her casket (or in some versions, her jar) of new wonders, "scattered pains and evils among men."[2] In the working out of Greek culture, its peoples came increasingly to believe that Pandora stood for an element of their *own* natures; culture founded on man-made things risks continual self-harm.

Something nearly innocent in human beings can produce this risk: men and women are seduced by sheer wonder, excitement, curiosity, and so create the fiction that opening the casket is a neutral act. About the first weapon of mass destruction, Arendt could have cited a diary note made by Robert Oppenheimer, director of the Los Alamos project. Oppenheimer reassured himself by asserting, "When you see something that is technically sweet, you go ahead and do it and you argue about what to do about only after you have had your technical success. That is the way it was with the atomic bomb."[3]

The poet John Milton told a similar story about Adam and Eve, as an allegory for the dangers of curiosity, with Eve taking the Oppenheimer role. In Milton's primal Christian scene, the thirst for knowledge, rather than for sex, leads human beings to harm themselves. Pandora's image remains potent in the writings of the modern theologian Reinhold Niebuhr, who observes that it is human nature to believe that anything that seems possible should therefore be tried.

Arendt's generation could put numbers to the fear of self-destruction, numbers so large as to numb the mind. At least seventy million people perished in wars, concentration camps, and gulags in the first fifty years of the twentieth century. In Arendt's view, these numbers represent the compound of scientific blindness and bureaucratic power—bureaucrats minded just to get the job done, embodied for her by the Nazi death-camp organizer Adolf Eichmann, to whom she attached the label "the banality of evil."

Today, peacetime material civilization posts equally numbing figures of self-made self-harm: one million, for instance, represents the number of years Nature took to create the amount of fossil fuel now consumed in a single year. The ecological crisis is Pandoric, man-made; technology may be an unreliable ally in regaining control.[4] The mathematician Martin Rees describes a revolution in microelectronics that creates at least the possibility of a robotic world beyond the powers of ordinary human beings then to rule; Rees envisions such exotica as self-replicating microrobots intended to clean smog that might instead devour the biosphere.[5] A more urgent example is genetic engineering of both crops and animals.

Fear of Pandora creates a rational climate of dread—but dread can be itself paralyzing, indeed malign. Technology itself can seem the enemy rather than simply a risk. Pandora's environmental casket was too easily closed, for instance, in a speech given by Arendt's own teacher, Martin Heidegger, near the end of his life, at Bremen in 1949. On this infamous occasion Heidegger "discounted the uniqueness of the Holocaust in terms of the 'history of man's misdeeds' by comparing 'the manufacture of corpses in the gas chambers and the death camp' to mechanized agriculture." In the historian Peter Kempt's words, "Heidegger thought that both should be regarded as embodiments of the 'same technological frenzy' which, if left unchecked, would lead to a world-wide ecological catastrophe."[6]

If the comparison is obscene, Heidegger speaks to a desire in many of us, that of returning to a way of life or achieving an imaginary future in which we will dwell more simply in nature. As an old man Heidegger wrote in a different context that "the fundamental character of dwelling is this sparing and preserving," against the claims of the modern machine world.[7] A famous image in these writings of his old age invokes "a hut in the Black Forest" to which the philosopher withdraws, limiting his place in the world to the satisfaction of simple needs.[8] This is perhaps a desire that could be kindled in anyone facing the big numbers of modern destruction.

In the ancient myth, the horrors in Pandora's casket were not humans' fault; the gods were angry. Pandora-fear in a more secular age is more disorienting: the inventors of atomic weapons coupled curiosity with culpability; the unintended consequences of curiosity are hard to explain. Making the bomb filled Oppenheimer with guilt, as it did I. I. Raby, Leo Szilard, and many others who worked at Los Alamos. In his diary, Oppenheimer recalled the Indian god Krishna's words, "I am become Death, the destroyer of worlds."[9] Experts in fear of their own expertise: what could be done about this terrible paradox?

When Oppenheimer gave the Reith Lectures for the BBC, subsequently published as *Science and the Common Understanding,* in 1953—broadcasts intended to explain the place of science in modern society—he argued that treating technology as an enemy will only render humanity more helpless. Yet, consumed by worry over the nuclear bomb and its thermonuclear child, in this political forum he could offer his listeners no practical suggestions about how to cope with it. Though confused, Oppenheimer was a worldly man. He was entrusted at a relatively young age with the bomb project during the Second World War, he combined a first-class brain with the talent to manage a large group of scientists; his skills were both scientific and corporate. But to these insiders, too, he could provide no satisfying picture of how their work should be used. Here are his parting words to them on November 2, 1945: "It is good to turn over to mankind at large the greatest possible power to control the world and to deal with it according to its lights and its values."[10] The creator's works become the public's problem. As David Cassidy, one of Oppenheimer's biographers, has observed, the Reith Lectures thus proved "a huge disappointment for both the speaker and his listeners."[11]

If the experts cannot make sense of their work, what of the public? Though I suspect Arendt knew little about physics, she took up Oppenheimer's challenge: let the public indeed deal with it. She had a robust faith that the public could understand the material conditions in which it dwells and that political action could stiffen humankind's will to be master in the house of things, tools, and machines. About the weapons in Pandora's casket, she told me, there should have been public discussion about the bomb even while it was being made; whether rightly or wrongly, she believed that the secrecy of the technical process could have been protected even as this discussion occurred. The reasons for this faith appear in her greatest book.

The Human Condition, published in 1958, affirms the value of human beings openly, candidly speaking to each other. Arendt writes, "Speech and action . . . are the modes in which human beings appear to each other, not indeed as physical objects, but qua men. This appearance, as distinguished from mere bodily existence, rests on initiative, but it is an initiative from which no human being can refrain and still be human." And she declares, "A life without speech and without action is literally dead to the world."[12] In this public realm, through debate, people ought to decide which technologies should be encouraged and which should be repressed. Though this affirmation of talk may well seem idealistic, Arendt was in her own way an eminently realistic philosopher. She knew that public discussion of human limits can never be the politics of happiness.

Nor did she believe in religious or natural truths that could stabilize life. Rather, like John Locke and Thomas Jefferson, Arendt believed that a polity differs from a landmarked building or "world heritage site": laws should be unstable. This liberal tradition imagines that the rules issuing from deliberation are cast in doubt as conditions change and people ponder further; new, provisional rules then come into being. Arendt's contribution to this tradition turns in part on the insight that the political process exactly parallels the human condition of giving birth and then letting go of the children we have made and raised. Arendt speaks of natality in describing the process of birth, formation, and separation in politics.[13] The fundamental fact of life is that nothing lasts—yet in politics we need something to orient us, to lift us above the confusions of the moment. The pages of The Human Condition explore how language might guide us, as it were, to swim against the turbulent waters of time.

✳ ✳ ✳

As her student almost a half-century ago, I found her philosophy largely inspiring, yet even then it seemed to me not quite adequate to deal with the material things and concrete practices contained in Pandora's casket. The good teacher imparts a satisfying explanation; the great teacher—as Arendt was—unsettles, bequeaths disquiet, invites argument. Arendt's difficulty in dealing with Pandora seemed to me, dimly then and more clearly now, to lie in the distinction she draws a distinction between *Animal laborens* and *Homo faber*. (*Man* does not, clearly, mean just men. Throughout this book, when I have to deal with gendered language, I'll try to make clear when *man* refers generically to human beings and when it applies only to males.) These are two images of people at work; they are austere images of the human condition, since the philosopher excludes pleasure, play, and culture.

Animal laborens is, as the name implies, the human being akin to a beast of burden, a drudge condemned to routine. Arendt enriched this image by imagining him or her absorbed in a task that shuts out the world, a state well exemplified by Oppenheimer's feeling that the atomic bomb was a "sweet" problem, or Eichmann's obsession with making the gas chambers efficient. In the act of making it work, nothing else matters; *Animal laborens* takes the work as an end in itself.

By contrast, *Homo faber* is her image of men and women doing another kind of work, making a life in common. Again Arendt enriched an inherited idea. The Latin tag *Homo faber* means simply "man as maker." The phrase crops up in Renaissance writings on philosophy and in the arts; Henri Bergson had, two generations before Arendt, applied it to psychology; she applied it to politics, and in a special way. *Homo faber* is the judge of material labor and practice, not *Animal laborens*'s colleague but his superior. Thus, in her view, we human beings live in two dimensions. In one we make things; in this condition we are amoral, absorbed in a task. We also harbor another, higher way of life in which we stop producing and start discussing and judging together. Whereas *Animal laborens* is fixated in the question "How?" *Homo faber* asks "Why?"

This division seems to me false because it slights the practical man or woman at work. The human animal who is *Animal laborens* is capable of thinking; the discussions the producer holds may be mentally with materials rather than with other people; people working together certainly talk to one another about what they are doing. For Arendt, the mind engages once labor is done. Another, more balanced view is that thinking and feeling are contained within the process of making.

The sharp edge of this perhaps self-evident observation lies in its address to Pandora's box. Leaving the public to "sort out the problem" after the work is done means confronting people with usually irreversible facts on the ground. Engagement must start earlier, requires a fuller, better understanding of the process by which people go about producing things, a more materialistic engagement than that found among thinkers of Arendt's stripe. To cope with Pandora requires a more vigorous cultural materialism.

The word *materialism* should raise a warning flag; it has become debased, stained in recent political history by Marxism and in everyday life by consumer fantasy and greed. "Materialistic" thinking is also obscure because most of us use things like computers or automobiles that we do not make for ourselves and that we do not understand. About "culture" the literary critic Raymond Williams once counted several hundred modern usages.[14] This wild verbal garden divides roughly into two big beds. In one, culture stands for the arts alone, in the other it stands for the religious, political, and social beliefs that bind a people. "Material culture" too often, at least in the social sciences, slights cloth, circuit boards, or baked fish as objects worthy of regard in themselves, instead treating the shaping of such physical things as mirrors of social norms, economic interests, religious convictions—the thing in itself is discounted.

So we need to turn a fresh page. We can do so simply by asking—though the answers are anything but simple—what the process of making concrete things reveals to us about ourselves. Learning from things requires us to care about the qualities of cloth or the right way to poach fish; fine cloth or food cooked well enables us to imagine larger categories of "good." Friendly to the senses, the cultural materialist wants to map out where pleasure is to be found and how it is organized. Curious about things in themselves, he or she wants to understand how they might generate religious, social, or political values. *Animal laborens* might serve as *Homo faber*'s guide.

In my own old age I've returned mentally to that street on the Upper West Side. I want to make the case my juvenile self could not then make to Arendt, that people can learn about themselves through the things they make, that material culture matters. As she aged, my teacher became more hopeful that *Homo faber*'s powers of judgment could save humanity from itself. In my winter, I've become more hopeful about the human animal at work. The contents of Pandora's box can indeed be made less fearsome; we can achieve a more humane material life, if only we better understand the making of things.

The Project
The Craftsman; Warriors and Priests; the Foreigner

This is the first of three books on material culture, all related to the dangers in Pandora's casket, though each is intended to stand on its own. This book is about craftsmanship, the skill of making things well. The second volume addresses the crafting of rituals that manage aggression and zeal; the third explores the skills required in making and inhabiting sustainable environments. All three books address the issue of *technique*—but technique considered as a cultural issue rather than as a mindless procedure; each book is about a technique for conducting a particular way of life. The large project contains a personal paradox that I have tried to put to productive use. I am a philosophically minded writer asking questions about such matters as woodworking, military drills, or solar panels.

"Craftsmanship" may suggest a way of life that waned with the advent of industrial society—but this is misleading. Craftsmanship names an enduring, basic human impulse, the desire to do a job well for its own sake. Craftsmanship cuts a far wider swath than skilled manual labor; it serves the computer programmer, the doctor, and the artist; parenting improves when it is practiced as a skilled craft, as does citizenship. In all these domains, craftsmanship focuses on objective standards, on the thing in itself. Social and economic conditions, however, often stand in the way of the craftsman's discipline and commitment: schools may fail to provide the tools to do good work, and workplaces may not truly value the aspiration for quality. And though craftsmanship can reward an individual with a sense of pride in work, this reward is not simple. The craftsman often faces conflicting objective standards of excellence; the desire to do something well for its own sake can be impaired by competitive pressure, by frustration, or by obsession.

The Craftsman explores these dimensions of skill, commitment, and judgment in a particular way. It focuses on the intimate connection between hand and head. Every good craftsman conducts a dialogue between concrete practices and thinking; this dialogue evolves into sustaining habits, and these habits establish a rhythm between problem solving and problem finding. The relation between hand and head appears in domains seemingly as different as bricklaying, cooking, designing a playground, or playing the cello— but all these practices can misfire or fail to ripen. There is nothing inevitable about becoming skilled, just as there is nothing mindlessly mechanical about technique itself.

Western civilization has had a deep-rooted trouble in making connections between head and hand, in recognizing and encouraging the impulse of craftsmanship. These difficulties are explored in the first part of the book. It begins as a story about workshops—the guilds of medieval goldsmiths, the ateliers of musical instrument makers like Antonio Stradivari, modern laboratories—in which masters and apprentices, work together but as unequals. The craftsman's struggle with machines is portrayed in the eighteenth-century invention of robots, in the pages of that bible of the Enlightenment, Diderot's *Encyclopedia,* and in the nineteenth century's growing fear of industrial machines. The craftsman's consciousness of materials appears in the long history of making bricks, a history that stretches from ancient Mesopotamia to our own time, a history that shows the way anonymous workers can leave traces of themselves in inanimate things.

In its second part, the book explores more closely the development of skill. I make two contentious arguments: first, that all skills, even the most abstract, begin as bodily practices; second, that technical understanding develops through the powers of imagination. The first argument focuses on knowledge gained in the hand through touch and movement. The argument about imagination begins by exploring language that attempts to direct and guide bodily skill. This language works best when it shows imaginatively how to do something. The use of imperfect or incomplete tools draws on the imagination in developing the skills to repair and to improvise. The two arguments combine in considering how resistance and ambiguity can be instructive experiences; to work well, every craftsman has to learn from these experiences rather than fight them. A diverse group of case studies illustrates the grounding of skill in physical practice—the hand habits of striking a piano key or using a knife; the written recipes used to guide the neophyte cook; the use of imperfect scientific instruments like the first telescopes or puzzling instruments like the anatomist's scalpel; the machines and plans that can work with resistances of water, ambiguities on land. Developing skill in all these domains is arduous, but it is not mysterious. We can understand those imaginative processes that enable us to become better at doing things.

In its third part, the book addresses more general issues of motivation and talent. The argument here is that motivation matters more than talent, and for a particular reason. The craftsman's desire for quality poses a motivational danger: the obsession with getting things perfectly right may deform the work itself. We are more likely to fail as craftsmen, I argue, due to our inability to organize obsession than because of our lack of ability. The Enlightenment believed that everyone possesses the ability to do good work of some kind, that there is an intelligent craftsman in most of us; that faith stills makes sense.

Craftsmanship is certainly, from an ethical point of view, ambiguous. Robert Oppenheimer was a committed craftsman; he pushed his technical skills to the limit to make the best bomb he could. Yet the craftsman's ethos contains countervailing currents, as in the principle of using minimum force in physical effort. The good craftsman, moreover, uses solutions to uncover new territory; problem solving and problem finding are intimately related in his or her mind. For this reason, curiosity can ask, "Why?" and well as, "How?" about any project. The craftsman thus both stands in Pandora's shadow and can step out of it.

The book concludes by considering how the craftsman's way of working can give people an anchor in material reality. History has drawn fault lines dividing practice and theory, technique and expression, craftsman and artist, maker and user; modern society suffers from this historical inheritance. But the past life of craft and craftsmen also suggests ways of using tools, organizing bodily movements, thinking about materials that remain alternative, viable proposals about how to conduct life with skill.

The volumes that follow build on the character of craft set out in this first book. Pandora remains their provocation. Pandora is a goddess of aggressive destruction; the priest and the warrior are her representatives, and in most cultures they entwine. In the second volume of the project I explore what might inflame or tame their combined power.

Religion and war are both organized through rituals, and I investigate ritual as a kind of craft. That is, I'm less interested in the ideologies of nationalism or jihad than in the ritual practices that train and discipline the human body to attack or pray, or the rituals that cause groups of bodies to deploy on the battlefield or within sacred spaces. Again, codes of honor become concrete by choreographing movement and gesture within the physical containers of walls, military camps, and battlefields on one hand, and shrines, burial grounds, monasteries, and retreats on the other. Ritual requires skill; it needs to be done well. The priest-craftsman or warrior-craftsman will share the ethos of other craftsmen when seeking to do the work well for its own sake. The aura surrounding ritual suggests that it is mysterious in origin, veiled in operation. *Warriors and Priests* seeks to see behind this veil, by exploring how the craft of ritual makes faith physical. My aim in this study is to understand how the fatal marriage of religion and aggression might possibility be altered by changing the ritual practices in each. This is a speculative enterprise, to be sure—but it seems more realistic to explore how concrete behavior might change or be regulated than to counsel a change of heart.

The final book in the project returns to more certain terrain, the earth itself. In both natural resources and climate change, we are facing a physical crisis largely of our own human making. The myth of Pandora has become now a secular symbol of self-destruction. To deal with this physical crisis we are obliged to change both the things we make and how we use them. We will need to learn different ways of making buildings and transport and to contrive rituals that accustom us to saving. We will need to become good craftsmen of the environment.

The word *sustainable* is now used to convey this kind of craftsmanship, and it carries a particular baggage. *Sustainable* suggests living more at one with nature, as Martin Heidegger imagined in his old age, establishing an equilibrium between ourselves and the resources of the earth—an image of balance and reconciliation. In my view, this is an inadequate, insufficient view of environmental craft; to change both productive procedures and rituals of use requires a more radical self-critique. A stronger jolt to changing how we have used resources would come in imagining ourselves to be like immigrants thrust by chance or fate onto a territory not our own, foreigners in a place we cannot command as our own.

The stranger, remarks the sociologist Georg Simmel, learns the art of adaptation more searchingly, if more painfully, than people who feel entitled to belong, at peace with their surrounding. In Simmel's view, the foreigner also holds up a mirror to the society into which he or she enters, since the foreigner cannot take for granted ways of life that seem to natives just natural.[15] So great are the changes required to alter humankind's dealings with the physical world that only this sense of self-displacement and estrangement can drive the actual practices of change and reducing our consuming desires; the dream of dwelling in equilibrium and at peace with the world risks, in my view, leading us to seek escape in an idealized Nature, rather than confronting the self-destructive territory we have actually made. At least this is my starting point in trying to understand the techniques of environmental craft different kind, and why I've titled this third volume *The Foreigner*. That craft is now foreign to us.

This is in sum the project on material culture I envision. *The Crafts-man*, *Warriors and Priests*, and *The Foreigner* tell together a story about the declaration made by Shakespeare's Coriolanus: "I am my own maker." Materially, humans are skilled makers of a place for themselves in the world. Pandora hovers over this story in objects, in rituals, and in the earth itself. Pandora can never be laid to rest; the Greek goddess represents inextinguishable human powers of mismanagement, self-inflicted harm, and confusion. But these powers can perhaps be caged if understood materially.

I write within a long-standing tradition, that of American pragmatism, a tradition explained more fully at the end of this volume. Pragmatism has sought to join philosophy to concrete practices in the arts and sciences, to political economy, and to religion; its distinctive character is to search for the philosophic issues embedded in everyday life. The study of craft and technique is simply a logical next chapter in pragmatism's unfolding history.

A Note on History
The Shortness of Time

In this project my guide to using the record of history is a thought experiment proposed by the biologist John Maynard Smith. He asks us to imagine a two-hour film that clocks, greatly speeded up, evolution from the first vertebrates to the appearance of ourselves: "tool-making man would appear only in the last minute." Then he imagines a second two-hour film, charting the history of tool-making man: "the domestication of animals and plants would be shown only during the last half minute, and the period between the invention of the steam engine and the discovery of atomic energy would be only one second."[16]

The point of the thought experiment is to challenge the famous phrase that opens L. P. Hartley's novel *The Go-Between*: "The past is a foreign country." In the fifteen seconds of recorded civilization, there's no reason why Homer, Shakespeare, Goethe, or simply a grandmother's letters should be alien to our understanding. Culture's time in natural history is short. Yet in these same few seconds human beings have contrived enormously different ways to live.

In studying material culture, I've treated the historical record as a catalogue of experiments in making things, performed by experimenters who are not alien to us, whose experiments we can understand.

If in this way culture's time is short, in another way it is long. Because cloth, pots, tools, and machines are solid objects, we can return to them again and again in time; we can linger as we cannot in the flow of a discussion. Nor does material culture follow the rhythms of biological life. Objects do not inevitably decay from within like a human body. The histories of things follow a different course, in which metamorphosis and adaptation play a stronger role across human generations.

I might have conducted this exploration by writing a strict linear narrative, beginning with the Greeks, ending where we are now. Instead, I've preferred to write thematically, going between past and present, to assemble the experimental record. When I've judged that the reader needs detailed context, I've provided it; when not, not.

Material culture provides in sum a picture of what human beings are capable of making. This seemingly limitless view is bounded by self-inflicted harm whether occurring innocently, by intent, or by accident. Retreat into spiritual values is unlikely to furnish much help in coping with Pandora. Nature might be a better guide, if we understand our own labors as part of its being.

PART ONE   Craftsmen

CHAPTER ONE

The Troubled Craftsman

The Craftsman summons an immediate image. Peering through a window into a carpenter's shop, you see inside an elderly man surrounded by his apprentices and his tools. Order reigns within, parts of chairs are clamped neatly together, the fresh smell of wood shavings fills the room, the carpenter bends over his bench to make a fine incision for marquetry. The shop is menaced by a furniture factory down the road.

The craftsman might also be glimpsed at a nearby laboratory. There, a young lab technician is frowning at a table on which six dead rabbits are splayed on their backs, their bellies slit open. She is frowning because something has gone wrong with the injection she has given them; she is trying to figure out if she did the procedure wrong or there is something wrong with the procedure.

A third craftsman might be heard in the town's concert hall. There an orchestra is rehearsing with a visiting conductor; he works obsessively with the orchestra's string section, going over and over a passage to make the musicians draw their bows at exactly the same speed across the strings. The string players are tired but also exhilarated because their sound is becoming coherent. The orchestra's manager is worried; if the visiting conductor keeps on, the rehearsal will move into overtime, costing management extra wages. The conductor is oblivious.

The carpenter, lab technician, and conductor are all craftsmen because they are dedicated to good work for its own sake. Theirs is practical activity, but their labor is not simply a means to another end. The carpenter might sell more furniture if he worked faster; the technician might make do by passing the problem back to her boss; the visiting conductor might be more likely to be rehired if he watched the clock. It's certainly possible to get by in life without dedication. The craftsman represents the special human condition of being *engaged*. One aim of this book is to explain how people become engaged practically but not necessarily instrumentally.

Craftsmanship is poorly understood, as I noted in the Prologue, when it is equated only with manual skill of the carpenter's sort. German employs the word *Handwerk,* French the word *artisanal* to evoke the craftsman's labors. English can be more inclusive, as in the term *statecraft;* Anton Chekhov applied the Russian word *mastersvo* equally to his craft as a doctor and as a writer. I want first to treat all such concrete practices as like laboratories in which sentiments and ideas can be investigated. A second aim of this study is to explore what happens when hand and head, technique and science, art and craft are separated. I will show how the head then suffers; both understanding and expression are impaired.

All craftsmanship is founded on skill developed to a high degree. By one commonly used measure, about ten thousand hours of experience are required to produce a master carpenter or musician. Various studies show that as skill progresses, it becomes more problem-attuned, like the lab technician worrying about procedure, whereas people with primitive levels of skill struggle more exclusively on getting things to work. At its higher reaches, technique is no longer a mechanical activity; people can feel fully and think deeply what they are doing once they do it well. It is at the level of mastery, I will show, that ethical problems of craft appear.

The emotional rewards craftsmanship holds out for attaining skill are twofold: people are anchored in tangible reality, and they can take pride in their work. But society has stood in the way of these rewards in the past and continues to do so today. At different moments in Western history practical activity has been demeaned, divorced from supposedly higher pursuits. Technical skill has been removed from imagination, tangible reality doubted by religion, pride in one's work treated as a luxury. If the craftsman is special because he or she is an engaged human being, still the craftsman's aspirations and trials hold up a mirror to these larger issues past and present.

The Modern Hephaestus
Ancient Weavers and Linux Programmers

One of the earliest celebrations of the craftsman appears in a Homeric hymn to the master god of craftsmen, Hephaestus: "Sing clear-voiced Muse, of Hephaestus famed for skill. With bright-eyed Athena he taught men glorious crafts throughout the world—men who before used to dwell in caves in the mountains like wild beasts. But now that they have learned crafts through Hephaestus famous for his art they live a peaceful life in their own houses the whole year round."[1] The poem is contrary in spirit to the legend of Pandora, which took form at roughly the same time. Pandora presides over destruction, Hephaestus over the craftsman as a bringer of peace and a maker of civilization.

The hymn to Hephaestus may seem to celebrate no more than a cliché, that of civilization commencing when human beings began to use tools. But this hymn was written thousands of years after the fabrication of such tools as knives, the wheel, and the loom. More than a technician, the civilizing craftsman has used these tools for a collective good, that of ending humanity's wandering existence as hunter-gatherers or rootless warriors. Reflecting on the Homeric hymn to

Hephaestus, a modern historian writes that because craftwork "brought people out of the isolation, personified by the cave-dwelling Cyclopes, craft and community were, for the early Greeks, indissociable."[2]

The word the hymn used for craftsman is *demioergos*. This is a compound made between public (*demios*) and productive (*ergon*). The archaic craftsman occupied a social slice roughly equivalent to a middle class. The *demioergoi* included, in addition to skilled manual workers like potters, also doctors and lower magistrates, and professional singers and heralds who served in ancient times as news broadcasters. This slice of ordinary citizens lived in between the relatively few, leisured aristocrats and the mass of slaves who did most of the work—many of whom had great technical skills but whose talents earned them no political recognition or rights.[3] It was in the middle of this archaic society that the hymn honored as civilizers those who com-bined head and hand.

Archaic Greece, like many other societies that anthropologists until quite recently labeled "traditional," took it for granted that skills would be handed down from generation to generation. This assumption is more remarkable than it might appear. Social norms counted for more than individual endowments in the traditional "skills society." Developing one's talents depended on following the rules established by earlier generations; that most modern of words—personal "genius"—had little meaning in this context. To become skilled required, personally, that one be obedient. Whoever composed the hymn to Hephaestus accepted the nature of this communal bond. As with deeply held values in any culture, it seemed self-evident that people will identify with other craftsmen as fellow citizens. Skill would bind them to their ancestors as to their fellows. In their gradual evolution, traditional skills thus seem exempt from Hannah Arendt's principle of "natality."

If the artisan was celebrated in the age of Homer as a public man or woman, by classical times the craftsman's honor had dimmed. The reader of Aristophanes finds a small sign of this change in the contempt with which he treats the potters Kittos and Bacchios as stupid buffoons due the work they do.[4] A graver portent of the artisan's darkening fortunes appears in the writings of Aristotle on the nature of craft. In the *Metaphysics,* he declares, "We consider that the architects in every profession are more estimable and know more and are wiser than the artisans, because they know the reasons of the things which are done."[5] Aristotle abandons the old word for the craftsman, *demioergos,* and uses instead *cheirotechnon,* which means simply handworker.[6]

This shift had a particular, ambiguous meaning for women workers. From earliest times, weaving was a craft reserved for women that gave them respect in the public realm; the hymn singles out crafts like weaving as practices that helped civilize the hunter-gatherer tribes. As archaic society became classical, still the public virtue of women weavers was celebrated. In Athens, women spun a cloth, the *peplos,* that they then paraded through the city streets in an annual ritual. But other domestic crafts like cooking had no such public standing, and no craftwork would earn Athenian women in the classical era the right to vote. The development of classical science contributed to the gendering of skill that produced the word *craftsman* as applying to men. This science contrasted the man's hand dexterity to the inner-organ strength of women as childbearers; it contrasted the stronger arm and leg muscles of men to those of women; it supposed that men's brains were more "muscular" than those of women.[7]

This gender distinction sowed the seed of a still-living plant: most domestic crafts and craftsmen seem different in character than labor now outside the home. We do not think of parenting, for instance, as a craft in the same sense that we think of plumbing or programming, even though becoming a good parent requires a high degree of learned skill.

The classical philosopher most sympathetic to the archaic ideal of Hephaestus was Plato, who also worried about its demise. He traced skill back to the root word for "making," *poiein*. This is the parent word for *poetry,* and in the hymn, too, poets appear as just another kind of craftsman. All craftsmanship is quality-driven work; Plato formulated this aim as the *arete,* the standard of excellence, implicit in any act: the aspiration for quality will drive a craftsman to improve, to get better rather than get by. But in his own time Plato observed that although "craftsmen are all poets . . . they are not called poets, they have other names."[8] Plato worried that these different names and indeed different skills kept people in his day from understanding what they shared. In the five centuries between the Hymn to Hephaestus and his own lifetime, something seemed to have slipped. The unity in archaic times between skill and community had weakened. Practical skills still sustained the ongoing life of the city but were not generally honored for doing so.

※   ※   ※

To understand the living presence of Hephaestus, I ask the reader to make a large mental jump. People who participate in "open source" computer software, particularly in the Linux operating system, are craftsman who embody some of the elements first celebrated in the Hymn to Hesphaestus, but not others. The Linux technicians also represent as a group Plato's worry, though in a modern form; rather than scorned, this body of craftsmen seem an unusual, indeed marginal, sort of community.

The Linux system is a public craft. The underlying software kernel in Linux code is available to anyone, it can be employed and adapted by anyone; people donate time to improve it. Linux contrasts to the code used in Microsoft, its secrets until recently hoarded as the intellectual property of one company. In one current, popular Linux application, Wikipedia, the code kernel makes possible an encyclopedia to which any user can contribute.[9] When established in the 1990s, Linux sought to recover some of the adventure of the early days of computing in the

1970s. During these two decades, the software industry has morphed within its brief life into a few dominant firms, buying up or squeezing out smaller competitors. In the process, the monopolies seemed to churn out ever more mediocre work.

Technically, open-source software follows the standards of the Open Source Initiative, but the brute label "free software" doesn't quite capture how resources are used in Linux.[10] Eric Raymond usefully distinguishes between two types of free software: the "cathedral" model, in which a closed group of programmers develop the code and then make it available to anyone, and the "bazaar" model, in which anyone can participate via the Internet to produce code. Linux draws on craftsmen in an electronic bazaar. The kernel was developed by Linus Torvalds, who in the early 1990s acted on Raymond's belief that "given enough eyeballs, all bugs are shallow"—engineer-speak for saying that if enough people participate in the code-writing bazaar, the problems of writing good code can be solved more easily than in the cathedral, certainly more easily than in proprietary commercial software.[11]

This, then, is a community of craftsmen to whom the ancient appellation *demioergoi* can be applied. It is focused on achieving quality, on doing good work, which is the craftsman's primordial mark of identity. In the traditional world of the archaic potter or doctor, standards for good work were set by the community, as skills passed down from generation to generation. These heirs to Hephaestus have experienced, however, a communal conflict about the use of their skills.

The programming community is grappling with how to reconcile quality and open access. In the Wikipedia application, for instance, many of the entries are biased, scurrilous, or just plain wrong. A breakaway group now wants to apply editing standards, an impulse that runs smack up against the movement's desire to be an open community. The editor "elitists" don't dispute the technical proficiency of their adversaries; all the professional parties in this conflict feel passionately about maintaining quality. The conflict is equally strong in the generative

realm of Linux programming. Its members are grappling with a structural problem: how can quality of knowledge coexist with free and equal
exchange in a community?[12]

We'd err to imagine that because traditional craft communities
pass on skills from generation to generation, the skills they pass down
have been rigidly fixed; not at all. Ancient pottery making, for instance,
changed radically when the rotating stone disk holding a lump of clay
came into use; new ways of drawing up the clay ensued. But the radical
change appeared slowly. In Linux the process of skill evolution is
speeded up; change occurs daily. Again, we might think that a good
craftsman, be she a cook or a programmer, cares only about solving
problems, about solutions that end a task, about closure. In this, we
would not credit the work actually involved. In the Linux network,
when people squash one "bug," they frequently see new possibilities
open up for the use of the code. The code is constantly evolving, not a
finished and fixed object. There is in Linux a nearly *instant* relation
between problem solving and problem finding.

Still, the experimental rhythm of problem solving and problem
finding makes the ancient potter and the modern programmer members of the same tribe. We would do better to contrast Linux programmers to a different modern tribe, those bureaucrats unwilling to make
a move until all the goals, procedures, and desired results for a policy
have been mapped in advance. This is a closed knowledge-system. In
the history of handcrafts, closed knowledge-systems have tended toward short lifespans. The anthropologist André Leroi-Gourhan contrasts, for instance, the open, evolving, difficult, but long-lasting craft
of metal knife-making in preclassical Greece to the craft of wooden
knife-making—a more precise, economical, but static system of fab-
ricating knives that was soon abandoned for the problems of metal.[13]

Linux is most deeply "Greek" in its impersonality. In Linux online
workshops, it's impossible to deduce, for instance, whether "aristotle

@mit.edu" is a man or a woman; what matters is what "aristotle@mit .edu" contributes to the discussion. Archaic craftsmen experienced a kindred impersonality; the demioergoi were frequently addressed in public by the names of their profession. All craftsmanship, indeed, has something of this impersonal character. That the quality of work is impersonal can make the practice of craftsmanship seem unforgiving; that you might have a neurotic relation to your father won't excuse the fact that your mortise-and-tenon joint is loose. In one of the British-based Linux chat rooms to which I belong, the normal polite feints and indirections of British culture have disappeared. Gone are such locutions as "I would have thought that . . ."; in are "This problem is fucked-up." Looked at another way, this blunt impersonality turns people outward.

The Linux community might have served the mid-twentieth-century sociologist C. Wright Mills in his effort to define the character of the craftsman. Mills writes: "The laborer with a sense of craft becomes engaged in the work in and for itself; the satisfactions of working are their own reward; the details of daily labor are connected in the worker's mind to the end product; the worker can control his or her own actions at work; skill develops within the work process; work is connected to the freedom to experiment; finally, family, community, and politics are measured by the standards of inner satisfaction, coherence, and experiment in craft labor."[14]

If Mills's description seems impossibly idealistic, rather than reject it we might ask instead why craftsmanship of the Linux sort is so unusual. The question is a modern version of Plato's ancient worry; the Linux programmers are certainly grappling with fundamental issues like collaboration, the necessary relation of problem solving to problem finding, and the impersonal nature of standards, yet the community seems special if not marginal. Some cluster of social forces must be pushing these fundamental issues to the sidelines.

Weakened Motivation
Workers Demoralized by Command and by Competition

The modern world has two recipes for arousing the desire to work hard and well. One is the moral imperative to do work for the sake of the community. The other recipe invokes competition: it supposes that competing against others stimulates the desire to perform well, and in place of communal cohesion, it promises individual rewards. Both recipes have proved troubled. Neither has—in naked form—served the craftsman's aspiration for quality.

The problems with the moral imperative appeared to me personally and sharply on a visit my wife and I made to the communist empire in 1988, on the eve of its collapse. We'd received an invitation from the Russian Academy of Sciences to visit Moscow, a trip to be organized without the "support" of the foreign ministry and its resident spies; we were promised the freedom of the city. We toured Moscow churches previously locked, now overflowing, and the offices of an unauthorized newspaper where people smoked, talked, and at odd moments wrote. Almost as an afterthought, our hosts led us out to the Moscow suburbs, which I had never seen before.

These housing developments were built mostly in the decades after the Second World War. Laid out as enormous chessboards, the suburbs stretch to the horizon across flat land sparsely planted with birch and aspen. The architectural design of the suburban buildings was good, but the state had not been able to command good-quality work. The signs of poorly motivated workers appeared in the details of construction: in almost every building, concrete had been badly poured and sloppily reinforced, well-conceived, prefabricated windows had been set askew into the concrete shells, and little caulk had been applied to the seams joining window frames to concrete. In one new building we found the empty cartons of caulk for sealing the windows, but the contents had been sold, our guides said, on the black market. In a few apartment towers workers had stuffed pieces of newspaper between the window frames and walls, then painted over the seams to give the appearance—lasting only a season or two—that the buildings had been sealed.

Poor craftsmanship was a barometer of other forms of material indifference. The housing we saw was meant for relatively privileged citizens, the Soviet scientific class. These families were allotted individual apartments rather than forced to live in communal space. Yet the negligence of construction was mirrored in the inhabitants' neglect of their surroundings: window boxes and balconies were bare of plants; walls had crusted over with crayon graffiti or spray-painted obscenities that nobody had bothered to clean up. When I asked about the dilapidated state of these buildings, our tour guides gave us a sweeping explanation. "People"—in general—don't care; they are demoralized.

This broad condemnation could not apply generally in the empire, since Soviet construction workers had long proved capable of making high-quality scientific and military buildings. Still, the guides seemed bent proving the emptiness of the collective, moral recipe for craftsmanship. They led my wife and me from block to block with grim satisfaction, pointing out fraudulence and deception, taking almost a connoisseur's pleasure in contemplating the fake caulking that nature required mere winter to expose. When prodded, one of our guides coined "the ruins of Marxism" to explain the evidence both of demoralized workers and of inhabitants indifferent to their surroundings.

The young Karl Marx thought of himself a secular Hephaestus whose writings would set the modern craftsman free. In the *Grundrisse,* he framed craftsmanship in the broadest possible terms as "form-giving activity."[15] He emphasized that self and social relations develop through by making physical things, enabling the "all-round development of the individual."[16] Before Marx became an analyst of economic injustice, he was a Moses to workers, promising to realize the dignity of labor natural to people as part of a community. This utopian core of Marxism survived even as the older Marx hardened into a bitter, rigid ideologue. As late as his essay "The Gotha Program," he returned to the view that communism would rekindle the spirit of craftsmanship.[17]

On the ground, Russia's command economy seems to explain the ruin of Marxism. Economists note the abysmally low productivity of Russian civil society throughout the 1970s and 1980s. The construction industry suffered particular problems of centralized command: its central bureaucracy was bad at estimating the materials needed for a project; the movement of materials across Russia's vast distances was slow and followed irrational paths; factories and construction crews seldom communicated directly. And authorities overreacted to initiative on building sites, fearing that local self-management might germinate general resistance to the state.

For these reasons, the moral imperative, "Do a good job for your country!" rang hollow. The problems on the ground are hardly unique to Russia's construction industry. The sociologist Darren Thiel has found equally demoralized workers at many British building sites. The construction industry in free-market Britain suffers from low productivity; its craft workers are treated badly or indifferently; onsite initiative is discouraged.[18]

The moral imperative is not, though, inherently empty. In the same decades that Russia was rotting, Japan was prospering under a command economy suffused with its own cultural imperatives to work well for the common good. Japan has been called "a nation of craftsmen," which is a little like calling England a nation of shopkeepers or observing that New Zealanders are good at raising sheep.[19] Still, in the past half-century the Japanese manifested a practical creativity that brought the country back to life after the Second World War. In the 1950s the Japanese mass-produced cheap, simple goods; by the early 1970s they produced cheap, high-quality automobiles, radios, and stereos, as well as superb steel and aluminum for special applications.

Working precisely to high standards provided the Japanese during these years a sense of mutual and self-respect. In part they needed the collective goal because workers, particularly those in the middle ranks of organizations, spent long hours together laboring, seldom seeing their wives or children, in order to make ends meet. But the moral imperative worked because of how it was organized.

In the postwar years Japanese corporations embraced the nostrums of the business analyst W. Edwards Deming, who advocated, for the sake of "total quality control," that managers get their hands dirty on the shop floor and subordinates speak frankly to their superiors. When Deming spoke of "collective craftsmanship," he meant that the glue binding an institution is created by sharp mutual exchanges as much as by shared commitment. Caricatures of the Japanese frequently depict them as herd-loving conformists, a stereotype that hardly makes sense of how sharply critical Japanese at work in Toyota, Subaru, and Sony plants could be of one another's efforts.

Hierarchy governed the Japanese workplace, but the plain speaking of the Linux community was normal in these plants. Within the Japanese factories it was possible to speak truth to power, in that an adept manager could easily penetrate the codes of courtesy and deference in speech to get across the message that something was wrong or not good enough. In Soviet collectivism, by contrast, the ethical as well as the technical center was too far removed from life on the ground. Marx dealt with "the worker"; Deming and his Japanese followers dealt with the work.

Rather than become Japanese, this comparison asks us to think again about the triumphalism that greeted the collapse of the Soviet empire a generation ago, capitalism winning out as communism collapsed from within. A large part of the triumphalist story turned on contrasting the virtues of competition to the vices of collectivism—individual competition taken to be more likely to produce good work, competition to spur quality. Not only capitalists have subscribed to this view; in the "reform" of public services like health care, the effort has been to promote internal competition and markets to improve the quality of services. We need to look more deeply at this triumphalist view, because it obscures both the roles competition and cooperation actually play in getting good work done and, more largely, the virtues of craftsmanship.

✳ ✳ ✳

The making of the mobile telephone tells an illuminating story about the superiority of cooperation to competition in getting good work done.

The mobile phone is the result of the metamorphosis of two technologies, the radio and the telephone. Before these two technologies fused, telephone signals were broadcast by landline wires, radio signals emitted in the air. In the 1970s mobile phones of a sort existed in the military. These were large, clunky radios with dedicated bands for communication. Domestic versions of the mobile phone operated domestically in taxicabs, their range limited, their sound quality poor. The landline telephone's fixity was its defect, its virtue the clarity and security of transmission.

At the heart of this virtue lay the switching technology of the landline phone, elaborated, tested, and refined with care over several generations of use. It was this switching technology that had to change in order for the radio and telephone to amalgamate. The problem and its solution were clear enough. Much ambiguity lurked, however, in connecting the two.

The economists Richard Lester and Michael Piore have studied the firms that sought to create the switching technology, finding that cooperation and collaboration within certain companies allowed them to make headway on the switching technology problem, whereas internal competition at other corporations diminished engineers' efforts to improve the quality of the switches. Motorola, a success story, developed what it called a "technology shelf," created by a small group of engineers, on which were placed possible technical solutions that other teams might use in the future; rather than trying to solve the problem outright, it developed tools whose immediate value was not clear. Nokia grappled with the problem in another collaborative way, creating an open-ended conversation among its engineers in which salespeople and designers were often included. The boundaries among business units in Nokia deliberately ambiguous, because more than technical information was needed to get a feeling for the problem; lateral thinking was required. Lester and Piore describe the process of communication this entailed as "fluid, context-dependent, undetermined."[20]

By contrast, companies like Ericsson proceeded with more seeming clarity and discipline, dividing the problem into its parts. The birth of the new switch was intended to occur through "the exchange of information" among offices "rather than the cultivation of an interpretative community."[21] Rigidly organized, Ericsson fell away. It did eventually solve the switching technology problem, but with greater difficulty; different offices protected their turf. In any organization, individuals or teams that compete and are rewarded for doing better than others will hoard information. In technology firms, hoarding information particularly disables good work.

The corporations that succeeded through cooperation shared with the Linux community that experimental mark of technological craftsmanship, the intimate, fluid join between problem solving and problem finding. Within the framework of competition, by contrast, clear standards of achievement and closure are needed to measure performance and to dole out rewards.

Any musician would find the story of the mobile phone eminently clear: good chamber music and orchestral work can only improve, especially in rehearsal, in the same way. Listeners may sometimes imagine that working with a superstar conductor or soloist inspires orchestral players, the virtuoso setting a standard that lifts everyone's game, but this depends on how the star behaves. A soloist withdrawn from collegiality can actually diminish the will of orchestra players to perform well. Engineers, like musicians, are intensely competitive creatures; the issue for both is what happens when a compensating cooperation vanishes: the work degrades. The triumphalist story, however, has tended to be blind to this necessary balance.

The evidence of demoralized Russian workers that my wife and I encountered in the Moscow suburbs can be found closer to home. When I returned from this final trip to the empire, I began studying the demioergoi of the new American economy: middle-level workers whose skills should have earned them a secure place in the "new economy" in formation since the 1990s.[22] The label refers to labor in the high-technology, finance, and human services sectors, supported by global investors, conducted in institutions that are more flexible, responsive, and focused on the short-term than in the rigid bureaucratic cages of the past. My students and I focused on people who write computer code, do accounting in backoffices, or arrange shipments to local stores in a retail chain—all competent but without sexy job titles or showy incomes.

The world that their fathers and grandfathers knew was in a way protected from the rigors of competition. Skilled middle-class workers found a place, in twentieth-century corporations, in relatively stable bureaucracies that moved employees along a career path from young adulthood to retirement. The forebears of the people we interviewed worked hard for their achievements; they knew fairly well what would happen to them if they didn't.

It's no longer news that this middle-class world has cracked. The corporate system that once organized careers is now a maze of fragmented jobs. In principle, many new economy firms subscribe to the doctrines of teamwork and cooperation, but unlike the actual practices of Nokia and Motorola, these principles are often a charade. We found that people made a show of friendliness and cooperation under the watchful eyes of boss-minders rather than, as in good Japanese firms, challenging and disputing their superiors. We found, as have other researchers, that people seldom identified as friends the people with whom they worked in teams. Some of the people we interviewed were energized by this individualized competition, but more were depressed by it—and for a particular reason. The structure of rewards didn't work well for them.

The new economy has broken two traditional forms of rewarding work. Prosperous companies are intended, traditionally, to reward employees who work hard, at all levels. In these new economy firms, however, the wealth share of middle-level employees has stagnated over the past generation, even as the wealth of those at the top has ballooned. One measure is that in 1974 the chief executive officer of a large American corporation earned about thirty times as much as a median-level employee, whereas in 2004 the CEO earned 350 to 400 times as much. In these thirty years, real-dollar earnings at the median point have risen only 4 percent.

Sheer service to a company was, in an earlier generation, another reward for work, set in bureaucratic stone through automatic seniority increases in pay. In the new economy, such rewards for service have diminished or disappeared; companies now have a short-term focus, preferring younger, fresher workers to older, supposedly more ingrown employees—which means for the worker that, as his or her experience accumulates, it loses institutional value. The technicians whom I first began interviewing in Silicon Valley thought they could see themselves through this problem of experience by developing their skills, creating an inner armory that they could transport from company to company.

But craft does not protect them. In today's globalized marketplace, middle-level skilled workers risk the prospect of losing employment to a peer in India or China who has the same skills but works for lower pay; job loss is no longer merely a working-class problem. Again, many firms tend not to make long-term investments in an employee's skills, preferring to make new hires of people who already have the new skills needed rather than to engage in the more expensive process of retraining.

There are wrinkles in this gloomy picture. The sociologist Christopher Jencks has shown that economic "returns to skill" are robust at the upper reaches of the skills ladder but weaker lower down; crack systems designers are handsomely rewarded today, but low-level programmers often do no better and sometimes worse than people with manual service skills like plumbers and plasterers. Again, Alan Blinder argues, although many higher-skilled technical jobs in the West are being sent offshore to places in Asia and the Middle East, there are unexportable jobs that require face-to-face contact. If you live in New York, you can work with an accountant in Bombay, but you cannot usefully deal with a divorce lawyer there.[23]

Still, the trials of the craftsmen of the new economy are a caution against triumphalism. The growth of the new economy has driven many of these workers in America and Britain inside themselves. Those firms that show little loyalty to their employees elicit little commitment in return—Internet companies that ran into trouble in the early 2000s learned a bitter lesson, their employees jumping ship rather than making efforts to help the imperiled companies survive. Skeptical of institutions, new economy workers have lower rates of voting and political participation than technical workers two generations ago; although many are joiners of voluntary organizations, few are active participants. The political scientist Robert Putnam has explained this diminished "social capital," in his celebrated book *Bowling Alone,* as the result of television culture and the consumerist ethic; in our study, we found that withdrawal from institutions was tied more directly to people's experiences at work.[24]

If the work people do in new economy jobs is skilled and high pressure, requiring long hours, still it is dissociated labor: we found few among the technicians who believed that they would be rewarded for doing a good job for its own sake. The modern craftsman may hew inside him or herself to this ideal, but given the structuring of rewards, that effort will be invisible.

❋ ❋ ❋

From the social point of view, in sum, demoralization has many sides. It can occur when a collective goal for good work becomes hollow and empty; equally, sheer competition can disable good work and depress workers. Neither corporatism nor capitalism as crude labels get at the institutional issue. The forms of collective communication in Japanese auto plants and the practices of cooperation in firms like Nokia and Motorola have made them profitable. In other realms of the new economy, however, competition has disabled and disheartened workers, and the craftsman's ethos of doing good work for its own sake is unrewarded or invisible.

Fractured Skills
Hand and Head Divided

The modern era is often described as a skills economy, but what exactly is a skill? The generic answer is that skill is a trained practice. In this, skill contrasts to the *coup de foudre*, the sudden inspiration. The lure of inspiration lies in part in the conviction that raw talent can take the place of training. Musical prodigies are often cited to support this conviction—and wrongly so. An infant musical prodigy like Wolfgang Amadeus Mozart did indeed harbor the capacity to remember large swatches of notes, but from ages five to seven Mozart learned how to train his great innate musical memory when he improvised at the keyboard. He evolved methods for seeming to produce music spontaneously. The music he later wrote down again seems spontaneous because he wrote directly on the page with relatively few corrections, but Mozart's letters show that he went over his scores again and again in his mind before setting them in ink.

We should be suspicious of claims for innate, untrained talent. "I could write a good novel if only I had the time" or "if only I could pull myself together" is usually a narcissist's fantasy. Going over an action again and again, by contrast, enables self-criticism. Modern education fears repetitive learning as mind-numbing. Afraid of boring children, avid to present ever-different stimulation, the enlightened teacher may avoid routine—but thus deprives children of the experience of studying their own ingrained practice and modulating it from within.

Skill development depends on how repetition is organized. This is why in music, as in sports, the length of a practice session must be carefully judged: the number of times one repeats a piece can be no more than the individual's attention span at a given stage. As skill expands, the capacity to sustain repetition increases. In music this is the so-called Isaac Stern rule, the great violinist declaring that the better your technique, the longer you can rehearse without becoming bored. There are "Eureka!" moments that turn the lock in a practice that has jammed, but they are embedded in routine.

As a person develops skill, the contents of what he or she repeats change. This seems obvious: in sports, repeating a tennis serve again and again, the player learns to aim the ball different ways; in music, the child Mozart, aged six and seven, was fascinated by the Neapolitan-sixth chord progression, in fundamental position (the movement, say, from a C-major chord to an A-flat major chord). A few years after working with it, he became adept in inverting the shift to other positions. But the matter is also not obvious. When practice is organized as a means to a fixed end, then the problems of the closed system reappear; the person in training will meet a fixed target but won't progress further. The open relation between problem solving and problem finding, as in Linux work, builds and expands skills, but this can't be a one-off event. Skill opens up in this way only because the rhythm of solving and opening up occurs again and again.

These precepts about building skill through practice encounter a great obstacle in modern society. By this I refer to a way in which machines can be misused. The "mechanical" equates in ordinary language with repetition of a static sort. Thanks to the revolution in microcomputing, however, modern machinery is not static; through feed-back loops machines can learn from their experience. Yet machinery is misused when it deprives people themselves from learning through repetition. The smart machine can separate human mental under-standing from repetitive, instructive, hands-on learning. When this occurs, conceptual human powers suffer.

Since the Industrial Revolution of the eighteenth century, the ma-chine has seemed to threaten the work of artisan-craftsmen. The threat appeared physical; industrial machines never tired, they did the same work hour after hour without complaining. The modern machine's threat to developing skill has a different character.

An example of this misuse occurs in CAD (computer-assisted design), the software program that allows engineers to design physical objects and architects to generate images of buildings on-screen. The technol-ogy traces back to the work of Ivan Sutherland, an engineer at the Massachusetts Institute of Technology who in 1963 figured out how a user could interact graphically with a computer. The modern material world could not exist without the marvels of CAD. It enables instant modeling of products from screws to automobiles, specifies precisely their engineering, and commands their actual production.[25] In archi-tectural work, however, this necessary technology also poses dangers of misuse.

In architectural work, the designer establishes on screen a series of points; the algorithms of the program connect the points as a line, in two or three dimensions. Computer-assisted design has become nearly universal in architectural offices because it is swift and precise. Among its virtues are the ability to rotate images so that the designer can see the house or office building from many points of view. Unlike a physical model, the screen model can be quickly lengthened, shrunk, or broken into parts. Sophisticated applications of CAD model the effects on a structure of the changing play of light, wind, or seasonal temperature change. Traditionally, architects have analyzed solid buildings in two ways, through plan and section. Computer-assisted design permits many other forms of analysis, such as taking a mental journey, on-screen, through the building's airflows.

How could such a useful tool possibly be abused? When CAD first entered architectural teaching, replacing manual drawing by hand, a young architect at MIT observed that "when you draw a site, when you put in the counter lines and the trees, it becomes ingrained in your mind. You come to know the site in a way that is not possible with the computer. . . . You get to know a terrain by tracing and retracing it, not by letting the computer 'regenerate' it for you."[26] This is not nostalgia: her observation addresses what gets lost mentally when screen work replaces physical drawing. As in other visual practices, architectural sketches are often pictures of possibility; in the process of crystallizing and refining them by hand, the designer proceeds just as a tennis player or musician does, gets deeply involved in it, matures thinking about it. The site, as this architect observes, "becomes ingrained in the mind."

The architect Renzo Piano explains his own working procedure thus: "You start by sketching, then you do a drawing, then you make a model, and then you go to reality—you go to the site—and then you go back to drawing. You build up a kind of circularity between drawing and making and then back again."[27] About repetition and practice Piano observes, "This is very typical of the craftsman's approach. You think and you do at the same time. You draw and you make. Drawing . . . is revisited. You do it, you redo it, and you redo it again."[28] This attaching, circular metamorphosis can be aborted by CAD. Once points are plotted on-screen, the algorithms do the drawing; misuse occurs if the process is a closed system, a static means-end—the "circularity" of which Piano speaks disappears. The physicist Victor Weisskopf once said to his MIT students who worked exclusively with computerized

experiments, "When you show me that result, the computer understands the answer, but I don't think you understand the answer."[29]

Computer-assisted design poses particular dangers for thinking
about buildings. Because of the machine's capacities for instant erasure and refiguring, the architect Elliot Felix observes, "each action is
less consequent than it would be paper . . . each will be less carefully
considered."[30] Returning to physical drawing can overcome this danger; harder to counter is an issue about the materials of which the
building is made. Flat computer screens cannot render well the tex-
tures of different materials or assist in choosing their colors, though
the CAD programs can calculate to a marvel the precise amount of
brick or steel a building might require. Drawing in bricks by hand,
tedious though the process is, prompts the designer to think about
their materiality, to engage with their solidity as against the blank,
unmarked space on paper of a window. Computer-assisted design also
impedes the designer in thinking about scale, as opposed to sheer size.
Scale involves judgments of proportion; the sense of proportion on-
screen appears to the designer as the relation of clusters of pixels. The
object on-screen can indeed be manipulated so that it is presented, for
instance, from the vantage point of someone on the ground, but in this
regard CAD is frequently misused: what appears on-screen is impossibly coherent, framed in a unified way that physical sight never is.

Troubles with materiality have a long pedigree in architecture. Few
large-scale building projects before the industrial era had detailed
working drawings of the precise sort CAD can produce today; Pope
Sixtus V remade the Piazza del Popolo in Rome at the end of the
sixteenth century by describing in conversation the buildings and public space he envisioned, a verbal instruction that left much room for
the mason, glazier, and engineer to work freely and adaptively on the
ground. Blueprints—inked designs in which erasure is possible but
messy—acquired legal force by the late nineteenth century, making

these images on paper equivalent to a lawyer's contract. The blueprint signaled, moreover, one decisive disconnection between head and hand in design: the idea of a thing made complete in conception before it is constructed.

A striking example of the problems that can ensue from mentalized design appear in Georgia's Peachtree Center, perched on the edge of Atlanta. Here is to be found a small forest of concrete office towers, parking garages, shops, and hotels, edged by highways. As of 2004, the complex covered about 5.8 million square feet, which makes this one of the largest "megaprojects" in the region. The Peachtree Center could not have been made by a group of architects working by hand—it is simply too vast and complex. The planning analyst Bent Flyvbjerg explains a further economic reason why CAD is necessary for projects of this scope: small errors have large knock-on effects.[31]

Some aspects of the design are excellent. The buildings are laid out in a grid plan of streets forming fourteen blocks rather than as a mall; the complex pays allegiance to the street and is meant to be pedestrian friendly. The architecture of the three large hotels is by John Portman, a flamboyant designer who favors such dramatic touches as glass elevators running up and down forty stories of interior atriums. Elsewhere, the three trade marts and office towers are more conventional concrete-and-steel boxes, some faced outside with the Renaissance or Baroque detailing that has become the stamp of postmodern design. The project as a whole reaches for character rather than anonymity. Still, pregnant failures of this computer-driven project are evident on the ground—three failures that menace computer-assisted design more largely as a disembodied design practice.

The first is the disconnect between simulation and reality. In plan, the Peachtree Center populates the streets with well-designed sidewalk cafés. Yet the plan has not actually engaged with the intense Georgia heat: the outdoor seats of the cafés are in fact empty from late morning to late afternoon much of the year. Simulation is an imperfect substitute for accounting the *sensation* of light, wind, and heat on site. The designers would perhaps have done better to sit unprotected in the midday Georgia sun for an hour before going to work each day; physical discomfort would have made them see better. The large issue here is that simulation can be a poor substitute for tactile experience.

Hands-off design also disables a certain kind of relational understanding. Portman's hotel, for instance, emphasizes the idea of coherence, with its inner drama of all-glass elevators running up a forty-story atrium; the hotel's rooms look outward over parking lots. On-screen, the parking-lot issue can be put out of mind by rotating the image so that the sea of cars disappears; on foot, it cannot be disposed of in this way. To be sure, this is not the computer's inherent fault. Portman's designers could perfectly well have put in an image of all the cars and then viewed the sea, on-screen, from the hotel rooms, but then they'd have had a fundamental problem with the design. Whereas Linux is set up to discover problems, CAD is often used to hide them. The difference accounts for some of CAD's commercial popularity; it can be used to repress difficulty.

Finally, CAD's precisions bring out a problem long inherent in blueprint design, that of overdetermination. The various planners involved in the Peachtree Center rightly point with pride to its mixed-use buildings, but these mixtures have been calculated down to the square foot; the calculations draw a false inference about how well the finished object will function. Overdetermined design rules out the crinkled fabric of buildings that allow little start-up businesses, and so communities, to grow and vibrate. This texture results from underdetermined structures that permit uses to abort, swerve, and evolve. There is thus missing the informal and so easy, sociable street life of Atlanta's older neighborhoods. A positive embrace of the incomplete is necessarily absent in the blueprint; forms are resolved in advance of their use. If CAD does not cause this problem, the program sharpens it: the algorithms draw nearly instantly a totalized picture.

The tactile, the relational, and the incomplete are physical experiences that occur in the act of drawing. Drawing stands for a larger range of experiences, such as the way of writing that embraces editing and rewriting, or of playing music to explore again and again the puzzling qualities of a particular chord. The difficult and the incomplete should be positive events in our understanding; they should stimulate us as simulation and facile manipulation of complete objects cannot. The issue—I want to stress—is more complicated than hand *versus* machine. Modern computer programs can indeed learn from their experience in an expanding fashion, because algorithms are rewritten through data feedback. The problem, as Victor Weisskopf says, is that people may let the machines do this learning, the person serving as a passive witness to and consumer of expanding competence, not participating in it. This is why Renzo Piano, the designer of very complicated objects, returns in a circular fashion to drawing them roughly by hand. Abuses of CAD illustrate how, when the head and the hand are separate, it is the head that suffers.

Computer-assisted design might serve as an emblem of a large challenge faced by modern society: how to think like craftsmen in making good use of technology. "Embodied knowledge" is a currently fashionable phrase in the social sciences, but "thinking like a craftsman" is more than a state of mind; it has a sharp social edge.

Immured in the Peachtree Center for a weekend of discussions on "Community Values and National Goals," I was particularly interested in its parking garages. A standardized bumper had been installed at the end of each car stall. It looked sleek, but the lower edge of each bumper was sharp metal, liable to scratch cars or calves. Some bumpers, though, had been turned back, on site, for safety. The irregularity of the turning showed that the job had been done manually, the steel smoothed and rounded wherever it might be unsafe to touch; the craftsman had thought for the architect. The lighting in these aboveground car-houses turned out to be uneven in intensity, dangerous shadows suddenly appearing within the building. Painters had added odd-shaped white strip lines to guide drivers in and out of irregular pools of light, showing signs of improvising rather than following the plan. The craftsman had done further, deeper thinking about light than the designers.

These steel grinders and painters had evidently not sat in on design sessions at the start, using their experience to indicate problematic spots in the designs plotted on-screen. Bearers of embodied knowledge but mere manual laborers, they were not accorded that privilege. This is the sharp edge in the problem of skill; the head and the hand are not simply separated intellectually but socially.

Conflicting Standards
Correct versus Practical

What do we mean by good-quality work? One answer is how something should be done, the other is getting it to work. This is a difference between correctness and functionality. Ideally, there should be no conflict; in the real world, there is. Often we subscribe to a standard of correctness that is rarely if ever reached. We might alternatively work according to the standard of what is possible, just good enough—but this can also be a recipe for frustration. The desire to do good work is seldom satisfied by just getting by.

Thus, following the absolute measure of quality, the writer will obsess about every comma until the rhythm of a sentence comes out right, and the woodworker will shave a mortise-and-tenon joint until the two pieces are completely rigid, needing no screws. Following the measure of functionality, the writer will deliver on time, no matter that every comma is in place, the point of writing being to be read. The functionally minded carpenter will curb worry about each detail, knowing that small defects can corrected by hidden screws. Again, the point is to finish so that the piece can be used. To the absolutist in every craftsman, each imperfection is a failure; to the practitioner, obsession with perfection seems a prescription for failure.

A philosophical nicety is necessary to bring out this conflict. *Practice* and *practical* share a root in language. It might seem that the more people train and practice in developing a skill, the more practical minded they will become, focusing on the possible and the particular. In fact, the long experience of practice can lead in the opposite direction. Another variant of the "Isaac Stern rule" is: the better your technique, the more impossible your standards. (Depending on his mood, Isaac Stern worked many, many variations of "the Isaac Stern rule" on the virtue of repeated practice.) Linux can operate in a similar fashion. The people most skilled in using it are usually the ones thinking about the program's ideal and endless possibilities.

The conflict between getting something right and getting it done has today an institutional setting, one I shall illustrate in the provision of medical care. Many elderly readers will, like me, know only too well its outline.

In the past decade Britain's National Health Service (NHS) has new measures for determining how well doctors and nurses do their jobs—how many patients are seen, how quickly patients have access to care, how efficiently they are referred to specialists. These are numeric measures of the right way to provide care, but measures meant to serve patient interests humanely. It would be easier, for instance, if referral to specialists were left to the doctor's convenience. However, doctors as well as nurses, nurses' aides, and cleaning staff believe that these "reforms" have diminished the quality of care, using the guideline of what's practicable on the ground. Their sentiments are hardly unusual. Researchers in western Europe widely report that practitioners believe that their craft skills in dealing with patients are being frustrated by the push for institutional standards.

The National Health Service has a special context quite unlike American-style "managed-care" or other market-driven mechanisms. In the wake of the Second World War, the creation of the NHS was a source of national pride. The NHS recruited the best people, and they were committed; few departed for better-paying jobs in America. Britain has spent a third less of its gross domestic product on health than the United States, yet its infant mortality rate is lower, and its elderly live longer. The British system is "free" health care, paid for through taxes. The British people have indicated that they are happy to pay these taxes, or even contribute more, if only the service can improve.

In time, like all systems, the NHS has worn down. The hospitals physically aged, equipment needing replacement remained in use, waiting times for service lengthened, and not enough nurses were in training. To solve these ills, Britain's politicians turned a decade ago to a different model of quality, one established by Henry Ford in the American auto industry early in the twentieth century. "Fordism" takes the division of labor to an extreme: each worker does one task, measured as precisely as possible by time-and-motion studies; output is measured in terms of targets that are, again, entirely quantitative. Applied to health care, Fordism monitors the time doctors and nurses spend with each patient; a medical treatment system based on dealing with auto parts, it tends to treat cancerous livers or broken backs rather than patients in the round.[32] A particular wrinkle in British health care is the number of times the health service has been "reformed" along Fordist lines in the past decade: four major reorganizations reverse or depart from previous changes.

Fordism has acquired a bad name in private industry for reasons that Adam Smith first laid out in *The Wealth of Nations* in the eighteenth century. The division of labor focuses on parts rather than wholes; to the vivacity of merchants, Smith contrasted the dulled wits of factory laborers doing just one small thing, hour after hour, day after day. Smith believed, though, that this system would be more efficient than work done by hand in the preindustrial way. Henry Ford justified his procedures by arguing that strictly machine-built autos were of better quality than those cars that were in his time assembled in small workshops. The advent of microelectronics in manufacturing has provided a further support for this way of making things: microsensors do a much more rigorous, steady job of monitoring problems than human eyes or hands. In sum, by the absolute measure of quality in the thing itself, the machine is a better craftsman than a person.

Medical reform finds its place in this long debate about the nature and value of craftsmanship in a mechanical, quantitative society. In the NHS, the Fordist reformers can claim quality has indeed improved: in particular, cancers and heart diseases are better treated. Moreover, frustrated though they are, British doctors and nurses have not lost the will to do good work; theirs is not the story of the Soviet construction workers. Though fatigued by constant reform and angry at the system of targets, these health care providers have not become indifferent to doing high-quality work; Julian Legrand, an insightful analyst of the NHS, remarks on the fact that although staff are nostalgic for the old days of loose practice, if they were magically transported back two generations, they would be appalled by what they saw.[33]

Putting nostalgia aside, what is there about medical "craft" that is demeaned by these changes? Studies of nurses provide one answer.[34] In the "old" NHS, nurses listened to elderly patients' stories about their children as well as to complaints about aches and pains; in the hospital wards, nurses often stepped in when a patient crisis erupted, even if they were legally not qualified to do so. Obviously, a sick patient cannot be repaired like an automobile, but behind this stands a deeper point about the practice standard. To do good work means to be curious about, to investigate, and to learn from ambiguity. As with Linux programmers, nursing craft negotiates a liminal zone between problem solving and problem finding; listening to old men's chatter, the nurse can glean clues about their ailments that might escape a diagnostic checklist.

This liminal zone of investigation is important to doctors in another way. In the Fordist model of medicine, there must be a specific illness to treat; the evaluation of a doctor's performance will then be made by counting the time required to treat as many livers as possible and the number of livers that get well. Because bodily reality doesn't fit well inside this classifying model, and because good treatment has to admit experiment, a not insignificant number of doctors create paper fictions to buy themselves time from the bureaucratic monitors. Doctors in the NHS often assign a patient a disease in order to justify the time spent on exploring a puzzling body.

The absolutists working on standards for the system can claim that they've raised the quality of care. Nurses and doctors in practice argue against this numeric claim. Rather than fuzzy sentimentalism, they invoke the need for curiosity and experiment and would subscribe, I think, to Immanuel Kant's image of "the twisted timber of humanity" as applying to both patients and themselves.

This conflict came to a head on June 26, 2006, at the annual meeting of the British Medical Association in Belfast. The association's president, Dr. James Johnson, observed that the government's "favored method of raising quality and keeping prices down is to do what they do in supermarkets and offer choice and competition." To his colleagues he said, "You tell me that the breakneck pace and incoherent planning behind systems reform are seriously destabilising the NHS. The message I am getting from the medical profession is that the NHS is in danger and that doctors have been marginalised." To the government, Johnson appealed, "Work with the profession. We are not the enemy. We will help you find the solution." When government officials then took the stage, however, an icy, polite silence greeted their speeches.[35]

British doctors and nurses are today suffering from reform fatigue, an NHS decisively reformed several times in a decade. Any organizational reform takes time to "bed in"; people have to learn how to put the changes into practice—whom now to call, which forms to use, what procedures to follow. If a patient is having a heart attack, you do not want to reach for your "Manual of Best-Practice Performances" to discover the latest rules about what you are supposed to do. The process of bedding in takes longer the bigger and more complex the organization in which one works. The NHS, Britain's biggest employer, consists of more than 1.1 million people. It cannot turn like a sailboat. Both nurses and doctors are still learning the changes proposed a decade ago.

❋　❋　❋

Embedding stands for a process essential to all skills, the conversion of information and practices into tacit knowledge. If a person had to think about each and every movement of waking up, she or he would take an hour to get out of bed. When we speak of doing something "instinctively," we are often referring to behavior we have so routinized that we don't have to think about it. In learning a skill, we develop a complicated repertoire of such procedures. In the higher stages of skill, there is a constant interplay between tacit knowledge and self-conscious awareness, the tacit knowledge serving as an anchor, the explicit awareness serving as critique and corrective. Craft quality emerges from this higher stage, in judgments made on tacit habits and suppositions. When an institution like the NHS, in churning reform, doesn't allow the tacit anchor to develop, then the motor of judgment stalls. People have no experience to judge, just a set of abstract propositions about good-quality work.

Proponents of absolutist standards of quality, however, have many worries about the interchange between tacit and explicit knowledge—as long ago as in Plato's writings on craftsmanship, the experiential standard is treated with suspicion. Plato views it as too often an excuse for mediocrity. His modern heirs in the NHS wanted to root out embedded knowledge, expose it to the cleansing of rational analysis—and have become frustrated that much of the tacit knowledge nurses and doctors have acquired is precisely knowledge they cannot put into words or render as logical propositions. Michael Polanyi, the modern philosopher most attuned to tacit knowledge, has recognized the justice of this worry. Bedded in too comfortably, people will neglect the higher standard; it is by arousing self-consciousness that the worker is driven to do better.

Here, then, is an emblematic conflict in measures of quality, from which follow two different concepts of institutional craftsmanship. To take a generous view, the reformers of the NHS are crafting a system that works correctly, and their impulse to reform reflects something about all craftsmanship; this is to reject muddling through, to reject the job just good enough, as an excuse for mediocrity. To take an equally generous view of the claims of practice, it encompasses pursuing a problem—be it a disease, a bumper railing, or a piece of the Linux computer kernel—in all its ramifications. This craftsman must be patient, eschewing quick fixes. Good work of this sort tends to focus on relationships; it either deploys relational thinking about objects or, as in the case of the NHS nurses, attends to clues from other people. It emphasizes the lessons of experience through a dialogue between tacit knowledge and explicit critique.

Thus, one reason we may have trouble thinking about the value of craftsmanship is that the very word in fact embodies conflicting values, a conflict that in such institutional settings as medical care is, so far, raw and unresolved.

An ancient ideal of craftsmanship, celebrated in the hymn to Hephaestus, joined skill and community. Traces of that ancient ideal are still evident today among Linux programmers. They seem an unusual, marginal group because of three troubled ways in which craftsmanship is now organized.

The first trouble appears in the attempts of institutions to motivate people to work well. Some efforts to motivate good work for the sake of the group have proved hollow, like the degradation of Marxism in Soviet civil society. Other collective motivations, like those in postwar Japanese factories, have succeeded. Western capitalism has sometimes claimed that individual competition rather than collaboration most effectively motivates people to work well, but in the high-tech realm, it is firms that enable cooperation who have achieved high-quality results.

A second trouble lies in developing skill. Skill is a trained practice; modern technology is abused when it deprives its users precisely of that repetitive, concrete, hands-on training. When the head and the hand are separated, the result is mental impairment—an outcome particularly evident when a technology like CAD is used to efface the learning that occurs through drawing by hand.

Third, there is the trouble caused by conflicting measures of quality, one based on correctness, the other on practical experience. These conflict institutionally, as in medical care, when reformers' desire to get things right according to an absolute standard of quality cannot be reconciled with standards of quality based on embedded practice. The philosopher finds in this conflict the diverging claims of tacit and explicit knowledge; the craftsman at work is pulled in contrary directions.

We can understand these three troubles better by looking more deeply into their history. In the next chapter we explore the workshop as a social institution that motivates craftsmen. Following that, we look at the eighteenth-century Enlightenment's first efforts to make sense of machines and skills. Last, we look at tacit and explicit consciousness in the long history of crafting a particular material.

The Workshop

The workshop is the craftsman's home. Traditionally this was literally so. In the Middle Ages craftsmen slept, ate, and raised their children in the places where they worked. The workshop, as well as a home for families, was small in scale, each containing at most a few dozen people; the medieval workshop looked nothing like the modern factory containing hundreds or thousands of people. It's easy to see the romantic appeal of the workshop-home to socialists who first confronted the industrial landscape of the nineteenth century. Karl Marx, Charles Fourier, and Claude Saint-Simon all viewed the workshop as a space of humane labor. Here they, too, seemed to find a good home, a place where labor and life mixed face-to-face.

Yet this beguiling image is misleading. The medieval workshop-home did not follow the rules of a modern family guided by love. Organized into a system of guilds, the workshop provided other, more impersonal emotional rewards, most notably, honor in the city. "Home" suggests established stability; this the medieval workshops had to struggle for, since they could not assume they would survive. The workshop as home may also obscure this living scene of labor today. Most scientific laboratories are organized as workshops in the sense that they are small, face-to-face places of work. So, too, can workshop conditions be carved out of giant enterprises: modern auto plants combine the assembly line with spaces reserved for small, specialist teams; the auto factory has become an archipelago of workshops.

A more satisfying definition of the workshop is: a productive space in which people deal face-to-face with issues of authority. This austere definition focuses not only on who commands and who obeys in work but also on skills as a source of the legitimacy of command or the dignity of obedience. In a workshop, the skills of the master can earn him or her the right to command, and learning from and absorbing those skills can dignify the apprentice or journeyman's obedience. In principle.

To use this definition we need to take account of authority's antonym: autonomy, self-sufficing work conducted without the interference of another. Autonomy has its own seductive power. We might easily imagine that the Soviet construction workers described in the previous chapter would have worked more diligently if they had held more control over their own labor. The British nurses and doctors certainly believed that they could get on better with a difficult job if left alone. They should be masters of their own house. No one working alone could figure out, however, how to glaze windows or to draw blood. In craftsmanship there must be a superior who sets standards and who trains. In the workshop, inequalities of skill and experience become face-to-face issues. The successful workshop will establish legitimate authority in the flesh, not in rights or duties set down on paper. In the failed workshop, subordinates like the Russian construction workers will become demoralized or, like British nurses at the medical convention, grow angry in the physical presence of those whom they must nonetheless obey.

The social history of craftsmanship is in large part a story of the efforts of workshops to face or duck issues of authority and autonomy. Workshops do have other aspects, in their dealings with markets, their quest for funds and profits. The social history of workshops emphasizes how the institutions have organized themselves to embody authority. A significant moment in the history of workshops occurred at the end of the medieval era—a particularly illuminating passage for the problems of authority today.

The Guild House
The Medieval Goldsmith

The medieval craftsman's authority rested on the fact that he was a Christian. Early Christianity had from its origins embraced the dignity of the craftsman. It mattered to theologians and laymen alike that Christ was the son of a carpenter, God's humble origins sending a signal about the universality of his message. Augustine thought Adam and Eve "fortunate to work in a garden. . . . Is there any more marvelous sight than the sowing of seeds, the planting of cuttings, the transplanting of shrubs?"[1] The religion embraced the work of the craftsman, moreover, because these labors could counteract the human propensity for self-destruction. As in the hymn to Hephaestus, craftwork seemed peaceable and productive rather than violent. For this reason, in the Middle Ages there appeared new craftsmen-saints. In Anglo-Saxon Britain, for instance, Saints Dunstan and Ethelwold were both metalworkers, venerated for their calm industry.

Although it respected craftwork, medieval Christian doctrine also feared the human Pandora, a fear that can be traced back to the faith's origins. Pagan Rome—in its belief that the work of one's hands can reveal much about the soul—represented a monumental folly. Augustine argued in the *Sermons* that *confessio* means "accusation of oneself; praise of God."[2] The principle of Christian retreat was founded on the conviction that the further a person can get from obsessing about material things, the closer he or she will come to discovering a timeless inner life not of human making. Doctrinally, the craftsman represents Christ's appearance to humankind but not his being.

The early medieval Christian craftsman found his spiritual home on earth in monasteries such as that of Saint Gall in what is now Switzerland, a walled mountain refuge within which monks gardened, practiced carpentry, and concocted herbal medicines as well as prayed. Saint Gall harbored lay craftsmen whose lives were almost equally subject to monastic discipline. In a nearby nunnery, nuns in strict seclusion nonetheless spent much of each day in the practical activities of weaving and sewing. Saint Gall and kindred monasteries were largely self-sufficient communities, "sustainable" we would say, producing most of what they needed for survival. The workshops of Saint Gall followed the precepts of authority according to the dual canon of the faith: the Holy Spirit can appear to men and women under these conditions; the Spirit is not, however, contained within the walls.

As cities developed in the twelfth and thirteenth centuries, the workshop became a different sort of space both sacred and profane. A contrast of the parish surrounding the Cathedral of Notre-Dame in Paris in 1300 to the monastery at Saint Gall three hundred years earlier, in 1000, shows some of the differences. The urban episcopal parish contained many private houses—"private" in that a workshop leased or bought premises from the parish and in that monks and religious officials could not enter these houses at will. The Bishop's Landing on the south side of the Seine served the religious community as a door for goods; Saint Landry's Landing on the north side served the intermingled lay community. When Jehan de Chelles began the final phase of building this urban community in the mid-thirteenth century, the State appeared in its inaugural celebrations as the equal partner of the Church. Together and equally these two authorities celebrated "the building trades, feting the carvers, glassblowers, weavers and carpenters who did the manual labor, and the bankers who financed the work."[3]

The guilds were corporations that attempted to translate the principle *rex qui nunquam moritur*—the king never dies—into profane terms.[4] Legal documents partly sustained the guilds, but even more the hands-on transmission of knowledge from generation to generation aimed to make them sustainable. This "knowledge capital" was intended as the source of the guild's economic power. The historian Robert Lopez pictures the urban guild as "a federation of autonomous workshops, whose owners [the masters] normally made all decisions and established the requirements for promotion from the lower ranks [journeymen, hired helpers, or apprentices]."[5] The *Livre des métiers* of 1268 lists about a hundred crafts organized in this way, divided into seven groups: foods, jewelry, metals, textiles and clothiers, furs, and building.[6]

Still, religious authority of a hierarchical sort moved to town. Not only did religious rituals shape the daily routine of urban workers in guilds, but the master of each of Paris's seven major guilds claimed moral stature akin to that of an abbot. In the city, sheer necessity in part prompted this claim. There were no effective police in medieval towns, whose streets were violent both day and night. The equilibrium of the monastery was absent in the city; violence on the streets seeped into and among the workshops. The Latin word *auctoritas* stands for a personage who inspires fear and awe and so submission: the master of a workshop had to inspire such sentiments to keep order in his house.

Christian morality most shaped the "man" in the urban Christian craftsman. Early Church doctrine generally viewed free time as a temptation, leisure as an invitation to sloth. This fear applied particularly to women. Eve was the temptress, distracting man from his work. The Church Fathers imagined women as specifically prone to sexual license if they had nothing to occupy their hands. This prejudice bred a practice: female temptation could be countered by a particular craft, that of the needle, whether in weaving or embroidery, the woman's hands kept ever busy.

The needle as a remedy for female idleness traces traced back to the early Church Father Jerome. As is the way of prejudices that mature in time, this sexual negative became by the early Middle Ages also a source of honor. As the historian Edward Lucie-Smith points out, "queens were not ashamed both to weave and to sew"; Edith, queen of Edward the Confessor, sewed simple clothes, as did Matilda, queen of William the Conqueror.[7]

Still, the "man" in craftsmanship excluded women from formal membership in guilds, even though women cooked and cleaned in the houses of the city's workshops.

In the medieval guild, male authority was incarnate in the three-tiered hierarchy of masters, journeymen, and apprentices. Contracts specified the length of an apprenticeship, usually seven years, and the cost, usually borne by the young person's parents. The stages of progress in a guild were marked out first by the apprentice's presentation of the *chef d'oeuvre* at the end of his seven years, a work that demonstrated the elemental skills the apprentice had imbibed. If successful, now a journeyman, the craftsman would work for another five to ten years until he could demonstrate, in a *chef d'oeuvre élevé,* that he was worthy to take the master's place.

The apprentice's presentation focused on imitation: learning as copying. The journeyman's presentation had a larger compass. He had to show managerial competence and give evidence of his trustworthiness as a future leader. The difference between brute imitation of procedure and the larger understanding of how to use what one knows is, as we saw in the previous chapter, a mark of all skill development. The medieval workshop was distinctive in the authority invested in the teachers and judges of this progress. The master's verdicts were final, without appeal. Only rarely would a guild interfere in the judgments of individual masters in a workshop, for in his person the master united authority and autonomy.

Medieval goldsmithing is a good craft to study in this regard, because this craft had a peculiarity that makes it comprehensible rather than foreign to us. The apprentice goldsmith was place-bound while learning how to smelt, purify, and weigh precious metals. These skills required hands-on instruction from his master. Once the apprentice had locally presented his chef d'oeuvre, however, he could move from city to city as a journeyman, responding to opportunities.[8] The traveling goldsmith journeyman made his presentation elévé to the corporate body of master craftsmen in foreign cities. Through his managerial talents and moral behavior he had to convince these strangers that he could become one of them. The sociologist Alejandro Portes observes about modern economic migrants that they tend to be entrepreneurial in spirit; the passive stay home. This migratory dynamism was built into medieval goldsmithing.

It was for this reason that the goldsmith appealed in his own time to Ibn Khaldun, the first and still one of the greatest of sociologists. He was born in what is now Yemen but traveled extensively in Spanish Andalusia, at the time a mixed society of Jews, Christians, and Muslims, the last who ruled tenuously. The *Muqaddimah,* a vast enterprise, is in part a close observation of craftwork. In Andalusia Ibn Khaldun observed the wares of local Christian guilds, as well as the work of itinerant goldsmiths. The goldsmiths seemed to him like Berbers, made strong by travel and mobility. Sedentary guilds, by contrast, appeared to him inert and "corrupt." The good master, in his words, "presides over a travelling house."[9]

On the other side of the coin, migrant labor and the flow of international trade in the medieval era provoked some of the same fears we experience today. The great worry of urban guilds was a market flooded with fresh goods the guilds had not made. Guilds of medieval London and Paris in particular mounted defensive actions against the growth of trade in northern Europe. This threat they warded off by imposing punishing tolls and tariffs at the gates of cities and by strictly regulating the operations of fairs within cities. Itinerant guilds such as the goldsmiths sought contracts that would maintain the same conditions of labor wherever a goldsmith worked. Like ancient Greek weavers, these medieval craftsmen sought to hand down craft practices intact from generation to generation. Hannah Arendt's rhythm of "natality" and extinction was their enemy, for reasons of keeping the craft practice internationally coherent.

The *Livre des métiers* mentions in passing masters who become journeymen "either on account of poverty or by choice."[10] The first kind of downward mobility we easily comprehend; failed masters become other people's servants. The second is perhaps explained by the wandering goldsmith—a master in other crafts who renounces his place in the hierarchy of guilds in one city in order to travel in search of opportunity.

If adult goldsmiths formed a kind of analogue to modern flexible workers, moving to where the work is, still guild members forged a strong sense of community. The guild network provided contacts for workers on the move. Equally important, the guilds emphasized the migrant's obligations to newly encountered goldsmiths. Elaborate ritual did the work of binding the guild members to one another. Many goldsmithing guilds had, moreover, associated fraternities that included women, the fraternities supplying help for workers in need, from organizing social occasions to buying burial plots for the dead. In an age when written contracts between adults had little force, when informal trust instead underpinned economic transactions, "the single most pressing earthly obligation of every medieval artisan was the establishment of a good personal reputation."[11] This was especially an urgent matter for itinerant goldsmiths, who were strangers to many of the places in which they worked. The ritual life of guilds and their fraternities provided a frame to establish their probity.

"Authority" means something more than occupying a place of honor in a social web. For the craftsman, authority resides equally in the quality of his skills. And in the goldsmith's case, the good skills that established the master goldsmith's authority were inseparable from his ethics. This ethical imperative appeared in the very technological activity, the assay, that gave goldsmithing its economic value.

Corrupt, shaved, and false coins assailed the medieval economy. The goldsmith's role was to tell the truth about disguised substances, as well as to smelt gold from raw ore. The honor of the guild was meant to reinforce honesty; goldsmiths discovered to be dishonest were violently punished by other guild members.[12] The repute of the truthful craftsman mattered politically as well as economically, for he certified that the wealth of a nobleman or of a city government was genuine. To strengthen the craftsman's ethical sense, the gold assay by the thirteenth century became a religious rite, sanctified by special prayers, in which the content of gold was sworn by a master craftsman in the name of God. We may not now believe that faith makes for truth in chemistry; our forebears did.

The procedures of the gold assay were not scientific in the modern sense. Metallurgy was still yoked to the ancient belief in nature's four basic elements. Only at the end of the Renaissance could metallurgists effectively deploy the single test of "cupellation," in which a sample is scorched with hot air, oxidizing impurities like lead.[13] Before that, the medieval goldsmith had to use many tests to arrive at the judgment that the material he held in his hand was indeed gold.

In the assay, "hands-on" was no mere figure of speech to the goldsmith. The most important of his tests depended on his sense of touch. The goldsmith rolled and squeezed the metal, trying to judge from its consistency its nature. The sense of touch was itself in the Middle Ages endowed with magical, indeed religious properties, as in the "king's touch," the king laying hands on a subject to cure scrofula and leprosy.

In craft practice, the slower and more searchingly the goldsmith worked with his hands, the more truthful he appeared both to his peers and to his employers. Instant results employing a single test were suspect.

Ethics also shaped the relationship between goldsmiths and alchemists. Alchemy was not quite in the fourteenth and fifteenth centuries the foolishness we now take it for, because people believed that all solid elements shared the same fundamental "earth." Nor were those who practiced alchemy crooks—even in the late seventeenth century eminent figures like Isaac Newton dabbled in alchemy. "Most of the leading alchemists," the historian Keith Thomas writes, "thought of themselves as pursuing an exacting spiritual discipline, rather than a crude quest for gold."[14] They were in search of the principles of purification by which a substance of "noble value" could be extracted from crude earth, a model in turn for purification of the soul. Thus the goldsmith and the alchemist were often two faces, as it were, of the same coin, engaged in the same quest for purity.

Still, the medieval goldsmith served as the practical critic of alchemical claims, just as he was the counterfeiter's God-sworn enemy. Alchemical treatises abounded in the Middle Ages, some merely fanciful, other deeply serious investigations using the science of the time. In the assay, the goldsmith tested theory literally with his hands. His relation to the alchemical theorists resembles that of the modern British nurse, faced with a stack of paper "reforms," judging them in substance, in practice.

Goldsmithing is perhaps most revealing in what it tells about the workshop conceived as a craftsman's home—a place that unites family and labor. All medieval guilds were based on the hierarchy of the family, but these were not necessarily blood ties. The master craftsman legally stood in loco parentis to the journeymen and apprentices below him even if they were not his kin. A father entrusted his sons to the master craftsman as a surrogate parent most notably by transferring the right to punish misbehavior with physical violence.

Making the workplace into a surrogate family, however, also restrained the authority of the surrogate father. The master was enjoined by a religious oath that no father had ever to swear in words, that of improving the skills of his charges. This contract, notes the historian S. R. Epstein, protected apprentices against "the opportunism of their masters. They were [otherwise] liable to be exploited as cheap labor" without any benefit to themselves.[15] Correspondingly, the apprentice was contracted by religious oath to keep the secrets of his master. These legal and religious bonds brought emotional rewards that the biological bond could not furnish: they guaranteed the good apprentice that he could carry emblems or flags of the guild in civic parades and that he could enjoy a privileged place at banquets. The guilds' religious oaths established reciprocal *honor* between surrogate father and son rather than simple filial obedience.

Today, the dozen years or so of childhood are succeeded by an adolescence that seems to stretch out, agonizingly, another decade. Historians of childhood like Philippe Ariès have argued that in the Middle Ages there was no such stretched-out time of youth: children were treating as young adults from the age of six or seven, fighting alongside older people, frequently marrying before puberty.[16] Though Ariès's account has factual flaws, it explains the relations of authority and autonomy in guild life, for these relations turned on treating the child as an incipient adult.

Historical records show that many guilds privileged the biological sons of masters, but blood sons did not enjoy this privilege securely. Durable family businesses were the exception rather than the rule. By one large estimate, in the 1400s only about half of family businesses passed from generation to generation in the dense European belt of workshops from Bruges to Venice. By the end of the 1600s, only a tenth of artisan sons took their father's place.[17] More precisely, about half the sons of barrel masters in Bruges took over their fathers workshops in 1375; by 1500, nearly none did.[18] Paradoxically, the surrogate father's sworn oath to pass on a skill was a surer guarantee than the biological father's power to pass on a business that the young adult could be master in his own house.

Surrogacy, as people experienced it eight hundred years ago, is not entirely a "foreign country," to recall the phrase of L. P. Hartley. Surrogate parenting is a modern reality in schools, where teachers dominate an ever-increasing portion of the human life cycle. Divorce and remarriage create another kind of surrogate parenting.

The medieval workshop was a home held together more by honor than by love. The master in this house based his authority, concretely, on the transference of skills. This was the surrogate parent's role in child development. He did not "give" love; he was paid to do his particular kind of fathering. As a mirror held up to ourselves, in loco parentis is both an inspiring and an unsettling image of fatherhood: the guild master had a clear role as a father figure, one that expanded a child's horizons beyond the accidents of birth. Moreover, in goldsmithing, the child was inducted into an adult code of honor that widened his horizons beyond that of the individual house, beyond the confines of a particular loved parent. The medieval surrogate father could be affectionate to his charges, but he had no need to love them. Love, in its inner twists and turns, in its sheer generosity, is not the point of craftsmanship. The surrogate father, we might be tempted to say, was a stronger father figure.

In sum, the medieval craftsman was both brother and stranger to the present. His work was migrant, yet he also sought stability through shared skill. Ethical behavior was implicated in his technical work. His craft was hands-on, like a clinical practice. His surrogate parenting reveals still-puissant virtues. Yet his workshop did not endure. Of the many reasons for the decline of the medieval workshop, none is more important that its foundation of authority, the knowledge it could pass on by imitation, ritual, and surrogacy.

The Master Alone
The Craftsman Becomes an Artist

Probably the most common question people ask about craft is how it differs from art. In terms of numbers this is a narrow question; professional artists form a mere speck of the population, whereas craftsmanship extends to all sorts of labors. In terms of practice, there is no art without craft; the idea for a painting is not a painting. The line between craft and art may seem to separate technique and expression, but as the poet James Merrill once told me, "If this line does exist, the poet himself shouldn't draw it; he should focus only on making the poem happen." Though "what is art?" is a serious and endless question, lurking in this particular definitional worry may be something else: we are trying to figure out what autonomy means—autonomy as a drive from within that impels us to work in an expressive way, by ourselves.

This at least is how the historians Margot and Rudolf Wittkower saw the matter in their absorbing history *Born under Saturn,* which recounts the emergence of the Renaissance artist from the community of medieval craftsmen.[19] "Art" does a lot of heavy lifting in this version of cultural change. First of all, it stands for a new, larger privilege accorded subjectivity in modern society, the craftsman outward turned to his community, the artist inward turned upon himself. The Wittkowers emphasize Pandora's reappearance in the shift; self-destructive subjectivity was evinced by such suicides as the artists Francesco Bassano and Francesco Borromini.[20] In the minds of contemporaries, their genius drove these men to despair.

This version of change is not quite a tight story; the dark consequences of subjectivity were applied in Renaissance thinking more broadly than to working artists, whether geniuses or not. Robert Burton's *Anatomy of Melancholy* (1621) explored the "saturnine temperament" as a human condition, rooted in the biology of the body, when the brooding, introspective "humour"—a "humour" being closest to what modern medicine would conceive as a glandular secretion—is allowed to flourish. Isolation, Burton explained, stimulated this secretion. His rambling masterpiece returned again and again to the fear that subjectivity turns to melancholy. The "artist" to him is but one instance of the risk of depression entailed by the workings of the human body in solitude.

Art seemed to the Wittkowers to place the artist on a more autonomous footing in society than the craftsman, and this for a particular reason: the artist claimed originality for his work; originality is the trait of single, lone individuals. Few Renaissance artists in fact worked in isolation. The craft workshop continued as the artist's studio, filled with assistants and apprentices, but the masters of these studios did indeed put a new value on the originality of the work done in them; originality was a value that was not celebrated by the rituals of medieval guilds. The contrast still informs our thinking: art seems to draw attention to work that is unique or at least distinctive, whereas craft names a more anonymous, collective, and continued practice. But we should be suspicious of this contrast. Originality is also a social label, and originals form peculiar bonds with other people.

The patrons of Renaissance artists and the market for their art changed as court society grew at the expense of medieval communes. Clients had an increasingly personal relationship to connection to the masters of the studios. Often they did not understand what the artists were attempting to achieve, yet they just as often asserted their authority to judge the work's worth. If original in his labors, the artist lacked a collective shield, as the member of a community, against these verdicts. The artist's only defense against intrusion was, "You do not understand me," a not entirely enticing selling point. Again there is a modern resonance: who is fit to judge originality? Maker or consumer?

The most famous goldsmith of the Renaissance, Benvenuto Cellini, confronted these issues in his *Autobiography*, which he began writing in 1558. His book opens confidently, with a sonnet boasting of two accomplishments. The first is about his life: "I have been involved in astounding exploits and I have lived to tell the tale." Born in Florence in 1500, Cellini was variously imprisoned for sodomy and the father of eight children; an astrologer; poisoned deliberately, once by powdered diamonds and later by a "delicious sauce" prepared by a "vicious priest"; the murderer of a postman; a naturalized French citizen who loathed France; a soldier who spied for the army he fought against; . . . the catalogue of such amazing incidents is endless.

The second advertisement is for his work. He boasts: "In my art / I have surpassed many and arrived at the level of the / only one who was my better."[21] One master—Michelangelo—and no equals; none of his peers is able to rise to his level nor is as original. A famous golden saltcellar that Cellini made in 1543 for Francis I of France (now in the Kunsthistorisches Museum, Vienna) served as evidence for this boast. Not even that haughty monarch could casually have taken salt from it. The bowl holding the salt is submerged in a golden clutter. On its crown male and female golden figures represents the Sea and the Earth (salt belonging to both realms), while on the ebony base bas-reliefs of figures represent Night, Day, Twilight, and Dawn plus four Winds (Night and Day pay direct homage to Michelangelo's sculpting of these same figures on the Medici tombs). This glorious object was meant to provoke amazement and it did.

Before inquiring into what might make this a work of art rather than a piece of craft, we should place Cellini among his fellows. Throughout the Middle Ages there were masters as well as journeymen who, as the

Livre des métiers noted, wished to set up on their own as individual entrepreneurs. These craft entrepreneurs wanted simply to pay assistants without being obliged to train them. Their prosperity depended on making a name for their goods as what we today would call a "brand label."

This last fact sent an ever-more personal signal of distinction. Medieval guilds did not tend to emphasize individual differences within a town's workshops; the guild's collective effort of control names where a cup or coat was made rather than who made it. In the material culture of the Renaissance, naming the maker became increasingly important to the sale of a wide variety of goods, even the most prosaic. Cellini's saltcellar falls within this general, branding pattern. The very fact that a dish to hold salt had become an elaborate object transcending any mere functional purpose called attention to it and to its maker.

Around 1100, a change in the relation of goldsmiths to other craftsmen slowly appeared, one remarked in Alan of Lille's *Anticlaudianus* in the early 1180s. Before this time, the forms of working gold into decorative objects had set the pace for painting and glassmaking, the gold frame orienting the objects within it. About this time, the craft historian T. E. Heslop observes, the process slowly began to reverse: "What we would call naturalism, most readily associated with painting and sculpture, came to dominate to such an extent that goldsmiths had to cultivate the arts of drawing and modelling as never before."[22] Cellini's pictures in gold are one result of this process: they are a "new" kind of goldsmithing, in part simply because they incorporate into metalwork another craft practice, that of drawing.

Cellini kept a certain allegiance to the craft workshops from which his art emerged. He was never ashamed of the foundry, its dirt, noise, and sweat. Moreover, he hewed to the traditional craft value placed on truthfulness. In the *Autobiography* he recounts the struggle to extract gold, real gold and lots of it, from masses of raw ore—whereas even his richest patrons would have been content with the illusion of surface gilding. In carpenter's terms, Cellini hated veneers. He wanted "honest gold" and held to this same standard of truthfulness in the other materials he worked with, even in cheap metals like brass. It had to be pure, so that things would look what they are.

We'd thus risk vulgarizing Cellini's autobiography to see it simply as self-serving. Indeed, though in the economy of the time artisans of all sorts advertised the individual merits of their work, Cellini's book itself does not fall into the category of publicity. He chose not to publish the *Autobiography* in his lifetime; he wrote it for himself and left it to posterity. Yet, like many other goods, his saltcellar was taken to have public value because it exposed and expressed the inner character of its maker. Francis I certainly thought so, exclaiming, "Here is Cellini himself!"

Distinction of this sort carried material rewards. As the historian John Hale points out, many artists prospered thanks to the distinctiveness of their work: Lucas Cranach the Elder's house in Wittenberg was a small palace, as was Giorgio Vasari's in Arezzo.[23] Lorenzo Ghiberti, Sandro Botticelli, and Andrea del Verrocchio all trained as goldsmiths. So far as we can determine, they were wealthier than their peers who remained strictly within the guild orbit of assay and raw material production.

Authority in the generic sense relies on a basic fact of power: the master sets out the terms of work that others do at his direction. The Renaissance artist's atelier differed little in this from the medieval workshop or the modern scientific laboratory. In an artist's atelier, the master made the overall design in the painting and then filled in the most expressive parts, such as the heads. But the Renaissance studio existed in the first place because of the master's distinctive talents; the point was not to produce pictures as such but rather to create *his* pictures or pictures in his manner. Originality gave a particular importance to face-to-face relations in the studio. Unlike goldsmith assayers, the artist's assistants had to remain in the physical presence of their masters; originality is hard to write down in a rulebook you might pack in your luggage.

"Originality" traces its origins back one Greek word, *poesis*, which Plato and others used to mean "something where before there was nothing." Originality is a marker of time; it denotes the *sudden* appearance of something where before there was nothing, and because something suddenly comes into existence, it arouses in us emotions of wonder and awe. In the Renaissance, the appearance of something sudden was connected to the art—the genius, if you will—of an individual.

We'd certainly err by imagining that medieval craftsmen were entirely resistant to innovation, but their craftwork changed slowly and as the result of collective effort. For instance, the immense Salisbury Cathedral began, in 1220–1225, as a set of stone posts and beams that established the Lady Chapel at one end of the future cathedral.[24] The builders had a general idea of the cathedral's eventual size, but no more. However, the proportions of the beams in the Lady Chapel suggested a larger building's engineering DNA and were articulated in the big nave and two transepts built from 1225 to about 1250. From 1250 to 1280, this DNA then generated the cloister, treasury, and chapter house; in the chapter house the original geometries, meant for a square structure, were now adapted to an octagon, in the treasury to a six-sided vault. How did the builders achieve this astonishing construction? There was no one single architect; the masons had no blueprints. Rather, the gestures with which the building began evolved in principles and were collectively managed over three generations. Each event in building practice became absorbed in the fabric of instructing and regulating the next generation.

The result is a striking building, a distinctive building embodying innovations in construction, but it is not original in the sense that Cellini's saltcellar is: an amazing blow, a painting in pure gold. As earlier remarked, the "secret" of originality here is that the two-dimensional practice of drawing has been transferred to the three dimensions of gold, and Cellini pushed this transfer to an extreme that his contemporaries had not imagined possible.

But originality carried a price. Originality could fail to provide autonomy. Cellini's *Autobiography* is a case study of how originality could be new kinds of social dependence and, indeed, humiliation. Cellini left the guild realm of assay and metal production only to enter court life with all its intrigues of patronage. With no corporate guarantee for the worth of his work, Cellini had to charm, hector, and plead with kings and princes of the Church. These were unequal trials of strength. Confrontational and self-righteous as Cellini could be to patrons, ultimately his art depended on them. There was in Cellini's life a telling moment when this unequal trial of strength became clear to him. He sent Philip II of Spain the sculpture of a naked Christ in marble, to which the king rather wickedly added a fig leaf made of gold. Cellini protested that the distinctive character of the Christ was spoiled, to which Philip II replied, "It's mine."

We would say now this is a matter of integrity—the integrity of the thing in itself—but it's also a matter of the maker's social standing. Cellini, as he repeatedly stresses in his autobiography, was not to be measured like a courtier, by a formal title or a post at court. But any person who stands out still has then to *prove* him or herself to others. The medieval goldsmith furnished proof of his worth through communal rituals, proof about the work's worth through the process of proceeding slowly and carefully. These are irrelevant standards for judging originality. Put yourself in Philip II's elegant shoes: faced with an original and so unfamiliar object, how would you evaluate its worth? Confronted with Cellini's declaration, "I am an artist! Don't touch what I've done!" you, in your kingly majesty, might well think, "How dare he?"

A final, signal fact about Cellini's *Autobiography* is that his experiences of unrequited dependency and misunderstanding heightened his self-consciousness. Again and again in these pages, humiliation at the hands of a patron drives the writer to bouts of introspection. This condition was just the opposite of the passive, and so brooding isolates pictured in the pages of Burton's *Anatomy of Melancholy.* Here the Renaissance artist may well be the emblematic first modern man: active, and so suffering, driven inward, searching for a refuge in his "autonomous creativity." In this view, creativity lies within us, no matter how society treats us.

That belief became powerfully grounded in Renaissance philosophy. It appeared in the writings of the philosopher Pico della Mirandola, who envisaged *Homo faber* to mean "man as his own maker." Pico was one of Hannah Arendt's (unacknowledged) sources; his *Oration on the Dignity of Man* of 1486 was based on the conviction that, as the force of custom and tradition wanes, people have to "make experience" for themselves. Each person's life is a narrative in which the author does not know how the story will turn out. Pico's figure for *Homo faber* was Odysseus, voyaging through the world, not knowing where he would land. A kindred idea of man as his own maker also appears in Shakespeare, when Coriolanus asserts, "I am my own maker," and thus defies the adage of Augustine, who warned, "Hands off the self! Touch it and you make a ruin!"[25]

Art plays a particular role in this life voyage, at least for artists. The work of art become like a buoy at sea, marking out the journey. Unlike a sailor, though, the artist charts his own course by making these buoys for himself. This is how, for instance, Giorgio Vasari proceeds in *The Lives of the Artists* (1568), one of the first books ever written to chart artistic careers. Vasari's "lives" concern artists who develop within, who brought forth works despite all impediments, artists whose creative urge is autonomous. Works of art are the evidence of an inner life sustained even in the face of humiliation and incomprehension—as indeed Cellini sometimes faced. Renaissance artists discovered that originality does not provide a solid *social* foundation of autonomy.

The scorned or misunderstood artist has a long trajectory in Western high culture, in all the arts. Cellini is the troubled ancestor of

Mozart in his dealings with the bishop of Salzburg in the eighteenth century, of Le Corbusier's struggles with a stodgy Harvard University in trying to construct the Carpenter Center for the Visual Arts in the twentieth. Originality brings to the surface the power relations between artist and patron. In this regard, the sociologist Norbert Elias reminds us that in court societies the bond of mutual obligation was distorted. The duke or cardinal paid the tradesmen's bills when it suited him, if at all; Cellini, like many others, died with large uncollected royal debts.

Cellini's story does, in sum, enable a certain a sociological contrast between craft and art. The two are distinguished, first, by agency: art has one guiding or dominant agent, craft has a collective agent. They are, next, distinguished by time: the sudden versus the slow. Last, they are indeed distinguished by autonomy, but surprisingly so: the lone, original artist may have had less autonomy, be more dependent on uncomprehending or willful power, and so be more vulnerable, than were the body of craftsmen. These differences still matter in their content to people who are not among the small band of professional artists.

Unmotivated workers like the Soviet construction workers, depressed workers like the British doctors and nurses suffer not so much from the work they do as by how it is organized. This is why we should not give up on the workshop as a social space. Workshops present and past have glued people together through work rituals, whether these be shared cup of tea or the urban parade; through mentoring, whether the formal surrogate parenting of medieval times or informal advising on the worksite; through face-to-face sharing of information.

The historical turn is for these reasons more complicated than a story of decline; a new, disturbing set of work values was added to the sociable workshop. Modern managerial ideology urges even the lowliest worker to work "creatively" and evince originality. In the past the satisfaction of this command proved a recipe for distress. The Renaissance artist still needed a workshop, and his assistants in it undoubtedly learned from the example of their master. The master's own mastery changed in content; claims for his distinctiveness and originality now posed a motivational problem for him. He would need the will to fight in order to validate these claims. His honor took on an adversarial character. The workshop would serve him as a refuge from society.

"His Secrets Died with Him"
In Stradivari's Workshop

In the *Autobiography,* Cellini says that the "secrets of his art would die" with him.[26] His daring and innovation certainly could not be passed down through pageants, feasts, and prayers of earlier times; the value of the work lodged in its originality. So here was a concrete limit placed on the long-term viable life of the workshop. In modern parlance, knowledge transfer became difficult; the master's originality inhibited the transfer. This difficulty remains, in scientific laboratories as much as in artist's studios. Although in a lab the neophyte can be readily inducted in procedures, it's harder for a scientist to pass on the capacity to look suspiciously for new problems in the course of solving old ones or to explain the intuition formed from experience that a problem is likely to wind up a dead-end.

The difficulty of knowledge transfer poses a question about *why* it is should be so difficult, why it becomes a personal secret. This isn't the case in music conservatories, for instance; both through individual and master classes, and in workshop discussions, expression is constantly analyzed and refined. In the famous Class 19 conducted by Mstislav Rostropovich at the Moscow Conservatory in the 1950s and 1960s, the great cellist used all manner of weapons—novels, jokes, and vodka, as well as strict musical analysis—to bludgeon his pupils into becoming themselves more individually expressive.[27] Yet in the fabrication of musical instruments, the secrets of masters like Antonio Stradivari or Guarneri del Gesù have indeed died with them. Mountains of cash and endless experiments have failed to prize out the secrets of these masters. Something in the character of these workshops must have inhibited knowledge transfer.

When Antonio Stradivari began making violins, he formed part of a tradition whose standards on carving the belly, backs, and peg boxes of stringed instruments had been set by Andrea Amati a century earlier. Subsequent luthiers (the word represents makers of varied stringed instruments) paid fealty to these Cremona masters and their Austrian neighbor Jacob Stainer. Many trained in the workshops of their disciples; others learned by repairing old instruments that came into their hands. Carving books existed from the origins of *lutherie* in the Renaissance, but the texts were expensive to produce and few in number; technical training involved hands-on contact with the instruments and on spoken explanation passed generation to generation. The young luthier would have held in his hands, copied, or repaired an Amati original or prototype. This was the method of knowledge transfer that Stradivari inherited.

Inside, the workshop of Stradivari also looked back in that, like that of other luthiers, the physical house was both a place of work and a home, filled with Stradivari's family and many young male apprentices and journeymen lodgers. Labor dominated all waking hours. The workshop operated from dawn to dusk, with the work team literally rooted to the benches, since the unmarried apprentices slept underneath them on bags of straw. As in the past, Stradivari's male children learning the business were subjected to the same formal rules as lodger apprentices.

Youngsters at work usually did such preparatory labor as soaking wood in water, rough molding, and rough cutting. Journeymen higher up did finer belly cutting and neck assembly, and the master himself took charge of the ultimate installation of the parts and of varnishing, the protective coating of the wood being the ultimate guarantor of its sound. The master, however, was everywhere present in the production. We know, thanks to the researches of Tony Faber, that Stradivari occupied himself with the smallest details in the production of his violins. Though he rarely traveled, in the house he was in constant motion, not confined to an office—an imperious, even hectoring character who sometimes threw spectacular tantrums, oozing instructions and exhortations.[28]

Yet the medieval goldsmith would not have felt at home here. Like Cellini's, the Stradivari workshop revolved around the extraordinary talents of an individual. But Cellini might also have trouble understanding it: the master now presented himself to the open market, rather than to one or a few patrons. The number of luthiers and the volume of instruments had by Stradivari's time also radically expanded. Supply began to exceed demand. Even Stradivari, famous as he early on became, had to worry about markets because he dealt with many private clients and this market patronage proved fickle, especially at the end of his long life. In the general economic decline of the 1720s his workshop had to trim costs, and much of its output went into stock.[29] Cracks in the workshop hierarchy widened owing to the uncertainties of the open market; ambitious apprentices, seeing that even so famous a master had an uncertain fate, began to buy out or beg off the last years of their contracts. What was unusual in the time of the *Livre des métiers* had now become normal: the open market shrank the time frame of the master's dominion.

The market also deepened those inequalities whose seed was planted in the Renaissance branding of craft goods. As early as 1680, Stradivari's success put pressure on other families like the Guarneri, whose business was founded by Andrea Guarneri. The grandson Bartolomeo Giuseppe, known as "del Gesù," worked in the shadow of

Stradivari. "In contrast to Antonio Stradivari's vast international cli-
entele," Guarneri's biographer tells us, his "customers were by and
large . . . humble Cremonese players who [performed in] palaces and
churches in and around Cremona."[30] As great a maker as Stradivari,
del Gesù could sustain his workshop for only fifteen years; he had even
more trouble holding onto the best apprentices.

When Antonio Stradivari died, he passed on the business to his two
sons, Omobono and Francesco, who never married and who spent
their adult lives in their father's house as his servant-heirs. They were
able to trade on his name for several years, but the business eventually
foundered. He had not taught, he could not teach either of them how
to be a genius. (The work of theirs I've held and played is excellent, but
no more than that.)

This is the brief outline of a workshop death. For nearly three
centuries luthiers have struggled to revive this corpse in order to recover the secrets of Stradivari and Guarnieri del Gesú that died with
them. Even while the Stradivari sons were alive, this investigation of
originality began. Guarnieri del Gesú's imitators set to work about
eighty years after his death, abetted by the false story that he made his
greatest violins while in prison. Today analysis of the masters' work
proceeds on three fronts: exact physical copies of the instruments'
form; chemical analyses of the varnish; and work that reasons backward from the sound (the idea here being that one could copy the
sound in instruments that do not look like a Strad or a Guarneri). Even
so, as the violinist Arnold Steinhardt of the Guarneri String Quartet
has remarked, the professional musician can almost instantly distinguish between the original and any copy.[31]

Missing in these analyses is a reconstruction of the workshops of
the master—more precisely, one element that has irretrievably gone
missing. This is the absorption into tacit knowledge, unspoken and
uncodified in words, that occurred there and became a matter of habit,
the thousand little everyday moves that add up in sum to a practice.

The most significant fact we know about Stravidari's workshop was that he was all over it, popping up unexpectedly everywhere, gathering in and processing those thousands of bits of information that could not signify in the same way to assistants who were doing just one part. The same thing has been true in scientific labs run by idiosyncratic geniuses; the master's head becomes stuffed with information only he or she can see the point of. This is why the secrets of the physicist Enrico Fermi as a great experimenter can't be fathomed by poring over the minutiae of his lab procedures.

To put this observation abstractly: in a workshop where the master's individuality and distinctiveness dominates, tacit knowledge is also likely to dominate. Once the master dies, all the clues, moves, and insights he or she has gathered into the totality of the work cannot be reconstructed; there's no way to ask him or her to make the tacit explicit.

In theory the well-run workshop should balance tacit and explicit knowledge. Masters should be pestered to explain themselves, to dredge out the assemblage of clues and moves they have absorbed in silence within—if only they could, and if only they would. Much of their very authority derives from seeing what others don't see, knowing what they don't know; their authority is made manifest in their silence. Would we then sacrifice Stradivari's cellos and violins for the sake of a more democratic workshop?

In the seventeenth century the person most alive to the problem of knowledge transfer was the poet John Donne. He couched the problem of singularity in terms of scientific discovery, imagining the innovator as a phoenix rising from the ashes of received truth and tradition, in these famous lines:

> Prince, Subject, Father, Son, are things forgot,
> For every man alone thinks he hath got
> To be a Phoenix, and that then can be
> None of that kind, of which he is, but he.[32]

Today the difficulty of recovering the secrets of genius illuminates the contrast we made in the first chapter between the two craft standards of quality: the absolute standard versus quality of practice. The masters set an absolute standard, one that often proves impossible to reproduce. But the democratic question just posed should be taken seriously. Why try to recover someone else's originality? The modern luthier wants to get on with the business of making violins; the luthier wants to make the best violins possible according to his or her bright-enough lights rather than be immobilized, imprisoned by fruitless imitation. This is the claim of practice against correctness. And yet. The Stradivarius Davidoff cello defines what a cello can be, what is possible; it sets a standard that, once you've heard it, you can never forget, particularly if you happen to be making a cello.

"His secrets died with him" casts a particular shadow in science. The sociologist Robert K. Merton sought to explain knowledge transfer in science by invoking the famous image of "standing on the shoulders of giants."[33] By that he meant two things: first, that the work of great scientists sets the terms of reference, the orbits, within which lesser standard scientists revolve; and second, that knowledge is additive and accumulative; it builds up in time as people stand on the giants' shoulders, like those human pillars in the circus.

In craftwork, Merton's idea would apply to the makers of Salisbury Cathedral, whose labors worked within the orbit of their forebears—whether giants or not. The idea would make sense of the rituals of the medieval goldsmiths; these celebrated the standards set by the monastic founders of the guild as fathers. Though his model illuminates medieval masons and goldsmiths, it is harder to apply to the more modern realm of Stradivari's workshop. The desire to stand on the luthier's shoulders has certainly existed ever since his death; finding a footing has proved frustrating; thinking about a giant can prove paralyzing. In practice we do something that is distinctive whenever we solve thorny practical issues, no matter how small. And yet a scientist can no more forget Einstein's ambition than an instrument maker a Stradivarius's sound.

✳   ✳   ✳

The history of the workshop shows, in sum, a recipe for binding people tightly together. The essential ingredients of this recipe were religion and ritual. A more secular age replaced these ingredients with originality—a condition separate in its practical terms from autonomy, originality implying in the workshop a new form of authority, an authority frequently short-lived and silent.

One mark of the modern world is that we have become as worried about paying obeisance to authority in this personalized form as to authority of an older, more religious sort. To quote just one instance of this worry: Cellini's near-contemporary Étienne de La Boétie was one of the first to question submission to higher authority through either admiration or imitation. In his view, people are more capable of freedom. In the *Discourse of Voluntary Servitude,* he wrote: "So many men, so many villages, so many cities, so many nations sometimes suffer under a single tyrant who has not other power than the power they give; who could do them absolutely no injury unless they preferred to put up with him rather than contradict him. . . . It is therefore the inhabitants themselves who permit, or rather, bring about their own servitude."[34] Servitude through admiration or tradition must be cast off. If correct, then the workshop cannot be a comfortable home for the craftsman, for its very essence lies in the personalized, face-to-face authority of knowledge. And yet it is a necessary home. Since there can be no skilled work without standards, it is infinitely preferable that these standards be embodied in a human being than in a lifeless, static code of practice. The craftsman's workshop is one site in which the modern, perhaps unresolvable conflict between autonomy and authority plays out.

CHAPTER THREE

Machines

The greatest dilemma faced by the modern artisan-craftsman is the machine. Is it a friendly tool or an enemy replacing work of the human hand? In the economic history of skilled manual labor, machinery that began as a friend has often ended up as an enemy. Weavers, bakers, and steelworkers have all embraced tools that eventually turned against them. Today the advent of microelectronics means that intelligent machines can invade realms of white-collar labor like medical diagnosis or financial services once reserved for human judgment.

The seduction of CAD lies in its speed, the fact it never tires, and indeed in the reality that its capacities to compute are superior to those of anyone working out a drawing by hand. Yet people can pay a personal price for mechanization; misuse of CAD programming diminished the mental understanding of its users. This seems a sad story, but perhaps it can be told in a different way. Might we, in our very comparative imperfection, learn something positive about being human?

Workers as much as writers struggled with this philosophical question at the dawn of the Industrial Age in the eighteenth century. Their observations and arguments were based on an experience of material culture that had long predated machine production.

As early as the fifteenth century, Europe had been suffused by what the historian Simon Schama has called "an embarrassment of riches," a new cornucopia of material goods.[1] In the Renaissance, trade with non-Europeans and the ever-greater number of artisans working in towns swelled the goods at people's disposal. Jerry Brotton and Lisa Jardine evoke the "tide of new material objects" first flooding into Italian homes in the fifteenth century.[2] By the early 1600s in the Netherlands, Britain, and France, "there was an unprecedented demand for desks, tables, sideboards, sets of hanging shelves and cupboards, all suited to the housing and display of new possessions," in the words of John Hale.[3] As material abundance seeped downward, it extended to the most ordinary matters, like possessing several pots to cook with, different plates to eat off, more than a single pair of shoes to wear, and different clothes for varying seasons. Things that we now taken for granted as necessities were increasingly available to ordinary people.[4]

It was in chronicling this flood tide of things that Schama applied the phrase "an embarrassment of riches" to the sixteenth- and seventeenth-century Dutch, who were long used to scrimping and saving. The phrase can be misleading, since at the dawn of the modern era anxiety was often people's reaction to the wealth of things at their disposal. The enriched world of objects prompted intense theological worry in both Reformation and Counter-Reformation circles about material seduction; beneath the theological horizon, this fear attached even to such innocuous objects of daily life as children's toys.

In the late sixteenth and early seventeenth centuries European children first began to enjoy an abundance of toys. Previously—and strangely to us—adults amused themselves with dolls, toy soldiers, and the other artifacts of childhood; such toys were few in number and costly. As the cost went down the number of toys increased. In this process toy objects also became the distinctive property of children. The increase in toys introduced the first discussions—indeed the very concept—of "spoiling" children.

The advent of machines in the eighteenth century only increased the anxiety of riches. Age-old questions of deprivation and lack did not go away—the masses of Europeans still lived in a scarcity society—but machine production of tableware, clothing, bricks, and glass added to this other dimension of worry: how to use these goods well, what abundance might be for, how not to be spoiled by possessions.

On balance, the eighteenth century embraced the virtue of abundance, mechanically produced, and so should we. As consumers the machine then promised and by the twenty-first century has infinitely improved the quality of our lives; more and better medicines, houses, food—an endless list. The material quality of life for the European working poor in modern times is in many ways higher than of the bourgeois classes of the seventeenth century. Even Martin Heidegger eventually installed electricity and modern plumbing in his Black Forest hut. What Enlightenment writers worried more about was the machine's productive side, its influences on the experience of making—and these worries remain.

To some figures in the Enlightenment, the superiority of machines was no cause for human despair. Isaac Newton had after all depicted all of nature as a giant machine, a view taken to an extreme in the eighteenth century by writers like Julien Offray de la Mettrie. Other writers subscribed to views of rational improvement, progress, and the "perfectibility of Man," modeled on the efficiency of new machinery like James Watt's steam engine. But still others thought in a different way about this model, and not as traditionalists refusing the new: rather, the comparison of man and machine caused them to think more about man. Human virtues of restraint and simplicity came to the fore as man's contribution to human culture; none of these sentiments could be called mechanical. People so minded had a particular interest in craftsmanship: it seemed to mediate between machined abundance and the modestly humane.

Socially, craftsmen took a new turn. Watt's eighteenth-century steam engine, originally built in workshop conditions that resembled the studio of Antonio Stradivari, soon came to be fabricated, and then deployed, in a radically different social setting. The recipe for making a steam engine became entirely codifiable by 1823 in documents; the master—and Watt himself behaved like a Stradivari of engineering—no longer had secrets to keep. This mirrors a larger change in nineteenth-century engineering that has already appeared to us in the history of the blueprint: a movement from hands-on knowledge to the dominant authority of explicit knowledge. Workshop work of course continued in various forms, in the arts, in everyday commerce, as in the sciences, but the workshop seemed increasing merely the means to establishing another institution: the workshop as a way station to the factory.

As machine culture matured, the craftsman in the nineteenth century appeared ever less a mediator and ever more an enemy of the machine. Now, against the rigorous perfection of the machine, the craftsman became an emblem of human individuality, this emblem composed concretely by the positive value placed on variations, flaws, and irregularities in handwork. Eighteenth-century glassmaking had foreshadowed this change in cultural values; now the writings of John Ruskin, the great Romantic analyst of craft, regretted the loss of the workshops of the preindustrial past and made of the craftsman's labors in his own age a blazon of resistance—resistance to capitalism coupled with resistance to machines.

These cultural and social changes remain with us. Culturally we are still struggling to understand our limits positively, in comparison to the mechanical; socially we are still struggling with anti-technologism; craftwork remains the focus of both.

The Mirror Tool
Replicants and Robots

A mirror-tool—my coinage—is an implement that invites us to think about ourselves. There are two kinds of mirror-tools. These are the replicant and the robot.

The modern name for the first comes from the film *Blade Runner*, which features copies of human beings. The perfect women created in Ira Levin's novel *The Stepford Wives* are also replicants. In the real world, pacemakers for the heart serve as replicant machines, providing the energy charge needed for the heart to function as it should biologically. All these artifices mirror us by mimicking us.

By contrast, a robotic machine is ourselves enlarged: it is stronger, works faster, and never tires. Still, we make sense of its functions by referring to our own human measure. The little iPod possesses, for instance, the memory of a robot; currently, the machine is capable of containing more than thirty-five thousand minutes of music, nearly the entire written output of J. S. Bach, which is more than any human brain can remember. The robot is like a mirror in a fun fair, enlarging human memory to giant size. Yet this giant memory is organized technically to serve the small human measure of songs or other music of comprehensible length. iPod listeners never use the full memory capacity of the machine at a given moment.

An ambiguous zone exists between replicant and robot, between mimicking and enlarging. In the film *Blade Runner* the replicant copies of human beings enlarge the particularly brutal, vicious aspects of everyday life. Conversely Mary Shelley's *Frankenstein* recounts the story of a man-made giant who wants to be a replicant, treated just as a normal human being. But, in general, the replicant shows us as we are, the robot as we might be.

Size and scale provide two measures of how large is "enlarged." In architecture, very large buildings can seem on an intimate human scale, whereas some small-sized structures feel very big. To the historian Geoffrey Scott, vast Baroque churches seem intimate in scale because their undulating walls and decor mimic the motions the human body makes, whereas Bramante's motionless little Tempietto feels as big, as enlarged, as the Pantheon on which it is modeled.[5] Just the same distinction between size and scale applies to machines; the kidney dialysis machine is a large replicant, the atmosphere-eating robots in the astrophysicist Martin Rees's cabinet of horrors are microrobots.

In the Enlightenment, when precise replicants began to be constructed, the machines seemed at first benign toys. In 1738 a shop in Paris displayed an extraordinary automaton constructed by Jacques de Vaucanson, a Jesuit-educated mechanical inventor. Vaucanson's Flute Player was a life-size figure five and a half feet tall that played the flute. The wonder was the flute itself, for a mechanical figure could much more easily play the harpsichord, which would require the machine only to strike a key. The problem with playing a flute is that the tone comes through breathing as well as finger action. Soon after, Vaucanson created his Shitting Duck, a mechanical creature that appeared to ingest grains with its mouth and defecate in short order at its anus. The Shitting Duck proved to be a fraud (the anus was stuffed), though an interesting one; the Flute Player was genuine.[6]

To make the Flute Player work, Vaucanson created, at the figure's base, a complicated system of nine bellows that passed into the robot's chest through three pipes, which provided the breath; a separate set of levers operated a mechanical tongue, and another set moved the lips in and out. The whole thing was a mechanical marvel. Voltaire evoked the awe it aroused in calling Vaucanson "the modern Prometheus."

But this machine remained a replicant because the Flute Player was no god. Vaucanson's automaton played no faster than a human flutist. As an artist it was limited, producing only simple loud-soft contrasts and unable to play legato, where one note dissolves liquidly into the next. So this was a reassuring replicant; its workings could be measured by the standards of human music making. The imaginative stimulus it afforded visitors to Vaucanson's shop lay in wondering about the means of mimicry: how could nine bellows attached to three pipes be akin to human breathing?

This replicant, unfortunately, bred a robot. Louis XV, though not scientifically minded, suspected that Vaucanson's talents could be put to better use than making an intriguing toy. In 1741 he gave the inventor charge of French silk manufacturing. The silk produced in early-eighteenth-century France, particularly in Lyon, was not of uniformly good quality: the tools were poor, the weavers poorly paid and often on strike. Drawing on his knowledge of the replicant, Vaucanson sought to produce a robot that would eliminate the human problem.

Vaucanson transferred the knowledge of breathing tension he had gained in The Flute Player to weaving machines that had to hold threads in tension. The shuttle action in his machines moved by minutely, precisely measuring the tension, and so the tightness, of weave; previously workers proceeded by "feel" and visual inspection. His loom in turn increased the number of colored strands of silk that could be held in equal tension during the weaving process, far more strands than could previously be managed by two human hands.

In Lyon, as elsewhere, investment in such machines became cheaper than investment in labor, as well as doing better work. Gaby Wood gets at the conundrum in observing that whereas the Flute Player "was designed for man's entertainment," Vaucanson's looms in Lyons were "meant to show man that he was dispensable."[7] Lyonnais weavers assaulted Vaucanson in the streets whenever in the 1740s and 1750s he dared appear. He provoked them further by designing a machine to weave an intricate design of flowers and birds, this complicated loom powered by a donkey.

Thus began the classic story of displacement of craftsman by the machine. Vaucanson's machines seem an economic germ that has sickened the modern artisan; the robot rather than the replicant taught this negative, threatening story of human limits. What kindlier mirror-tools would show a more positive image?

The Enlightened Craftsman
Diderot's Encyclopedia

To unpack this question we will need to plunge into the word *Enlightenment* itself, and we could easily drown in the process. Literally, *enlightenment,* German *Aufklärung,* and French *éclaircissement* all mean "to shed light on"; one French phrase for the historical Enlightenment, *siècle des Lumières,* is "century of luminaries." Understood as the process of casting the light of reason over the manners and mores of society, Enlightenment became a buzzword in the eighteenth century (much as "identity" is today), the word becoming current in Paris in the 1720s and reaching Berlin a generation later. There was a midcentury American Enlightenment whose leading light was Benjamin Franklin and a Scottish Enlightenment composed of philosophers and economists seeking for mental sunlight in the mists of Edinburgh.

Perhaps the most concise way to frame "the Enlightenment's" relation to material culture, and in particular to the machine, is to travel mentally to Berlin. In December 1783, the theologian Johann Zöllner invited readers of the *Berlinische Monatsschrift* to respond to the question, "What is Enlightenment?" This newspaper series then ran for twelve years. Many contributors answered his question by invoking progress and improvement. The energy for Enlightenment lay in these words; man could take greater control over his material circumstances. Pastor Zöllner found quite troubling these responses, which celebrated the expansion of human powers rather than their limitation. His parishioners seemed studiously polite when he read out in church the Bible's stories about human sins; they were merely courteous when he spoke to them about the dangers facing their immortal souls. Tolerance had become the urbane cousin of condescension; confident reason was in a way worse than the fire-breathing, satanic heresies of the past.

The leading writers who responded to his appeal had a passion of their own: this was the human adult's capacity to live without dogma. The greatest statement of this passionate conviction came from Immanuel Kant, who wrote in the September 30 issue of the *Berlinische Monatsscrift* of 1784: "Enlightenment is mankind's exit from its self-incurred immaturity. *Immaturity* is the inability to make use of one's own understanding without the guidance of another. *Self-incurred* is this inability, if its cause lies not in the lack of understanding but rather in the lack of resolution and the courage to use it without the guidance of another. *Sapere aude!* Have the courage to use your own understanding! is thus the motto of enlightenment."[8] The emphasis here is on the *act* of reasoning. Freedom in reasoning improves the mind by casting off childish certainties.

Reasoning of this free sort has nothing mechanical about it. The eighteenth century, it is sometimes said, took too much to heart Newtonian mechanics. Voltaire did so by asserting that the machinery of nature explicated in Newton's pages, precise and exactly balanced, should serve as a model for the social order, physics providing society an absolute standard. This was not Kant's way of reasoning. He hoped of course that destructive superstitions would lose their hold on the adult mind but did not imagine the machine's routines as a substitute for prayer. The free mind will always subject its own regulations and rules to critical judgment and therefore change them; Kant's focus is on judging and reflection upon rather than on planning order. Can free reason degrade, then, to the opposite pole of disorder? As the French Revolution darkened, even political activists like Johann Adam Bergk wondered if disembodied free reasoning played a role in the collective chaos. In 1796, the *Berlinische Monatsschrift* shut down the subject.

The few sentences above allude to an immense sea in which reason, revolution, and tradition form the main currents. Lost in these currents are those pages of the newspaper's debate in which culture of a more everyday material sort was discussed. The most Enlightening of these discussions came from Moses Mendelssohn. By origin a poor Jewish migrant to Berlin, intending there to become a rabbi, Mendelssohn came to reject the Talmudic training of the shuls as too narrow; he made himself into a philosopher who read German, Greek, and Latin. In 1767 he wrote *Phaidon,* a book breaking the faith of his fathers in order to declare his belief in a religion of Nature, a materialist Enlightenment. Mendelssohn's contribution to the newspaper debate about Enlightenment built on this materialism.

He devised an equation: *Bildung* = *Kultur* + *Aufklärung.*[9] *Bildung* implies at once education, the formation of values, and the behavior by which one steer's one's course in social relations. *Aufklarüng* is Kant's free reason. *Kultur,* says Mendelssohn, denotes the practical realm of "things done and not done," rather than good manners and refined taste.[10] Mendelssohn took a wide and generous view of practical culture. He believed that ordinary "things done and not done" are as worthy as any abstraction; in rationally reflecting upon them, we improve ourselves.

Bildung = *Kultur* + *Aufklärung* was a distillation of reading Mendelssohn had done in a remarkable book.[11] This was *The Encyclopedia, or Dictionary of Arts and Crafts,* edited principally by Denis Diderot. Appearing from 1751 to 1772, the thirty-five-volume *Encyclopedia* became a best-seller read by every one from Catherine the Great in Russia to merchants in New York.[12] Its volumes exhaustively described in words and pictures how practical things get done and proposed ways to improve them. There was a great difference in emphasis between the *encyclopédistes* and the German writers: for the French, daily practices of laboring are the focus rather than Kantian self-understanding or Mendelssohnian self-formation. From this emphasis followed the *Encyclopedia*'s credo. It celebrated those who are committed to doing work well for its own sake; the craftsman stood out as the emblem of

Enlightenment. But over these exemplary men and women hung the specter of Vaucanson's robots, their Newtonian ghosts.

To understand this bible of craftsmanship one has to understand its author's motives. Diderot was a poor provincial who migrated to Paris, where he talked endlessly, had too many friends, and spent other people's money.[13] Much of Diderot's life was wasted in literary hackwork to pay his debts; the *Encyclopedia* seemed to him at first just another way to stave off his creditors. The project began as a translation into French of Ephraim Chambers's English *Universal Dictionary of Arts and Sciences* (1728), a charming and rather disorganized collection of pieces by a "virtuoso" of the sciences—a "virtuoso" meaning in the mid-eighteenth century an amateur with a lively curiosity. One trade of the literary hack consisted in feeding the curiosity of the virtuoso, providing digestible bits of information and perhaps a few well-turned phrases the virtuoso could produce as his own in polite conversation.

The prospect of translating several hundred pages of such tasty morsels quite rightly depressed a man of Diderot's gifts. Once launched into the work, he transformed it. Chambers's text was soon cast aside; collaborators were enlisted to provide longer and deeper entries.[14] The *Encyclopedia* aimed, it is true, at the general reader rather than serving as a technical manual for practitioners. Diderot's wanted to stimulate the philosopher rather than the virtuoso in his readers.

In large, how could the *Encyclopedia* assert that the craftsman's labors were icons of Enlightenment?

First and foremost, by putting manual pursuits on an equal footing with mental labors. The general idea had a sharp edge; the *Encyclopedia* scorned hereditary members of the elite who do no work and so contribute nothing to society. By restoring the manual laborer to something like his archaic Greek honor, the encyclopédistes mounted a challenge equal in force to Kant's attack on traditional privilege but different in character: useful labor rather free reason challenges the past. The very march of the alphabet aided the *Encyclopedia*'s belief in the ethical equivalence of manual work to supposedly higher pursuits. In French *roi* (king) lies near *rôtisseur* (a roaster of meats or fowl), just as in English "knit" follows upon "king." As the historian Robert Darnton observes, the *Encyclopedia* seized on such couplings as more than happy accidents; these take the authority of a monarch down a peg by making it prosaic.

The pages of the *Encyclopedia* then look more particularly at usefulness and uselessness. In one telling plate, a maid appears industriously at work on a lady's coiffure. The maid radiates purpose and energy while her mistress languishes in ennui; the skilled servant and her bored mistress compose a parable of vitality and decadence. Diderot believed boredom to be the most corrosive of all human sentiments, eroding the will (Diderot continued throughout his life to explore the psychology of boredom, culminating in his novel *Jacques the Fatalist*). In the *Encyclopedia*, Diderot and his colleagues celebrated the vitality rather than dwelled on the sufferings of those deemed socially inferior. Vigor was the point: the encyclopédistes wanted ordinary workers to be admired, not pitied.

This positive emphasis was grounded in one of the eighteenth century's ethical touchstones, the power of sympathy. As our forebears understood sympathy, it did not quite conform to the biblical moral injunction to "treat thy neighbor as thyself." As Adam Smith observed in *The Theory of Moral Sentiments:* "As we can have no immediate experience of what other men feel, we can form no idea of the manner in which they are affected by conceiving what we ourselves should feel in a like situation."[15] Entering into others' lives requires therefore an act of *imagination*. David Hume made the same point in his *Treatise of Human Nature:* "Were I present at any of the more terrible operations of surgery, 'tis certain, that even before it began, the preparation of the instruments, the laying of the bandages in order, the heating of the irons, with all the signs of anxiety and concern in the patient and assistants, would have a great effect upon my mind, and excite the strongest sentiments of pity and terror."[16] For both philosophers, "empathy" meant imagining oneself as another, in all his or her difference, rather than simply likening him or her to ourselves. Smith thus invokes in *The Theory of Moral Sentiments* the "Impartial Spectator," a figure who judges others not by his own interests but rather by the impressions they make on him. It is this imaginative work of sympathy rather than reason that first enlightens us about people.

In Mendelssohn's Berlin, sympathy of this outward sort was made into a method in a parlor game current in the city's bourgeois salons. People spent the evening impersonating a famous character in literature or from history, trying to stay in character throughout the soirée. We are in Berlin, not in the Carnival at Venice, where it might have been no more than amusing for the Renaissance queen Marie de' Medici, heavily jeweled, to drink a glass of wine with a nearly naked, flabby Socrates; in Berlin, we are training ourselves to imagine what it is like to be another person, how they think, feel, and behave.[17] In Paris, the *Encyclopedia* aimed socially lower and asked readers in salons not to imitate but to admire ordinary people bustling at work.

The *Encyclopedia* sought to get its readers out of themselves and into the lives of artisan craftsmen in order, next, to clarify good work itself. Throughout, the volumes illustrate people engaged sometimes in dull, sometimes in dangerous, sometimes in complicated labor; the expression on all the faces tends to the same serenity. About these plates the historian Adriano Tilgher remarks on the "sense of peace and calm which flows from all well-regulated, disciplined work done with a quiet and contented mind."[18] These illustrations appeal to the reader to enter into a realm in which contentment with ordinary things made well reigns.

In ancient times, the gods' craft skills were glorified as weapons in an eternal warfare for mastery. Hesiod's *Works and Days* or Virgil's Georgics portray human labor reflecting some of this divine glory, work appearing as a heroic struggle. So, too, in our times, worker warriors appear in Nazi and Soviet kitsch art as titans of the forge or the plow. Philosophes during the mid-eighteenth century sought to break this warrior spell. The economic historian Albert Hirschmann found the counting house to be one scene that calmed the warrior spirit, the counting house replacing violence impulse by diligent reckoning.[19] Even more was this spell meant to be broken in the craftsman's workshop.

Diderot likened the pleasures of craftsmanship more to marital sex than to the excitements of an affair. The serenity appearing on the faces of Diderot's glassblowers and papermakers radiates also in Jean-Baptiste-Siméon Chardin's still-lifes—a quiet, steady satisfaction in material things well composed, well contrived.

This too-brief summary of the *Encyclopedia*'s origins and general aims sets the stage for probing what it is that people learn by learning their limits. The question of human limits was posed to Diderot the moment he, as it were, rose from his armchair. His method for finding out how people worked was, like a modern anthropologist, to ask them: "We addressed ourselves to the most skilled workers in Paris and the kingdom at large. We took the trouble to visit their workshops, to interrogate them, to write under dictation from them, to follow out their ideas, to define, to identify the terms peculiar to their profession."[20] The research soon ran into difficulty, because much of the knowledge craftsmen possess is tacit knowledge—people know how to do something but they cannot put what they know into words. Diderot remarked of his investigations: "Among a thousand one will be lucky to find a dozen who are capable of explaining the tools or machinery they use, and the things they produce with any clarity."

A very large problem lurks in this observation. Inarticulate does not mean stupid; indeed, what we can say in words may be more limited than what we can do with things. Craftwork establishes a realm of skill and knowledge perhaps beyond human verbal capacities to explain; it taxes the powers of the most professional writer to describe precisely how to tie a slipknot (and is certainly beyond mine). Here is a, perhaps *the,* fundamental human limit: language is not an adequate "mirror-tool" for the physical movements of the human body. And yet I am writing and you are reading a book about physical practice; Diderot and his collaborators compiled a set of volumes nearly six feet thick on this subject.

One solution to the limits of language is to substitute the image for the word. The many plates, by many hands, that richly furnish the *Encyclopedia* made this assist for workers unable to explain themselves in words, and in a particular way. In illustrations of glassblowing, for instance, each stage of blowing a glass bottle appears in a separate image; all the junk of an ordinary workshop has been eliminated, and the viewer focuses on just what hands and mouth need to do at this moment to transform the molten liquid into a bottle. The images, in other words, illuminate by clarifying and simplifying movement into a series of clear pictures of the sort the photographer Henri Cartier-Bresson called "decisive moments."

It might be possible to imagine an experience of enlightenment strictly as a visual experience following this photographic procedure, one that enables our eyes to do the thinking about material things. In silence, as in a monastery, communication among people would be reduced to a minimum for the sake of contemplating how an object is made. Zen Buddhism follows this nonverbal path, taking the craftsman to be an emblematic figure who enlightens by showing rather than telling. Zen counsels that to understand the craft of archery you need not become an archer; instead, silently compose its decisive moments in your mind.

The Western Enlightenment followed both the photographic procedure and another path to understanding. The limits of language can be overcome through active involvement in a practice. Diderot's solution to the limits of language was to become himself a worker: "There are machines so hard to describe and skills so elusive that . . . it has often been necessary to get hold of such machines, set them in operation, and lend one's hand to the work."[21] A real challenge for a man used to salons. We don't know precisely what manual skills Diderot attempted, though in his professional circumstances they were likely those of setting type and pulling etchings. His plunge into manual labor was logical if unusual for a culture in which the ethos of sympathy urged people to get out of themselves, enter other lives. However, enlightenment through practice—or as modern educators have it, learning by doing—raises the question of one's talent to act and so the possibility of learning little, because one is not good at actually doing the work.

Many of Diderot's collaborators were scientists for whom trial and error was a guiding method of experiment. Nicolas Malebranche, for example, imagined the process of trial and error as following a path from many to fewer errors, a steady and progressive improvement through experiment. "Enlightenment" dawns as error decreases. The commentary Diderot provides on his experiences in workshops seems at first to echo this scientific version of failure corrected: "Become an apprentice and produce bad results so as to be able to teach people how to produce good ones." "Bad results" will cause people to reason harder, and so improve.

But trial and error can lead to quite a different result if one's talents prove insufficient to ensure ultimate mastery. So it was for Diderot, who found that by plunging into practice, many of his faults and errors proved "irremediable." Exposing oneself to practice, daring to doing it, one may have then to make sense of *failure* rather than of *error*, reckon limits on skill one can do nothing about. In this light, learning by doing, so comforting a nostrum in progressive education, may in fact be a recipe for cruelty. The craftsman's workshop is indeed a cruel school if it activates our sense of inadequacy.

To the social philosopher, the intersection of practice and talent poses a general question about agency: we are minded to believe that engagement is better than passivity. The pursuit of quality is also a matter of agency, the craftsman's driving motive. But agency does not happen in a social or emotional vacuum, particularly good-quality work. The desire to do something well is a personal litmus test; inadequate personal performance hurts in a different way than inequalities of inherited social position or the externals of wealth: it is about you. Agency is all to the good, but actively pursuing good work and finding you can't do it corrodes one's sense of self.

Our ancestors too often turned a blind eye to this problem. The progressive eighteenth century strongly proclaimed the virtues of "careers open to talent"—talent rather than inheritance the just foundation of upward mobility in society. Proponents of this doctrine could easily neglect, in their drive to destroy inherited privilege, the fate of the losers in competition based on talent. Diderot was unusual in paying attention to such losers, from his earliest books to mature works like *Rameau's Nephew* and *Jacques the Fatalist*; in them, the inadequacy of talent rather than social circumstance or blind chance begets the most grinding form of ruin. Still, the effort of exposure and engagement has to be made. In a letter, Diderot remarks that only the rich can afford to be stupid; for others, ability is a necessity, not an option. Talent then runs its race. This is the outline of a tragedy, but in Diderot's pages the losers can gain something as well. Failure can temper them; it can teach a fundamental modesty even if that virtue is gained at great pain.

"Salutary failure" had earlier appeared in Michel de Montaigne's essays, pages in which God disciplines humanity through showing us what we cannot do. For Diderot, as for Montesquieu and—oddly—for

Benjamin Franklin, mere ordinariness could occasion the sentiment of salutary failure, in a dramatic way.

✳   ✳   ✳

The machine creates this dramatic occasion both as a fact and as a figure in Diderot's *Encyclopedia*. The replicant teaches nothing about salutary failure, but the robot—just possibly—can. The replicant may stimulate reasoning about ourselves, about our own internal machinery. The more powerful, tireless robot may set the standard against which all human beings fail. Should we be depressed by this outcome?

Papermaking suggests not. Enlightened papermaking appears in the *Encyclopedia* at a factory, L'Anglée, about sixty miles distant from Paris near the town of Montargis. Paper pulping was in the eighteenth century a messy and stinking operation, the rags used often stripped from corpses, then further rotted in vats for two months to break down their fibers. The entry for L'Anglée shows how the craft could be improved, human and robot cooperating in the effort.

First something simple: mirroring the eighteenth century's obsession with sanitation, the floors are swept spotless. Next, no worker appears on the verge of vomiting, because the illustrator has drawn vats with hermetic seals—anticipating an innovation that in fact came into being a generation later. Then, in the room where the fibers are beaten to a pulp—the messiest of all activities—there are no human beings at all, just a stamping mill tending itself, a robot that seems to modern eyes a primitive sort of automation but a machine that, again, was shortly to be realized by the steam engine. Finally, in the room where the trickiest human division of labor occurred, the pulp in vats scooped into thin sheets of material set in tray molds, three craftsmen work with balletic coordination, their faces serene, even though this scooping operation was backbreaking work; the laborers have sorted out this task through rational analysis.

This portrait, a narrative composed of a sequence of still images, is curious, just because it anticipates real innovations at L'Anglée. The writer and engraver's imagination has edited the papermaking process so that mechanical tools eliminate the most "bestial" labors; correspondingly, they show machines that enable human judgment and cooperation to come to the fore. The general principle for machine use here is that, if the human body is frail, the machine should aid it or supplant it. The robot is an alien body; this stamping mill works nothing like the human arm in stretching, compressing, and stamping the pulp. Alien, machinery superior to ourselves, but not inhumane.

If such a machine shows how to overcome human limits, still the productive outcome is successful. Here the relation between human and machine is one of relative inadequacy. Against this model of enlightened inequality, papermaking with its friendly robots, the *Encyclopedia* probes the craft of glassblowing in order to plumb salutary failure proper. To understand the relation of human and machine in this contrast, we need to know something about the substance of glass itself.

Glassmaking has been practiced for at least two thousand years. Ancient recipes combined sand with iron oxide, which produced a blue-green hue, the glass translucent rather than transparent. Eventually trial and error succeeded in making glass more transparent through the addition of fern-ash, potash, limestone, and manganese. Even so, glass was not of good quality, and its fabrication arduous. Medieval windows were fashioned by blowing the molten glass through a stem, twirling it rapidly so to produce a plate shape; this hot plate was then pressed down on a stone slab and cut into small square bits. So slow and costly was the process, however, that it proved uneconomic; because glass panes were so precious, the duke of Northumberland had them removed from his castle windows whenever he took a trip. In the Middle Ages, as in antiquity, oiled paper usually served instead of glass in the windows of most prosaic buildings.

The quest for clear, large windows has been driven by the need to bring into houses while protecting them from wind, rain, and noxious street smells. In the late seventeenth century French glassmakers learned how to make larger sheets of glass, at the Saint-Germain glass-works under the direction of Abraham Thévart, who in 1688 cast sheets in one piece eighty to eighty-four inches high and forty to forty-seven inches wide. This was, the historian Sabine Melchior-Bonnet remarks, "a size heard of previously only in fairy tales," though the glass itself remained in its medieval chemical formula.[22] Technical change in siz-ing glass now speeded up: in the early eighteenth century the ovens used for heating glass improved. A more refined craft labor followed, in the manner of pouring, flattening, and refiring the glass. By the time the Abbé Pluche came to describe the results in his *Spectacle of Na-ture* of 1746, the making of big glass panels for windows had become economically feasible; these French innovations enabled the Saint-Gobain works in France to pull ahead of its long-standing rivals in Venice, the glassmakers of the island of Murano.

Whereas the traditional eighteenth-century glassmaker poured his glass into molds, like making bricks, the modern glassmaker wanted to roll his glass into sheets. This is what the *Encyclopedia* seeks to portray, drawing on contemporary experiments in Paris. The illustrator presents a study in contrasts. First he shows the traditional way of twirling, then flattening, a molten gob of glass into a windowpane; against it, we see another image of a glassblower working with a rolling machine to flatten the pane. This machine procedure set a higher standard of a perfectly flat pane than the glassblower could ever achieve by working tradi-tionally; the machine rollers made the glass absolutely, uniformly thick.

In this latter version, the machine sets the terms of quality, raising the game to a standard the human hand and eye cannot achieve. We might here usefully draw a comparison to the work of goldsmithing presented in the last chapter, where goldsmiths' guilds were places for hands-on learning about quality. The apprentice goldsmith imbibed his craft by imitating the master at work; in the new way of making a pane of glass, the glassworker cannot imitate the machine. Not only does the roller function differently than the eye, but it works to a standard that the glassblower could never achieve by visual inspection.

So glass seems just another material that Vaucanson's looms and their progeny would colonize for profit at the expense of the skilled artisan. What could the glassblower, or the *Encyclopedia*'s readers, find salutary about the new technology?

To answer this question we will digress, as is the philosopher's wont, to a general observation and then to a seemingly unrelated subject. The general issue lies in what we conceive the purpose of a model to be. Any model shows how something ought to be done. The model embodied by a perfect machine suggests that the work can indeed be done flawlessly; if the glass roller is more "talented" than the human eye, then the career of window-making ought, in all justice, to be the exclusive preserve of the machine. But this line of thinking mistakes the purpose of a model. A model is a proposal rather than a command. Its excellence can stimulate us, not to imitate, but to innovate.

To make sense of this formula, we should quit for a moment the eighteenth-century workshop and enter its children's nurseries. One of the everyday achievements of the Enlightenment lay in explaining parenting as a craft. The *Encyclopedia* is but one of hundreds of books that explained how to feed and to keep babies clean, how to medicate sick children, how to toilet-train toddlers efficiently, and, above all, how to stimulate and educate children from an early age. Folk wisdom about these matters was deemed inadequate; like all traditional knowledge, it seemed only to pass on prejudice, which in parenting seemed particularly malign since medical advances now made it possible for more babies to survive infancy if parents would only change their own practices. A generation after the *Encyclopedia,* inoculation became the focus of debate between parents who refused this medical advance on traditional grounds and parents who accepted the strict schedule of repeated inoculations that medicine then required.[23]

The matter of the model appeared in the training required to produce an enlightened child. In Jean-Jacques Rousseau's writings, notably in his novel *Julie: ou, la nouvelle Héloïse*, the "craft" of both parents teaching children to be free is seen in the mother encouraging the young to act spontaneously on natural feelings like sympathy and the father encouraging both boys and girls to think rationally rather than rely on received authority. The undertow of Rousseau's writing is, however, that each parent in his or her own way should behave as an exemplary model—"I am the adult you ought to become." Imitate me.

Diderot's friend Louise d'Épinay, in her letters of advice to her granddaughter, *Conversations d'Émilie,* confronted this version of model parenthood.[24] She disputed first of all Rousseau's parental division of labor. A mother who trusts to her own instincts alone will not do enough to form a child's character; a father who acts as a stern man of reason risks driving the child inside him- or herself. More to our purposes, she challenges Rousseau's ideal of the exemplary model-parent. She believes that adults need to accept being "good enough" parents rather than "perfect parents"—as does her heir, Benjamin Spock, author of the most useful guide to parenting in modern times. As matter of common sense, parents need to accept their limitations, a lesson that, in any event, independent-minded children will teach them. But the real issue is self-image that parents hold up to their children: rather than convey "be like me," better parental advice should be more indirect. "This is how I lived" invites the child to reason about that example. Such advice omits, "Therefore you should . . . ." Find your own way; innovate rather than imitate.

I don't mean to push Madame d'Épinay into the arms of philosophy, but her forgotten little book is largely provocative. It contains the same force as Kant's famous image of the "twisted timber of humanity," a call to recognize and accept limits. Returning in the direction of the glassworks, this call matters as much in the workshop as in the nursery or the library. The challenge in the workshop is be to treat the ideal model as something people might use on their own terms, according to their own lights. The machined object, like the parent, makes a proposal about how something might be done; we ponder the proposal rather than submit to it. The model becomes a stimulus rather than a command.

That connection was drawn by Voltaire. He contributed anonymously to the *Encyclopedia*, though sporadically. The same Voltaire who subscribed to Newton's mechanical universe doubted that many of the machines depicted and described in its pages could themselves, alone, lead to Progress. Humankind has first to accept its own weakness and propensity to make a mess of things; if people really take to heart the fault lines in themselves, the perfect machine will seem less a commanding remedy; indeed, we will actively seek out an alternative to it. This view Voltaire advanced with panache in his novel *Candide*.

Voltaire's parable recounts one tale after another of rape, torture, slavery, and betrayal. The source of these disasters is Dr. Pangloss, a literary stand-in for the philosopher G. W. Leibniz, serving as a caricature of the man of reason who has no truck with mere mess. But Pangloss, like his real-life counterpart, is brilliant; he is a mechanist-celebrant of perfection whose explanations of why "all is for the best in the best of all possible worlds" are impeccable. The young Candide, an Odysseus in breeches and a wig, is dull-witted. Still, he eventually recognizes that the nostrums of his teacher are too dangerous. He finally, famously, concludes, "Il faut cultiver notre jardin"—simple work is good medicine for those battered by life.

Candide/Voltaire has certainly given good advice in counseling gardening rather than grieving. But the advice is not quite so simple. Of course, neither Candide nor Pangloss was likely to know how to fertilize a garden or even how to hold a shovel; they, too, were creatures of the salon; this novel is no policy brief for vocational training. Even if it were, the *Encyclopedia* had in any event shown the *salonier* that manual labor is much more complicated that it might seem looking out the windows of the Palais Royal. The nub of the advice is to prefer what one can manage for oneself, to prefer what is limited and concrete, and so human. Voltaire's point is that only someone who accepts that he or she is likely to fall short of perfection is likely to develop realistic judgments about life, to prefer what is limited and concrete and so human.

The spirit of that advice is what Voltaire's era was beginning to encompass in its encounter with machines. In the article on glassblowing, the *Encyclopedia* argues that imperfect, handmade glass has virtues: these are irregularity, distinctiveness, and what the writer refers to vaguely as "character." The two sets of images for glassblowing are thus inseparable; only by understanding how something might be done perfectly is it possible to sense this alternative, an object possessing specificity and character. The bubble or the uneven surface of a piece of glass can be prized, whereas the standard of perfection allows no room either for experiment, for variation—and the pursuit of perfection, Voltaire adjures his fellow philosophes, may lead human beings to grief rather than to progress.

The *Encyclopedia* tacks back and forth in its different articles between the poles represented by the paper factory and the glassmaker's workshop, the one a reconciliation of human and robot, the other an affirmation of work that is other than perfect; perfect work should serve as a foil for another sort of labor that aims at a different kind of result. By a very different route than the Renaissance celebration of artistic genius, then, the Enlightened craftsman could both celebrate and achieve individuality. But to follow this path, the good craftsman had to take on board Voltaire's caution; he had to accept imperfection in himself.

✳   ✳   ✳

Modernity's first encounter with the power of machines produced a dense and contradictory culture. Machines stuffed that cornucopia of goods that began to fill in an earlier time. More materially endowed, now the Enlightenment idealized human beings as self-empowering, about to cast off submission to tradition; the promise that humanity might cast off these shackles appeared in the pages of the *Berlinische Monatsschrift*. Would the machine prove an alternative power demanding submission? And what sort of machine? People wondered at replicants and feared robots, those alien contrivances superior to the bodies of their makers.

Diderot's *Encyclopedia* plunged into this matter by acknowledging from the outset the most basic of human limits, those of language to encompass the workings of the human body, especially the craftsman's body at work. Neither the worker nor the analyst of labor can really explain what's happening. Engaging in the process of craft labor to inform himself, Diderot discovered a further limit, that of talent; he could not understand intellectually work he could not do well practically. He had entered the robot's dangerous lair, in which the machine's "talents" provide a model of perfection against which human beings measure their own inadequacy.

Only a generation after the *Encyclopedia* appeared, Adam Smith had concluded that machines would indeed end the project of enlightenment, declaring in *The Wealth of Nations* that in a factory "the man whose whole life is spend in performing a few simple operations . . . generally becomes as stupid and ignorant as it is possible for a human creature to become."[25] Diderot's circle reached for another conclusion, which I would formulate as follows:

The enlightened way to use a machine is to judge its powers, fashion its uses, in light of our own limits rather than the machine's potential. We should not compete against the machine. A machine, like any model, ought to propose rather than command, and humankind should certainly walk away from command to imitate perfection. Against the claim of perfection we can assert our own individuality, which gives distinctive character to the work we do. Modesty and an awareness of our own inadequacies are necessary to achieve character of this sort in craftsmanship.

The reader will be aware that I have, like Diderot in the workshop, now spoken for him, and this is because the implications of Enlightenment are perhaps evident only two and a half centuries later. Sound judgment about machinery is required in any good craft practice. Getting things right—be it functional or mechanical perfection—is not an option to choose if it does not enlighten us about ourselves.

The Romantic Craftsman
John Ruskin Battles the Modern World

By the mid-nineteenth century, as the modern economic system crystallized, the enlightened hope dimmed that artisans could find an honored place in the industrial order. The long lines of labor's dealings with machinery are clearest in America and Britain, whose governments early on encouraged mechanical experiment for industrial development. In both countries the creation of machinery for large-scale production gradually threatened the standing of the most skilled laborers and increased the number of semi- or unskilled workers, the machinery tending to replace high-cost skilled labor rather than aiming, as the enlightened papermaking mill at L'Anglée, to eliminate unskilled, noisome tasks.

Steelworkers in the United States represented the change that occurred in many other basic industries. Steel is an alloy of iron and carbon hardening agents. The Bessemer converter, which came into use after 1855, mass-produced this alloy by a new kind of giant, oval oxidation chamber. Between 1865 and 1900 industrial design then focused on such technical feats as substituting sampling technology for the costly human skills that had judged and regulated the addition of materials for steel in the flow of the production process. Machinery of a very clever sort was also devised to substitute absolute numbers for human judgment about how to manage the cooling of the liquid metal.[26]

In the nineteenth-century steel industry, skilled artisans faced two potential futures because of technological change: deskilling or dismissal. The first meant they at least remained employed. In American steel mills by 1900, about half its artisans had accepted this fate, the other half seeking careers as metalworkers of other sorts. The skills involved in making steel did not easily "transfer," however, to other foundry labor—a signal fact for many basic industries, then and now.

Highly specialized skills represent not just a laundry list of procedures but a culture formed around these actions. Steelworkers in 1900 had developed a set of communal understandings that allowed large groups of workers to labor in a deafeningly noisy, poorly lit environment. These ways of working safely did not transfer to small, tight spaces as in a specialized machine shop, where the worker had to focus more on his individual body. This was a different sort of problem than the difficulties of technology transfer faced by the eighteenth-century luthiers of Cremona. In the luthier's intimate workshop, the transmission of individual talent was the issue; in the metal factory, it was adapting an established skill to a new spatial culture. As I've elsewhere documented, a kindred problem was faced in 1995 by programmers displaced from working on mainframe machines to personal computers and gaming devices. The norms of the workplace rather than computation formed the difficulty of change.[27]

Craft workers have fought technological change on three fronts: the employers, the unskilled laborers who took their jobs, and the machines. The American Federation of Labor (AFL) became an emblematic union in this regard. Over its long life its various craft unions fought well against their employers: many unions came to an understanding with the largely immigrant, unskilled workers whom employers preferred. But on the third front they did not fight well against the machine. The unions under the AFL umbrella failed to invest in alternative strategies of mechanical design; the craftsmen did not sponsor research or themselves design machines that would keep a large body of skilled operatives necessary. Mechanical change came *to* the labor force rather than from within the labor movement.

Failure on this third front has magnified the symbolic threat of the machine. Skilled operatives live with and through machines but rarely create them in modern industry. Technological advance comes in this way to seem inseparable from domination by others.

There was no more passionate Victorian protest against such mechanical domination than the English writer John Ruskin, who appealed to his readers to scorn the very idea of a mechanical civilization. Manual workers in medieval guilds seemed to him to lead better lives, in higher-quality institutions, than they do in modern factories. The radical nature of Ruskin's vision was to assert that modern society as a whole should and could return to the preindustrial past.

Ruskin was an unlikely champion of craft workers or indeed of any physical activity. Born into a prosperous, tight-knit family, he was an inward boy; his became the adult life of a sensitive, vulnerable man who found a refuge in the cloisters of Oxford but no inner peace. In part, physical objects and artisanal work served him as a release from self— but he in no way fitted the stereotype of a fussy aesthete. Ruskin's great modern biographer, Tim Hilton, presents him as a man who early on foreshadowed E. M. Foster's dictum "only connect," which in Ruskin's case meant connecting to other people through hand-made things.[28]

In early trips to Italy, particularly to Venice, Ruskin found an unexpected beauty in its rough-hewn medieval buildings. The gargoyles, arched doorways, and windows hewn by stonemasons appealed to him more than the abstract geometries of later Renaissance architecture or the perfect workmanship of eighteenth-century cabinetmakers. He drew these rough objects in the same spirit as he found them, beautifully evoking the irregularities of the stones of Venice in free-flowing lines on paper; by drawing, he discovered the pleasures of touch.

Ruskin's writing is intensely personal; he draws ideas and precepts from his own sensations and experience. The appeal he made we might formulate today as "get in touch with your body." His prose at its best has an almost hypnotic tactile power, making the reader feel the damp moss on an old stone or see the dust in sunlit streets. As his work progressed, his contrast of past and present became even more po- lemic: Italian cathedrals contrasted to British factories, Italians' ex- pressive labor to English dull industrial routine. At Oxford in the 1850s and 1860s Ruskin put the command "get in touch with your body" into practice. He led troops of gilded youth out to the suburbs to work on road construction, their sore, callused hands virtuous signs of connect- ing to Real Life.

If "Ruskinism" involved an appreciation of rough-hewn beauty, and more than a tinge of eroticism in hard physical labor, it clarified an apprehension Ruskin's readers could name only with difficulty. The industrial age consummated the cornucopia, the machine pouring forth a cornucopia of clothes, domestic utensils, books and news- papers, machines to make other machines. Like their predecessors Victorians both wondered and felt anxious about this material abun- dance. The machine introduced a new element concerning the relation of quantity and quality. For the first time, the sheer quantity of uniform objects aroused concerns that number would dull the senses, the uni- form perfection of machined goods issuing no sympathetic invitation, no personal response.

This inverse relation between quantity and quality expressed itself through waste—a problem only dreamed of by scarcity societies. We can work backward to this problem through the numbers that repre- sent waste today, in products thrown out long before the end of their practical life. By one count, 92 percent of used cars on sale in Britain in 2005 had a serviceable future life of at least five years; 86 percent of the buyers of new computers in 2004 ran the same programs they ran on their old computers. One explanation for such waste is that consumers buy the potential power of new objects rather than power they actually use; the new automobile can speed a hundred miles an hour, even though the driver is usually stuck in traffic. Another explanation of modern waste is that consumers are more aroused by anticipation than by operation; getting the latest thing is more important than then making durable use of it.[29] Either way, being able so easily to dispose of things desensitizes us to the actual objects we hold in hand.

Ruskin was not the first Victorian to perceive that sheer quantity might diminish the tactile qualities of material things. The problem of waste earlier appeared in Benjamin Disraeli's novel *Sybil, or the Two Nations,* in 1845. The point of this political tract cum novel was to attack the deprivation in which the masses of English people lived, a point sharpened by Disraeli's pictures of wealth as waste—half-consumed joints of beef, wines of which only a glass in a bottle might be tasted, clothes worn once or twice for the season and then cast aside. Many Victorian writers had depicted the horrors of poverty in itself. Disraeli's distinctive voice appears in how in this, and in the other two novels of which Sybil forms a part, he portrays waste as the negligence of privilege. Ruskin rang a bell in this overstuffed era on this account; the rooms he liked to live in were, for their time, relatively bare. As the good Victorian he was, he contrived a moral for this aesthetic spareness: the fewer things we display, the more we care about each one.

Quantity is measured by how big as well as how much. Big was symbolized to Ruskin's generation by one machine presented at the Great Exposition of 1851, the century's great celebration of the industrial cornucopia.

Conceived by the Prince Regent, the exposition itself was a massive display of modern machinery and industrial products set within a giant greenhouse designed and executed by Joseph Paxton. It encompassed everything from sophisticated steam engines and steam-driven tools to porcelain toilets and machine-made hairbrushes. Objects made by hand were included, prominent in the sections devoted to crafts from Britain's colonies. The things made in Britain were presented to show the variety that an industrial "type-form" like a flush toilet could take, its bowl cast variously as a simple cup, a decorated urn, or (my favorite) a kneeling elephant.[30] In the first, heady burst of consumer industrial production, there was no strict correlation between function and form.

Paxton's immense greenhouse housing this paean to the industrial machine, inaccurately called the Crystal Palace, was itself a product of the innovations in glassmaking foreshadowed in the pages of the *Encyclopedia*. To achieve large panes of rolled glass that were sturdy enough for construction required a reformation of the material's soda-lime proportions and the invention of cast-iron rollers tolerant of constant high heat—requirements entirely foreign to crystal. These innovations finally appeared in the 1840s.[31] The arcades of Paris begun earlier in the century had glass roofs, but the panes of the arcades were smaller and the roof panels leakier. At the exposition, everything was glass—glass held tightly in metal frames. The building embodied an aesthetic possible only thanks to the work of the machine, an aesthetic of pure transparency, the visual division between inside and outside abolished.

The single object in the Great Exposition of 1851 that most dramatically defined the machine's dominion was a robot called Count Dunin's Man of Steel, named after its creator, a robot given pride of place in the Crystal Palace at the base of the speaker's rostrum. Seven thousand pieces of steel, forged into plates and springs, composed a metal man in the shape of the Apollo Belvedere whose one arm stretches out before him as for a handshake. At the turn of a crank this metal figure began to expand, the springs and wheels within him pushing out concealed plates, so that he retained the perfection of the Apollo Belvedere's form but became the size of a welcoming Goliath. It took only thirty seconds to inflate Count Dunin's Man of Steel to double life-size or to shrink him down again to normal scale.[32]

Unlike Vaucanson's Parisian replicants, the metal Greek did not imitate any human function; unlike Vaucanson's Lyonnais robots, the Man of Steel produced nothing save the impression of his own power. The ethos of the overpowered automobile was embodied in this Victorian robot: big, but for not purpose.

That impression of sheer mechanical power, the whole point of the Great Exposition, Ruskin sought to deflate. This was the radical, energetic context of his nostalgia; he felt anger rather than sighed in regret. His writings issued a call to arms to combat the modern cornucopia, to reinvigorate sensate reaction to objects. Equally, in his call to arms, he exhorted artisans to reassert their claims on society's respect.

In the mid-1850s Ruskin helped create a Working Men's College in a house in London's Red Lion Square. In a letter to his friend Pauline Trevelyan he described its students: "I want to give short lectures to about 200 at once in turn, [to] shop decorators—and writing masters—and upholsterers—and masons—and brickmakers, and glassblowers and pottery people." The purpose of his lectures was in part to strip away the decorative masks of type-form, to make his students aware of the essential uniformity of mechanical production. "I want to explode printing; and gunpowder—the two great curses of the age—I begin to think that abominable art of printing is the root of all mischief—it makes people used to have everything of the same shape." Ruskin proposed to wake up the craftsmen's senses by creating a room where they could contemplate a few truly individual objects made in the past, "a room where anybody can go in all day and always see nothing in it but what is good."[33] As well as late medieval painting and sculpture, he wanted his students to savor the irregularities of handmade goods like eighteenth-century glass.

Behind the Working Men's College lay a positive conception of craftsmanship—broadly conceived, applicable to people who use their heads as well as their hands. This conception crystallized in the book that secured Ruskin's fame, *The Seven Lamps of Architecture,* in 1849. Gothic stonework, he says, is a "grammar," a "flamboyant" grammar, one form generating another sometimes by the stonemason's will, sometimes simply by chance; "flamboyance" is his cognomen for "experiment." In *The Stones of Venice* of 1851–1853 this word takes on a deeper cast. Now Ruskin is beginning to contemplate, as we have seen among Linux programmers, the intimate connection between problem solving and problem finding. A "flamboyant" worker, exuberant and excited, is willing to risk losing control over his or her work: machines break down when they lose control, whereas people make discoveries, stumble on happy accidents. The surrender of control, at least temporarily, now gives Ruskin a recipe for good craftsmanship and how it should be taught. In *The Stones of Venice* Ruskin invents this figure of a draftsman who has temporarily lost control of his work:

> You can teach a man to draw a straight line; to strike a curved line, and to carve it . . . with admirable speed and precision; and you will find his work perfect of its kind: but if you ask him to think about any of those forms, to consider if he cannot find any better in his own head, he stops; his execution becomes hesitating; he thinks, and ten to one he thinks wrong; ten to one he makes a mistake in the first touch he gives to his work as a thinking being. But you have made a man of him for all that, he was only a machine before, an animated tool.[34]

Ruskin's draftsman will recover, and his technique will be the better for the crisis he has passed through. Whether like the stonemason one leaves in the nicks and mistakes or whether like the draftsman one recovers the ability to make exact, straight lines, the craftsman is now become self-conscious. His is not the path of effortless mastery; he has had troubles, and he has learned from them. The modern craftsman should model himself or herself on this troubled draftsman rather than on Count Dunin's Man of Steel.

Ruskin's *Seven Lamps of Architecture* provided seven guides, or "lamps," for the troubled craftsman, guides for anyone who works directly on material things.[35] These seven are:

- "the lamp of sacrifice," by which Ruskin means, as I do, the willingness to do something well for *its* own sake, dedication;
- "the lamp of truth," the truth that "breaks and rents continually"; this is Ruskin's embrace of difficulty, resistance, and ambiguity;
- "the lamp of power," tempered power, guided by standards other than blind will;
- "the lamp of beauty," which for Ruskin is found more in the detail, the ornament—hand-sized beauty—than in the large design;
- "the lamp of life," life equating with struggle and energy, death with deadly perfection;
- "the lamp of memory," the guidance provided by the time before machinery ruled; and
- "the lamp of obedience," which consists of obedience to the example set by a master's practice rather than by his particular works; otherwise put, strive to be like Stradivari but do not seek to copy his particular violins.

As a vein of radical thought, Ruskin refuses the present, looks backward in order to look forward. Ruskin sought to instill in craftsmen of all sorts the desire, indeed the demand, for a lost space of freedom; it would be a free space in which people can experiment, a supportive space in which they could at least temporarily lose control. This is a condition for which people will have to fight in modern society. Ruskin believed that the rigors of the industrial age work against experiences of free experiment and salutary failure; had he lived long enough, he would have appreciated F. Scott Fitzgerald's observation that in America there are no second chances. For Ruskin, the craftsman serves as an emblem for all people in the very need of the opportunity for "hesitation . . . mistakes"; the craftsman must transcend working by the "lamp" of the machine, become in his or her doubts more than an "animated tool."

What would Diderot have made of the seven lamps guiding the craftsman? Certainly the encyclopédiste would have appreciated Ruskin's humanity, but he would insisted that reason could play a greater role in it, and that the modern machine, even a robot, serves a purpose in human self-understanding. Ruskin might reply that Diderot had not yet learned the hard truth of industrial power. Diderot might counter that Ruskin's lamps illuminate how craftsmen have done their work well but offer no real guidance about the materials the modern craftsman has to hand. Put in modern terms, we might compare Ruskin to Heidegger; Ruskin did not yearn to escape to a dream-hut; he sought instead another sort of material practice and another sort of social engagement.

In its time, Ruskin's craftsman appeared a Romantic figure, and as a Romantic trope the craftsman served as a counterweight to the Romanticism embodied in the emblem of the artist as technical virtuoso.

In the early eighteenth century a virtuoso like Chambers, with wide-ranging interests, rather prided himself on his amateurism. In Chambers's day Antonio Stradivari would not have been labeled a virtuoso; his genius ran in one channel only. In Britain, the gentleman amateur has retained a certain snobbish cachet, as has his opposite number, the gentleman who evinces effortless, casual mastery. Faced with complicated cancer surgery, you would not want to trust your body to either. But the specialist virtuoso also has an unsettling relation to technique.

In music, the virtuoso obsessed by technique took to the public stage in the mid-eighteenth century. Sheer finger dexterity became a display that audiences paid to hear in the new realm of public concert performances; the amateur listener began to applaud—as an inferior.

This situation marked a contrast to the performances in courts in which Frederick the Great, for instance, played the flute parts in the compositions he commissioned from his hired musicians or, earlier, the role as lead dancer Louis XIV frequently took in the spectacles mounted at Versailles. Both kings were highly skilled performers, but in courts the line between performer and audience, technical master and amateur, was blurred. Diderot's novel *Rameau's Nephew* marks the firmness of this new line as it began to be drawn in his time. This dialogue in part asks what is technical mastery and answers that it is the fruit of heroic struggle, man's battles with an instrument. The dialogue then poses the question whether technical flamboyance compromises artistic integrity. In the history of music the answer to that question became ever more pressing, from Niccolò Paganini to Sigismond Thalberg to Franz Liszt in their public appearances during the first half of the nineteenth century. They dramatized the heroics of technique, Paganini and Thalberg diminishing thereby the musical virtues of simplicity and modesty.

By the 1850s the musical virtuoso appeared to be someone whose technical skill had developed to such perfection that amateur players in an audience felt small, almost worthless in comparison. The rise of the virtuoso on stage coincided with silence and immobility in the concert hall, the audience paying fealty to the artist through its passivity. The virtuoso shocks and awes. In exchange, the virtuoso unleashed in listeners passions they could not produce using their own skills.[36]

Ruskin loathed this ethos of the Romantic virtuoso. The craftsman's hesitations and mistakes have nothing in common with such a performance; the musical analogue to Ruskin's celebration of the craftsman would be *haus-musik,* in which amateurs learned the classics on their own terms. But Ruskin shifted the scene in which the compromised virtuoso appears, from the concert hall to the engineering works.

Engineers like Isambard Kingdom Brunel—who will make a more extended appearance later in these pages—embodied for Ruskin the ills of technical virtuosity. An engineer of steel ships, of long-span bridges and viaducts, Brunel was a technical virtuoso whose work in one way conformed to Ruskin's "lamps": it was experimental, and much of the experiment proved flawed. And Brunel was a committed, not to say passionate craftsman who could have made more money by being more prudent. Yet his work celebrates sheer technical prowess, which to Ruskin was unforgivable. This refusal amounted to something like a religious mania: virtuosity employing machines is everywhere and always inhumane.

Ruskin, in sum, sought to assert the claims of work that is neither amateur nor virtuoso. This middle ground of work is craftsmanship. And this figure of the craftsman, as a worker both defiant and doomed, has passed down from Ruskin's time to our own, though the explicit label "Romantic" has disappeared.

A decade after Ruskin's death in 1900, the American sociologist Thorstein Veblen celebrated the Ruskinian virtues of the handmade over the machine-made in *The Spirit of Workmanship*, in characteristically ornate prose: "The visible imperfections of hand-wrought goods, being honorific, are accounted marks of superiority, of serviceability, or both."[37] The Great Exposition he saw firsthand, in Chicago in 1893, seemed to mark the craftsman's passing; most of the craftwork on display came from places and peoples Veblen called—with a sense of the irony involved—"primitive" or "undeveloped." The civilized goods dominated in their profuse, uniform, machined numbers. As befits an economist, Veblen tied the craftsman's demise to consumption patterns; the London Great Exposition of 1851 was for him an early foretaste event in machine-enabled "conspicuous consumption," a first exercise in mass advertising. The good craftsman is a poor salesman, absorbed in doing something well, unable to explain the value of what he or she is doing.[38]

To Veblen's heir, C. Wright Mills, the machine too seems the instrument by which the craftsman—though deeply fulfilled by work, embracing experiment and irregularity, modest in intent, careful and particular—is doomed. "This model of craftsmanship," Mills declares, "has become an anachronism."[39] This, too, is Ruskinian. Perhaps this cast of mind explains why craftsmen themselves, like the skilled American steelworkers, did not try to engage through their unions in technological innovation—or perhaps menaced workers cannot fight on all fronts. Still, a fundamental issue is posed by this history. Between the Enlightened and the Romantic views of craftsmanship we ought certainly, I believe, to prefer those of the earlier time, when working with machines rather than fighting was the radical, emancipatory challenge. It remains so.

CHAPTER FOUR

Material Consciousness

At the meeting of the British Medical Association in 2006
when the passions of doctors and nurses boiled over, a
room was found for the overflow of journalists, members
of the public like me, and medical people who could not
get into the hall. Some scientific presentation must have occurred in
this room previously, for left on the giant screen in front of our seats
was the full-color picture of a rubber-gloved hand lifting up a part of a
patient's large intestine in a surgical operation. The journalists occasionally glanced at this monster image only to look away as though it
were somehow obscene. The doctors and nurses in the room, however,
seemed to pay it more and more attention, particularly at those moments when the voices of government officials wafted through the
loudspeakers, droning on about reform.

Their rapt attention to whatever the gloved hand was doing to the
large intestine is material consciousness. All craftsmen have it, even
those who practice the most arcane art. The painter Edgar Degas is
once supposed to have remarked to Stéphane Mallarmé, "I have a
wonderful idea for a poem but I can't seem to work it out," whereupon
Mallarmé replied, "My dear Edgar, poems are not made with ideas,
they are made with words."

As might be imagined, "material consciousness" is a phrase that causes philosophers to salivate. Is our consciousness of things independent of the things themselves? Are we aware of words in the way we feel an intestine by touch? Rather than get lost in this philosophical forest, it might be better to focus on what makes an object interesting. This is the craftsman's proper conscious domain; all his or her efforts to do good-quality work depend on curiosity about the material at hand.

I want to make a simple proposal about this engaged material consciousness: we become particularly interested in the things we can change. The giant image of the human intestine on the screen was intriguing because the surgeons were, it transpired, doing something odd to it. People invest thought in things they can change, and such thinking revolves around three key issues: metamorphosis, presence, and anthropomorphosis. Metamorphosis can be as direct as a change in procedure, as when potters switch from molding clay on a fixed platter to building it up on a rotating wheel; potters who do both will be conscious of the difference in technique. Presence can be registered simply by leaving a maker's mark, such as a brickmaker's stamp. Anthropomorphosis occurs when we impute human qualities to a raw material; supposedly primitive cultures imagine that spirits dwell in a tree, and so in a spear cut from its wood; sophisticates personalize materials when using words like *modest* or *sympathetic* to describe finishing details on a cabinet.

In this chapter, I shall investigate each of these forms of material consciousness more in depth, among craftsmen working with clay.

Metamorphosis
The Potter's Tale

The simplest way to make a pot is to coil a rope of clay up around the edge of a flat disk.[1] A small innovation is to place a cut gourd under the flat disk so that the pot can be turned more easily in the potter's hands as the coil builds up around the sides. This small innovation suggests a much larger step, that of using a free-spinning wheel.

This step was taken about 4000 BCE in what is now Iraq and spread westward to the Mediterranean about 2500 BCE. Greek potters' wheels from about 1000 BCE onward were heavy wood or stone disks that rotated on a pointed stone support. A potter's assistant steadied and turned the wheel while the potter shaped the clay with both hands. The spinning wheel's momentum suggested an entirely new way of building up form than the rope coil; now the potter could raise a wet clay lump. If small, such a pot was structurally of one piece. Larger pots could be assembled by fitting together tubes shaped on the wheel. Whether small or large, the potter, after the pot began to dry, scraped off excess clay with a stylus while the pot turned on the wheel.

Archaic and ancient pottery certainly became more complex from about 800 BCE on. Sheer utility would not explain this logic, however, since rope building produced perfect serviceable objects, and it makes pots faster than wheel building. Nor would utility alone explain the decorative thinking that went into the surface of these pots.

All pottery can be decorated by the use of slips. These are highly refined clays of different colors that, once dried, can be mixed to create stronger colors and then be painted on the surface of a pot. Ancient slips differ from modern pottery glazes in lacking a high silica content. The Greeks, however, developed techniques for controlling firing in the kiln so that the surface achieved a vitreous shine. The modern potter Susanne Staubach has worked out how the Greek potter used the kiln as a chemistry laboratory to achieve these polychrome results. The kilns were heated to 900 degrees Celsius to oxidize the clay. Then sawdust was thrown into the kiln to begin the process of reduction. If left at this point, however, the slip would not register its distinctive color. The potter discovered a way to reoxidize the clay by opening the kiln's damper. The body of the pot now turned red while the figures painted in slip remained black. The same contrast appeared in reverse when the slip was painted as background.[2]

Changes in slip technique opened up expressive possibilities to the potters. The utilitarian pot used for storage and cooking, simply decorated, could now be painted with scenes that showed Greeks the nature of their myths and the significant events of their history. As Greek pottery evolved, these painted images became more than sheer representations, finally serving as social commentaries—the absurdities of lust in old age, for instance, depicted by fat, bald men with heavy, sagging genitals chasing nimble, tight-muscled youths.

Decoration of this sort did not lack economic value. The decorated pot became a "pictorial object which," the classicist John Boardman remarks, "might entertain, even instruct, buyers at home or abroad."[3] In time, pottery became an important element in Mediterranean trade. The potters who experimented centuries earlier with using a rotating stone in place of a gourd could not have foreseen its value.

We have no written record of what ancient potters thought about the potting wheel, we can only infer that they were conscious of what they were doing because their tools and practice changed and because potters in the early classical era used both procedures. We want to draw the inference that they knew what they were doing because it serves as a caution against the "just-so" stories that afflict accounts of technology.

The just-so account supposes that change has to happen in a just certain way, each step leading implacably to the next; the maker could do and think no other—as in "the single chisel wedge led *inevitably* to the dual hammer claw." This just-so explanation is entirely retrospective in character. Looking back in time, again, it appears perfectly logical that the free-spinning wheel would cause a change from rope coiling to drawing up a pot, but how could the person who first replaced his or her gourd with a stone know what we know? Perhaps the potter was puzzled, perhaps exhilarated—which are more engaged states of consciousness than "it had to happen just like this."

In the chapter on the workshop, the elapse of time proved one way to separate craft and art: craft practice is stretched out, art of the original sort is a more immediate event. The ancient potter dwelled in stretched-out time; after the wheel spinning on a pivot first appeared, centuries elapsed before the practice formed of drawing up clay was routinized. The bedding-in of a practice, in which the actions of the hand gradually become tacit knowledge, explains this *longue durée*. And throws up another cautionary flag.

Some followers of Adam Smith seized on the fact that most crafts take a long time to bed in as a sign that manual workers, in any one generation, are not particularly self-conscious, that they take procedures for granted and just get on with the work as they know it. John Ruskin's writings contested this dulled-wits view: Ruskin's sense of tradition is that the errors, imperfections, and variations that attend any practice are handed down from generation to generation; the mental provocation of these uncertainties is not rubbed away by time. There was by about 600 BCE great difference in the quality of pots produced around the Aegean. Ruskin's view is that the craftsmen themselves would have noted and cared about these differences. The shift from fixed disks to turning wheels suggests a kindred command of attention. Just because the craftsman's working time was slow, it couldn't be clear at any one moment what the range of variation in clay form as well as practice might be. Put as a principle, this is to say that metamorphosis arouses the mind.

Metamorphosis was a preoccupation of ancient mythology. The ancient world associated shifts in shape, the historian E. R. Dodds writes, with the irrational.[4] Magic raises the stakes of unforeseen events, gives changes in form a compelling power to command wonder and fear. Ovid declared at the outset of *The Metamorphoses*: "My purpose is to tell of bodies which have been transformed into shapes of a different kind," and he achieves his purpose famously in the story of Acteon, who broke divine law by eyeing a naked goddess, the gods then suddenly transforming Acteon into a stag torn apart by his own dogs. Wonder and fear governed the myth of Pandora, as in the perfume that, released from its jar, becomes a plague. This is arousal by magic.

Yet metamorphosis as the ancients conceived it was not entirely an irrational process. The myths drew on physics. Ancient materialists like Heraclitus and Parmenides believed that all physical reality is an endless recombination, an unceasing metamorphosis, of the four basic elements of nature: fire, water, earth, and air. Unlike the modern science of evolution, in which the arrow of change moves toward ever-increasing complexity, for these ancients, all natural processes seem to move toward entropy, the decay of form back into its simplest four elements, water to water, clay to clay, from which primal state new combinations, new metamorphoses would occur.[5]

The cultural challenge was how to resist this natural cycle of metamorphosis— how to combat decay. Plato found one philosophic solution in the famous image of a "divided line" in *The Republic,* a line of knowledge that becomes increasingly durable; though physical things decay, their form or idea endures.[6] In responding to his contemporaries on material flux, Plato asserted that a mathematical formula is an idea independent of the ink used to write it.[7] For the same reason, Aristotle argued, verbal expression is not bounded by the specific sounds of words—which is why we can translate from one language to another.

The desire for something more sustainable than decomposing materials is one of the sources in Western civilization for the supposed superiority of the head over the hand, the theorist better than the craftsman because ideas last. This conviction makes philosophers happy, but shouldn't. *Theoria* shares a root in Greek with *theatron,* a theater, which means literally a "place for seeing."[8] The philosopher can pay a certain price in the theater of ideas for durable ideas that the craftsman in the workshop does not.

In the archaic theater there was relatively little divide between spectator and performer, seeing and doing; people danced and spoke, then retired to a stone seat to watch others dance and declaim. By the time of Aristotle, actors and dancers had become a caste with special skills of costuming, speaking, and moving. Audiences stayed offstage, and so developed their own skills of interpretation as spectators. As critics, the audience sought to speculate then about what the stage-characters did not understand about themselves (though the chorus on stage sometimes also took on this clarifying role). The classicist Myles Burnyeat believes that here, in the classical theater, lies the origin of the phrase "seeing with the mind's eye."[9] Which is to say, understanding separated from doing, the "mind's eye" that of an observer rather than of a maker.

The craftsman, engaged in a continual dialogue with materials, does not suffer this divide. His or her arousal is more complete. Part of Plato's great ambivalence about craftsmen was that he knew this. The same philosopher who believed that an idea transcends the ink with which it is written commended craftsmen as demioergoi; they were equally engaged with material things and with one another. The workshop has a claim to make against the theater, practice against theory. But still, how could the craftsman guard against decay? Clay, that most philosophical of materials, shows three quite different ways in which its craftsmen could guide the metamorphosis of their craft.

Orderly metamorphosis can occur, first of all, through the evolution of a type-form. A "type-form" is technology-speak for a generic category of object; change occurs through the elaboration of its species. Once the ancient technology of slips was worked out, for instance, pots could be produced with red *or* black backgrounds. Each type-form can beget complicated species. We can think of some modern examples. The sociologist Harvey Molotch cites the modern example the example of the PT Cruiser, an automobile fitting twenty-first-century technology into a retro, 1950s-style body.[10] In the built environment of Britain, the village of Poundbury is a similarly evolved type-form, its houses composed of modern infrastructure sheathed in fake medieval, Elizabethan, or Georgian clothes. An even more complicated type-form evolution occurs when a new material condition suggests the new use of a new tool: to return to ancient clay-work, higher kiln temperature implied a different way to operate the kiln damper.

The historian of technology Henry Petroski rightly insists on the importance of salutary failure in the inner metamorphosis of type-form. When an object as simple as a pot cracks or as complicated as a bridge shifts, the analyst's first port of call is its details, its small parts. These clamor immediately for attention, and bits of the type-form may then change and evolve. This micro-address seems the sensible way to deal with failure or trial and error, and to Petroski the address bespeaks a healthy consciousness. Little can be learned by losing one's cool, which would be to imagine the whole project misguided because a bit doesn't work. (An example of losing one's cool was the British public's response to the Millennium Bridge, a footbridge designed by Ove Arup and Foster Partners to span the Thames. At first it swayed slightly; the public imagined it would fall down, which the bridge couldn't; a change in its cushioning mechanism set the sway right.) His observation takes us a step further in Madame d'Épinay's thinking about models. Failure might seem to demand an organic reconfiguration, the smallest change recomposing the relation of all the parts to one another, but technological fixes need not work like this: there's no need to change the whole type-form. As the species parts evolve, they can indeed make the generic type ever more viable.[11] A simple observation encapsulates this durability: ancient pots incorporated other visual practices but remained pots rather than metamorphosing into sculptures.

A second kind of man-made metamorphosis occurs when two or more unlike elements are joined, as in the combining of the technologies of the radio and the landline telephone. Here the craftsman has consciously to decide if the combination will best work like a com-pound, in which the whole becomes different than its parts, or like a mixture, in which the elements continue an independent coexistence. In the crafts we have so far studied, goldsmithing emphasized the importance of mixture, since in the foundry and in the assay the gold-smith sought to separate gold from the base metals with which it was often mixed; the honest goldsmith was suspicious of quack syntheses through alchemy. Glassmaking by contrast has required a more posi-tive embrace of synthesis. Clearing the tint in medieval glass required the glassmaker to introduce materials like manganese and limestone that rewrote the basic chemical formula for the substance; the synthe-sis was then tested practically by the glass's clarity. The ancient potter had to decide between these two procedures in mixing glazes. There are many shades of black in ancient pots: some were produced by chemical compounding, others by layering, then baking one glaze over another to produce blackness.

Perhaps the metamorphosis that most challenges the maker con-sciously to maintain form is the "domain shift." This phrase—my coin-age—refers to how a tool initially used for one purpose can be applied to another task, or how the principle guiding one practice can be ap-plied to quite another activity. Type-forms develop within, as it were, one country; domain shifts reach across borders. The ancient potter's experience of metamorphosis lay in the internal development of a type-form; to it, we might contrast weaving, the craft first celebrated in the hymn to Hephaestus; this was a craft that traveled across domains.

The archaic household loom consisted simply of two upright poles across which lay a beam. Threads, made taut by weights below, hung from this beam; the weaver worked across, starting at the top, con-tinually pushing the horizontal threads upward to tighten the cloth. "Weave closely; make good cloth, with many woof-threads in a short length of warp," the historian Hesiod counseled.[12] The cloth, tight at right angles, will then have a shapely form.

The cloth join of warp and woof shifted domains to the mortise-and-tenon joint in shipbuilding. In this joint, two pieces of wood are locked together, the end of one cut into the side of the other, the two pieces of wood sometimes pinned together, sometimes cut obliquely so that no pin is needed. The mortise-and-tenon joint is a way of weaving wood; both weaver and carpenter concentrate on making tight right-angle joints. So far as is known, archaic carpenters had long possessed the chisels at hand to make such joints but did not use them for this purpose. The shift occurred as Greek cities began to colonize settlements far from home base. The unmitered joints of older vessels, coated with tar, eroded on these long sea voyages, and in the sixth century BCE ship carpenters began using the mortise-and-tenon joint to cope with leaky hulls.

This metamorphosis proceeded into a further domain, as the locked orthogonal joints of both cloth and wood suggested a way to lay out streets. Older grid-plans had connected individual buildings, but the Greek city of Selinous, for instance, founded in Sicily in 627 BCE, was pure warp and woof; the corner itself was emphasized as the major design element. The image of an "urban fabric" was not here a casual metaphor, rather a direct description; similarly, Selinous had the tightness and compactness of a ship.

Like potting, these permutations in weaving occurred slowly, distilled by practice rather than dictated by theory. What endures, what does not decay, is the technique of focusing on the right angle. Domain shifts, when stated baldly, seem counterintuitive: at first glance it makes no sense to liken a ship to a cloth. But the craftsman's slow working through forges the logic and maintains the form. Many propositions that seem counterintuitive are not so; we just don't know their connections yet. Plodding craft labor is a means to discover it.

Domain shifts are the metamorphoses that most struck the anthropologist Claude Lévi-Strauss, the Ovid of modern anthropology; the subject of metamorphosis preoccupied him throughout his long life. The foundational craft for him is cooking rather than potting, weaving, or carpentry, but the logic of change in his view applies to all crafts. He presents change as a culinary triangle, in his words, a "triangular semantic field whose three points correspond respectively to the categories of the raw, the cooked, and the rotted."[13] The raw is the realm of nature, as human beings find it; cooking creates the realm of culture, nature metamorphosed. In cultural production, Lévi-Strauss famously declares, food is both good to eat (*bonne à manger*) and good to think with (*bonne à penser*). He means this literally: cooking food begets the idea of heating for other purposes; people who share parts of a cooked deer begin to think they can share parts of a heated house; the abstraction "he is a warm person" (in the sense of "sociable") then becomes possible to think.[14] These are domain shifts.

Clay would have served Lévi-Strauss equally well; clay, like meat, is good to think with. In pottery, raw clay is "cooked" both by the tools that shape it into a pot and by the kiln, which does the literal work of cooking. Cooked clay provides a medium for making images that, on a pot, create a narrative as the pot is turned. This narrative can travel, and it can be traded or sold as a cultural artifact. What Lévi-Strauss insists on is that symbolic value is inseparable from awareness of the material condition of an object; its creators thought the two together.

In sum, metamorphosis provokes material conscious in three ways: through the internal evolution of a type-form, in the judgment about mixture and synthesis, by the thinking involved in a domain shift. To say which of these three forms held the medical people rapt would require a professional knowledge of the large intestine that I unfortunately lack, but I suspect it was a domain shift, based on my neighbor's comment that she was seeing something "unconventional." She could recognize it as strange, yet she could attend to it and learn from it because she already had a craft to guide her in that foreign territory.

Presence
The Brickmaker's Tale

Maker's stamps on metal, wood, and clay evince a second category of material consciousness. The maker leaves a personal mark of his or her presence on the object. In the history of craftsmanship, these maker's marks usually have carried no political message, as a graffito scrawled on a wall can, merely the statement anonymous laborers have imposed on inert materials, *fecit:* "I made this," "I am here, in this work," which is to say, "I exist." The philosopher Anne Phillips would not scorn such a declaration as part of what she calls "the politics of presence," nor have historians of the labors and maker's marks of American slaves. Ancient brick stamps also bore this primal message, but to understand it requires understanding bricks themselves in some detail.

Mud bricks have been used in construction for nearly ten thousand years. Archaeologists have found pure-clay bricks of this age in the city of Jericho, and adobe bricks—clay tempered with straw or manure—in the same city dating from about 7600 BCE. Sun-fired bricks formed in molds are cheap and quick to make but are at the mercy of the weather, often degrading in prolonged rain. The invention of fired brick about 3500 BCE marked a turning point in brick construction, the blocks now strong in all seasons, serviceable in a variety of climates.

The invention of fired brick was inseparable from the invention of the oven; some evidence suggests that the same enclosures were first used for both cooking and constructing. In cooking bricks, the kiln walls do work no open-air fire could. Even within the earliest known kilns, temperatures could rise well above 1000 degrees Celsius. Bricks composed of 50 percent clay require from eight to fifteen hours of heat at this temperature and an equal time to cool slowly in order not to crack.

The character of brick varies in the amount of clay it holds. Unbaked mud bricks are usually composed of less than 30 percent clay; at the other, baked extreme, terracotta brick is usually about 75 percent clay. Sand, straw, and water bulk up the clay, but in fired brick, stone must be excluded from or crushed into the mix, because stone can explode in the high heat of a kiln.[15]

The brick, small and portable, radically influenced both the shape and the texture of large buildings. Egyptians at least since 3000 BCE contrived arches and vaults with fired bricks, thus adding curves to the right-angle beam-and-lintel system of more primitive structures. The Mesopotamians became masters of glazing and painting brick, so that permanent color became a feature of walls.

The Greeks were not great innovators of bricks stacked vertically. The availability and durability of architectural stone might partly explain why, though most Greek houses were too modest to be engineered in stone; in public buildings the Greeks wanted carved stone's plasticity. Greek contribution to clay-craft construction lay in the making of tiles laid horizontally. Terra-cotta roof tiles began to be fabricated sometime after 2600 BCE in the region around Argos, from which followed three different systems for overlapping tiles.

Roman bricks tended to be thin, though in other respects they varied widely in shape and size. The Romans were masters of firing brick, and this mastery permitted them to elaborate one of the great feats of all built form, the voussoired arch. In earlier arch making, the mortar joints between rectangular bricks were tapered so that the structure curved; tapered mortar, however, risks degrading endangering the structure. The Romans figured out ways to make wedge-shaped bricks, an innovation that allowed builders to produce the stable voussoired arch, and this form spread everywhere in Roman building, from aqueducts to houses. The wedged bricks needed more complicated molds, and they could not be fired as mechanically as uniformly sized blocks. The brickmaker had to do the equivalent of sautéing an almost-cooked brick to fire it evenly.

Roman brickwork can't be separated from an allied technical

achievement, the refinement of concrete. Primitive forms of concrete were merely a weak mortar made from lime and water. Romans transformed this traditional mortar into concrete by adding volcanic ash known as pozzolana (from Pozzuoli, near Mount Vesuvius), which interacted with lime to give better strength. With this sauce, thick walls of stone rubble could be constructed, the concrete gluing the stone securely.

By about the third century BCE, the technology of poured concrete admitted, in principle, an entirely new way of building. The vast warehouse complex known as the Porticus Aemilia (begun about 193 BCE) showed concrete's powers; here, a huge space was literally poured into being. Sometimes brick and concrete cooperated, as when a brick structure was slathered with concrete molded into forms to resemble cut stone or when parallel brick walls became casings for concrete poured between. In cities, these two materials more often went their separate ways, brick used for the infrastructure of roads, aqueducts, and modest houses, poured concrete the visible material of choice for ceremonial or majestic buildings. Facings were often contrived, as Frank Brown observes, to suggest that the buildings were marble or porphyry all the way through. The building appeared to be made of something that in substance it was not; its materiality was disguised.[16]

As soon as Roman legions captured a territory, Roman engineers began to build a city, based on the mother city. This empire the Romans made of brick, bricks used for roads, bridges, and aqueducts, as well as buildings. The act of making a Roman place or building was deeply encoded with religious symbolism, as the historian Joseph Rykwert has shown. Even the most mundane constructions, like granaries, carried a crust of significance referring to Rome's origins and gods; technology was inseparable from religion.[17] And from the state: every building held political significance; politics and politicians did not turn a blind eye even to the slum dwellings of Rome, in which storey after storey was precariously stacked atop shaky foundations.

These conditions shaped the Roman brick worker's craft. By the reign of the Emperor Hadrian, a century after Christ, the Roman architect had developed detailed, elaborate drawings—the blueprint in germ—and terra-cotta or plaster models to show in three dimensions what a structure should be.[18] Thereafter, matters were left to guilds of craftsmen, ranging from demolition teams to brick masons to carpenters (who made the molds into which concrete was poured) to painters and stucco workers. These guilds were themselves like ministates in their work rules, dictating precisely who did what when. Many of these technician brickmakers and masons were slaves with no rights of their own.

The historian Keith Hopkins reminds us that privileged Romans had a selective vision of those who stood below them. The privileged were indeed intensely aware of the lives of ordinary soldiers, and sheer proximity made them conscious of their household servants, whether free or slave.[19] Craftworkers, and especially slave craftworkers, dwelled in an anonymous space between warfare and personal service.

Romans drew on the Greek distinction between theory and practice to legitimate this domination. Aristotle reappears in Vitruvius's handbook when the Roman master architect declares, "The several arts are composed of two things—craftsmanship and theory." (In Latin this is *ex opera* versus *eius rationatione.*) He elaborates: "Craftsmanship belongs [only] to those who are trained . . . in the work; theory is share with all educated persons. All things are in common so far as theory is concerned . . . whereas work finely executed by hand or technical methods belongs to those who have been specially trained in a single trade."[20] This view, in which the educated generalist dominates the craftsman specialist, reflected a clear hierarchical structure in the Roman state. Vitruvius's *Ten Books of Architecture* (c. 20–30 BCE), the basic text for Roman building, at least contained sections about brick building;[21] other influential Roman architectural writers like Frontinus, Faventinus, and Palladius simply ignored this material of which

the Roman Empire was literally made.[22] "Who made this?" was perhaps a question best left unanswered.

Still the craftsmen found ways of leaving their mark in the work. In
part this was possible because in Roman building construction a gap
existed between command and execution. Like modern NHS medical
staff, a great deal of improvisation occurred on the ground. Many formal "errors" had to be committed to get the houses, roads, and sewers
to function. The thinking of menial workmen involved correction and
adaptation—and it was a dangerous form of thinking because many
guild masters treated these necessary variations as insubordination.
Some forms of improvisation were necessary simply because many
slaves were distant foreigners with no Roman models in their heads; for
these captives, the slave master's whip could not tell them what they
were supposed to do.

※　　※　　※

A maker's mark is a peculiar sign. The Greek maker's mark appeared
especially when potters were able to paint elaborate scenes; they then
began to sign their wares, sometimes with the name of the place in
which they lived, sometimes with their name. Such a signature could
add economic value. Marks left by the Roman slave builder would
attest only to his presence. In some Roman buildings in provincial
Gaul the impressed marks—rarely a name, more often a symbol identifying the place where the maker came from or the tribe to which he
belonged—are as dense in the brickwork as are the mason's marks in
the Taj Mahal, where the Mogul stamps create a huge decorative surface. Many of the adaptive irregularities in Roman brickwork modulated into expressive decoration, tiny flourishes like a figured tile mor-
tared in to cover over an imperfect joint behind the surface. These also
can be considered a maker's mark.

The story of these ancient bricks makes a particular connection
between craftwork and politics. "Presence," in the modern way of

thinking, seems self-referential, emphasizing the word "I." Ancient brickwork established presence through small details marking "it": the detail itself. In the lowly Roman craftsman's way, anonymity and presence could combine. The slave brickmaker had no thought of expression in any modern sense; nor was his realm like that of Ruskin's medieval mason, whose irregular work symbolized the free agency of the craftsman.

The size of bricks also matters in the message they send. The great historian of bricks, Alec Clifton-Taylor, observes that what most counts about them is their small size, which just suits the human hand laying a brick. A brick wall, he says, "is therefore an aggregation of small effects. This implies a human and intimate quality not present to the same extent in stone architecture." Clifton-Taylor further observes that brickwork imposes "a certain restraint . . . brick is anti-monumental . . . the smallness of the brick unit was not in tune with the grander . . . aspirations of the Classicist."[23] Ancient brick workers who labored on the classical empire's most grandiose projects still held in their hands a material with quite a different physical implication, and it was with this material that the anonymous slave brickmaker or mason made his presence known. The historian Moses Finlay wisely counsels against using a modern yardstick to read ancient maker's marks as sending signals of defiance; they declare, "I exist," rather than "I resist." But "I exist" is perhaps the most urgent signal a slave can send.[24]

Anthropomorphosis
Virtue Discovered in the Material

A third kind of material consciousness invests inanimate things with human qualities. "She's running real nice," my auto mechanic tells me about a transmission repair costing a thousand dollars. Bricks are an exemplary study of how anthropomorphosis happens; their makers at a certain moment in history began to invest cooked lumps of clay with human qualities of an ethical sort— as in the "honesty" of brick or the "friendliness" of certain brick walls. This humanizing language bred in turn one of the great dualisms of modern material consciousness: the contrast between naturalness and artificiality.

To understand this anthropomorphic turn, I'd ask the reader to make one of Maynard Smith's mental leaps in time. The Romans put their brick stamp everywhere they camped in Britain. When the empire ended and the Romans departed, English brickmaking went into decline for nearly a thousand years. During this millennium British builders instead cut forests or quarried stone, and only in the 1400s did something approaching the technological sophistication of Roman brick-building reappear. The resurgence of the craft became a necessity when, in 1666, the Great Fire of London consumed most of its wooden buildings; Christopher Wren, in beginning the task of rebuilding the city, made enlargement of the brick trade an urgent priority.

By the latter seventeenth century English brickmakers became adept at manufacturing large quantities of brick cheaply, but not in London. Development occurred largely thanks to the "cottage kiln," the small brickworks set up in villagers' backyards in communities with abundant sources of clay. Brickmaking was an ordinary skill of country life. Cottage kilns had given bricks a new aesthetic quality—color. English brickwork of the sixteenth and seventeenth centuries was largely red, but red of different shades depending on where the brick clay came from and on variations in firing practices from one backyard brickmaker to another.

Anthropomorphism started here; color issued the first invitation to think of bricks as possessing human qualities. Tudor and Stuart buildings, Clifton-Taylor remarks, resembled on their brick surfaces "the palette of the Impressionist painters," the subtle variations of red making the walls shimmer in the light.[25] These color qualities appeared to contemporaries in the eighteenth century variously as a building's "shining mane of hair" or its "mottled skin." Old brickwork in which red tones veered to brown or black was described as "an old man's weathered face."

There is nothing remarkable about the descriptions, as language. They deploy the power of metaphor, just as does "the rosy-fingered dawn," an anthropomorphizing metaphor, as does the single word *warmth* when it refers to a trait of personality rather than to a person running a fever. The puritan scorning such tropes would subject every adjective and adverb to a detective's suspicious scrutiny and thereby radically impoverish language. Still, rosy-fingered dawn reveals little about the balance between reflection and absorption of light in the cloud mist that determines its coloration. The attribution of ethical human qualities—honesty, modesty, virtue—into materials does not aim at explanation; its purpose is to heighten our consciousness of the materials themselves and in this way to think about their value.

Metaphoric richness of this sort infused the language of eighteenth-century English brickmaking as the printed book spread to the crafts-man's realm; the growth of literacy created a reading public among practitioners. Cookery books were written by working cooks; London's guilds had by the seventeenth century issued professional tomes. These latter were collectively distilled wisdom, though in a few cases individual craftsmen-authors identify themselves.[26] All contained far more technical know-how-to than Chambers's *Encyclopedia*, as technical as some of Diderot's volumes but without the philosophy. In the case of brickwork, the new genre of professions book provided patterns, explained procedures, and delved into the merits of bricks made in different provincial kilns.

It was in trying to assess the quality of good brickwork that metaphors of an ethical sort began to intrude: most fundamentally, "honest" brick is brick to which no artificial color has been added to the clay.[27] The medieval goldsmith also sought "honest" gold, but the older frame of reference was different; that word applied strictly to a chemical property, sheer purity of substance. "Honest" brick in the eighteenth century certainly refers to composition and to how bricks are used in construction. "Honest" brick describes brickwork in which all the bricks laid, say, in a Flemish bond course come from the same kiln, and even more, "honest" brick evokes a building surface in which the brickwork is exposed rather than covered over: no cosmetics, no "pots of whore's rouge" have been applied to its face. One reason for this shift was that masons were beginning to be aware of, and feel engaged in, debates about the meaning of naturalness as opposed to artifice—the great Enlightenment preoccupation about nature brought home to the proper use of a natural material.

The work these metaphors did on bricks can be understood through the attitudes we now harbor about organic food. Strictly speaking, organic food refers to purity of substance and minimal manipulation in production. Thus a free-range chicken can be described without anthropomorphizing as a healthy and even a happy bird, since it has been relieved of the stress of the battery cage. We take a step toward referring the nonhuman to the human by thinking more like Ruskin. Consider for instance an irregular tomato, its skin scarred by the traces of a predatory worm, the sort of vegetable sold expensively to consumers who dislike industrialized tomatoes like the Better Boy, perfectly uniform and shiny. Ruskin believes that we are saying something about ourselves in preferring a vegetable whose appearance seems rough-hewn, irregular; the organic tomato mirrors the values of "home" for us. (The Better Boy is, in fact, a tasty tomato.)

In 1756 the virtuoso Isaac Ware published *The Complete Body of Architecture,* a tome that tries to make sense of naturalness, which is for him the proposition that a building ought to look like on the outside the materials of which it is internally made; this makes the building honest—and again, rough-hewn and irregular. Ware loved the sensuous provocation of color emerging from the plebeian cottage kilns.

When Ware designed his own Wrotham Park in 1754, the house was of
simple, red brick (the stucco cement now slathered over this building
dates from the nineteenth century), and in London he admired the
"honest brick" that now marked buildings of the poor. But this arbiter
of eighteenth-century taste also and contradictorily thought that brick
seemed plebeian and therefore should be concealed; Ware warns "the
judicious architect" not to use brick to face the fronts of "dignified"
buildings. He saw the point of artifice in stucco, a material that contrasted to brick.

Stucco is a lime and fine-sieved sand mixture known since Roman
times. In 1677, British builders began using "glassis," a polishable mixture, and from 1773, "Liardet's cement," which admitted an even gloss-
ier surface; the 1770s saw also the appearance of Coade stone, whose
composition is akin to terra-cotta but can be made to look like marble.
In all variants, stucco is a flexible material, suitable for simulating
many things that it is not: ersatz columns can be poured in stucco,
statues, urns, woodcarvings . . . the builder's imagination could summon into being almost any construction the client desired.

Isaac Ware foreshadowed the modern historian John Summerson's
dislike of stucco as "a fake material," yet *The Complete Body of Architecture* addressed in detail such matters as how to mount cupids cast in
glassis over the door frame of a room; how inexpensively to simulate a
grotto filled with porpoises and water nymphs by painting on water-
proofed stucco, and how to tint and vein a polished stucco window
frame so that it looks like Carrara marble.

Stucco, it should be said, was the British social climber's material
of choice. The material permitted quick, cheap constructions of gran-
deur. Stucco imitations of imperial Rome later became a middle-class
tyranny. In the nineteenth century, in Regent's Park, for instance, the
leases for buildings required that "the color of such stucco [is] not to be
varied or changed at any time but always to be in imitation of Bath
stone."[28]

Yet the material dynamics ethics of stucco are those of play and fantasy; its ethics are those of freedom—at least they were to craftsmen. The *Builder's Magazine*, while invoking the virtues of "honest" brick, also showed how the artifices of stucco could give craftsmen more freedom to experiment in their work. In making fake interior columns, the stucco worker should begin with standard form-molds into which the stucco will be poured. Once the molds are removed, the stucco worker can add all manner of variations by hand. Workers adept at this became admired artisans in the trade; Jean André Rouquet used the French phrase *jeu de main*, "play of the hand," to describe such craftsmanship that elicits collegial admiration.

The sharp-eyed reader will have spotted that although "honest brick" is an anthropomorphic construction, the stuccoed column simulating cut stone doesn't make this animate claim. It's just an artificial column. Few clients for a backyard grotto imagined that their guests would be taken in; the pleasure would come in the self-conscious artifice of it all. Naturalness could be, in the hands of the craftsman, a more deceiving experience, as an artful construction that hid its art.

In the English garden of the late eighteenth century, for instance, seemingly jumbled plants were in fact selected to be seen to best advantage by human eyes; the paths were carefully laid out to compose a narrative of surprises for the stroller; the ha-ha, a fence sunk deep into a trough in the ground, separated animals in the field from observers roaming the garden but created the illusion that the cows and sheep ranged freely near the viewer: the wild English garden was anything but wild. Rather, it was sculpted like stucco.

In the realm of brick, the great modern debate about the virtues of naturalness and the contrary freedoms of fantasy-artifice crystallized as two different versions of craft. In Ware's time, brick seemed a building material that fit more largely in the search for authenticity as it appeared in the political writings of Rousseau. Brick embodied the

Enlightenment desires to live in harmony with simple things, a desire pictured by Chardin, and to show oneself as one really was, evinced by the revealing muslin dresses women wore at home. As in the garden, the painter and the seamstress sought to hide their presence. Clothing the body perhaps best makes the point. The eighteenth century was an age of wigs worn in public by the same men who preferred simple, "honest" clothes in private. These home clothes were anything but rags; they were artfully cut so as to bring out the weaver's best physical features, as artful as the miniature models of ships British and French women wore in their hair in public to mark the nation's triumph against an enemy in combat—the hair coated with grease and dyed blue to look like wavy seawater.[29]

Philosophers of varied stripes have long argued that the division between nature and culture is a false distinction. This brief excursion into brick's history suggests that such an argument rather misses the point. The distinction can be literally constructed, and the point is how to do it. In the craftsman's hand, baked clay became an emblem of natural rectitude; this natural virtue was made rather than found. As in the necessary pairing, in the French *Encyclopedia*, between two glassmaking procedures, so too in humanizing materials it was necessary to pair honesty and fantasy, brick and stucco; they played off each other. Again, the eighteenth century shows one technique for how to anthropomorphize, a technique that can be found in many other cultures at many different historical moments. When the natural and the artificial are set as opposites, human virtue can be attached to the first, freedom to the second. Craft skills are necessary to make these attachments and so heighten the conscious value of objects. Of the large number of bricks flooding into London from genuine cottage kilns, Ware the connoisseur-builder severely selected only the best of breed as embodying his values. The craftsman constructing an object that seems simple and honest is as thoughtful—might we say as cunning?—as the craftsman contriving a fantasy.

＊   ＊   ＊

As a pendent to this story, a word might be added about brickmaking since Isaac Ware's time. In the industrial era, these modest objects came to be involved in the debate about simulation. Is simulation dishonest? Is it destructive?—not an abstract question; as the trials of computer-aided design show, simulation can be a synonym for "design."

It was already evident in the eighteenth century that objects made by machine could be programmed to look traditionally handmade. Diderot's *Encyclopedia* notes the phenomenon of simulation, marveling at looms that industrially reproduced old tapestries, but these were high-cost, specialty reproductions. In brickmaking, it soon became clear that machines could simulate some of the qualities of "honest brick" cheaply, in immense quantities. The entrance of the machine would sustain debate about the integrity of this material up to our own time.

The sheer quantity of machined brick seemed, on one hand, to end any ethical debate based on brick's natural properties. A century after Ware, uniform bricks were produced that betrayed no hint of their local color variations. The variable color of clay was "corrected" by the addition of mineral dyes before the raw clay was further homogenized in steam-driven grinds and molders. The consistency of brick was further assured through the introduction of the Hoffmann kiln in 1858; in this kiln, heat could be maintained at a constant temperature, twenty-four hours a day, a steadiness that meant that the volume of brick produced increased dramatically in round-the-clock operations. The Victorians became engulfed by mountains of these manufactured, monotonous bricks, which Ruskin among many others hated.

But the same technical advances could be used for simulation: color could be added, clay-sand ratios altered to mimic the composition of traditional bricks from different locales. The pre-industrial brickmaker was not entirely innocent; one traditional means of making new brick look old consisted of coating laid bricks with pig-manure slime. In the factories, this effect could be achieved before the bricks arrived on site—quicker to use and with no need of pigs. Intellectuals imagine the "simulacrum" to be a product of "postmodernity"; brickworkers had to cope with simulacra long before. The traditional craftsman could only defend the brickmaking sphere by maintaining that he or she could detect the difference between real and simulated, but this was a matter for colleagues and cognoscenti. In fact, industrialized advances in brickmaking have made the differences ever harder to detect. As is true of the industrial factories now that mix, knead, and bake organic bread.

Arguably the greatest modern brick building that stresses the truth of materials on Isaac Ware's terms is Alvar Aalto's Baker House, a student residence constructed between 1946 and 1949 at the Massachusetts Institute of Technology. The building in form is a long, undulating wall, its curved walls giving student bedrooms different but equally fine views of the Charles River outside. The curved walls are made of brick, and in a self-consciously "primitive" way. Here's how Aalto describes his construction method: "The bricks were made of clay from topsoil exposed to the sun. They were fired in manually stacked pyramids, using nothing but oak for fuel. When the walls were erected all bricks were approved without sorting, with the result that the color shifts from black to canary yellow, thought the predominant shade is bright red."[30] This self-consciously traditional way of making bricks seems to take our story full circle. Aalto highlights the "honesty" of his brickmaking in a mark impressed on the wall surface; at intervals each course of brickwork includes an overburned, twisted brick. These blackened, twisted bricks make the viewer see the regular bricks fresh;

the contrast brings forward the character of both. We are thus disposed to think about what brick is—a reflection on the material that might not come to us were all the bricks imperturbably, uniformly perfect.

Simulation remains, in the craftsman's realm, just the same provocation it was in the eighteenth century: the negative we need to print a "real" positive. The industrialized simulacrum makes us think harder about nature. Aalto's positive print was the imperfect brick as an icon of virtue. The nature and virtue we are thinking of concerns ourselves.

The long history of crafting clay shows three ways of becoming aroused consciously by materials, in altering, marking, or identifying them with ourselves. Each act has a rich inner structure: metamorphosis can occur through development of a type-form, combination of forms, or domain shift. Marking an object can be a political act, not in the programmatic sense, but in the more fundamental matter of establishing one's presence, objectively. Anthropomorphosis reveals the power of metaphor and a technique for manufacturing symbols. In the history of clayware, none of these three processes proved as simple as these summary labels might suggest. The worker in clay coped slowly with technical change, with political oppression rendering him or her invisible, and with the clash of human attributes. We could of course treat clay simply as a material that is necessary for cooking and for shelter. But in this utilitarian spirit we would eliminate most of what has made this substance culturally consequent.

A Summary of Part One

It might be useful at this point to look at the path we've taken in Part One.

The craftsman is a more inclusive category than the artisan; he or she represents in each of us the desire to do something well, concretely, for its own sake. Developments in high technology reflect an ancient model for craftsmanship, but the reality on the ground is that people who aspire to be good craftsmen are depressed, ignored, or misunderstood by social institutions. These ills are complicated because few institutions set out to produce unhappy workers. People seek refuge in inwardness when material engagement proves empty; mental anticipation is privileged above concrete encounter; standards of quality in work separate design from execution.

The history of artisans has something to tell about these more general ills. We began in the medieval workshop, in which unequals, master and apprentice, were bound tightly together. The separation of art from craft in the Renaissance altered that social relation; the workshop further altered as the skills practiced in it became unique practices. This was a history in which individuation within the workshop produced only more dependency in society at large, a long sweep of change in which the handing on of skill and transfer of technology became troubled. The social space of the workshop thus became a fragmented space; the meaning of authority became problematic.

Progressive spirits in the mid-eighteenth century wanted to repair these fissures. To do so they had to address a distinctively modern tool, the industrial machine. They sought both a humane understanding of the machine and an equally enlightened sense of themselves in comparison to the machine's powers. A century later, the machine no longer seemed to admit this humanity; it appeared to dramatize the sheer fact of domination; the most radical way to contest machinery seemed, to some, to turn one's back to modernity itself. This Romantic gesture had the virtue of heroism, but it doomed the artisan, who could not work out how he or she might escape becoming the machine's victim.

From the origins of classical civilization, craftsmen have suffered mistreatment. What has kept them going humanly is belief in their work and their involvement with its materials. Material awareness has taken, over time, the three forms explored in this chapter, a consciousness sustaining work if not enriching the worker.

Perhaps the path we have traced ends logically in the poet William Carlos Williams's declaration in the 1930s that there should be "no ideas but in things." The poet was sick of soul talk; better to dwell in "things touched by the hands during the day."[31] This has been the craftsman's credo in the past. In Part Two, we turn to how the craftsman acquires and develops specific physical skills to do so.

PART TWO   Craft

CHAPTER FIVE

The Hand

Technique has a bad name; it can seem soulless. That's not how people whose hands become highly trained view technique. For them, technique will be intimately linked to expression. This chapter takes a first step in investigating the connection.

Two centuries ago Immanuel Kant casually remarked, "The hand is the window on to the mind."[1] Modern science has sought to make good on this observation. Of all the human limbs, the hands make the most varied movements, movements that can be controlled at will. Science has sought to show how these motions, plus the hand's varied ways of gripping and the sense of touch, affect how we think. That link between hand and head I will explore among three sorts of craftsmen whose hands become highly trained: musicians, cooks, and glassblowers. Advanced hand technique of their sort is a specialized human condition but has implications for more ordinary experience.

The Intelligent Hand
How the Hand Became Human
Grip and Touch

The image of "the intelligent hand" appeared in the sciences as early as 1833 when, a generation before Darwin, Charles Bell published

The Hand.[2] Bell, a devout Christian, believed the hand came from God the Creator perfectly designed, a fit-for-purpose limb like all of his works. Bell accorded the hand a privileged place in creation, using various experiments to argue that the brain receives more trustworthy information from the touch of the hand than from images in the eye—the latter so often yielding false, misleading appearances. Darwin dethroned Bell's conviction the belief that the hand was timeless in form and function. In evolution, Darwin surmised, the brains of apes became larger as their arms hands were used for other purposes than steadying the moving body.[3] With greater brain capacity, our human ancestors learned how to hold things in their hands, to think about what they held, and eventually to shape the things held; man-apes could make tools, humans make culture.

Until recently, evolutionists thought that it is the *uses* of the hand, rather than changes in its structure, that have matched the increasing size of the brain. Thus a half-century ago Frederick Wood Jones wrote, "It is not the hand that is perfect, but the whole nervous mechanism by which movements of the hand are evoked, coordinated, and controlled" which has enabled *Homo sapiens* to develop.[4] Today we know that, in the near history of our species, the physical structure of the hand has itself evolved. The modern philosopher and medical doctor Raymond Tallis explains part of the change by contrasting chimpanzee and human freedom to move the thumb at the trapezio-metacarpal joint: "As in chimpanzees, the joint is composed of interlocking concave and convex surfaces which form a saddle. The difference between ourselves and chimpanzees is that the saddle interlocks more in chimpanzees, and this restricts movement; in particular, it prevents opposition of the thumb to the other fingers."[5] Research by John Napier and others has shown how, in the evolution of *Homo sapiens*, the physical opposition between thumb and fingers has become ever more articulate; the opposition of thumb to other digits has combined with subtle changes occurred in the bones that support and strengthen the index finger.[6]

Such structural changes have allowed our species a distinctive physical experience of grip. Grips are voluntary actions; to grip is a decision, in contrast to involuntary motions like the blinking of the eyelids. The ethnologist Mary Marzke has usefully sorted out three basic ways we grip things. First, we can pinch small objects between the tip of the thumb and the side of the index finger. Second, we can cradle an object in the palm and then move it around with pushing and massaging actions between thumb and fingers. (Though advanced primates can perform these two grips, they cannot perform them as well as we can.) Third is the cupping grip—as when a ball or other biggish object is held by the rounded hand, thumb and index finger placed opposite the object—and is even more developed in our species. The cupping grip allows us to hold an object securely in one hand while we work on it with the other hand.

Once an animal like ourselves can grip well in these three ways, cultural evolution takes over. Marzke dates *Homo faber*'s first appearance on earth to the moment when, as it were, someone could grip things securely in order to work them over: "Most of the unique features of the modern human hand, including the thumb, can be related to . . . the stresses that would have been incurred with the use of these grips in the manipulation of stone tools."[7] Thinking then ensues about the nature of what one holds. American slang advises us to "get a grip"; more generally we speak of "coming to grips with an issue." Both figures reflect the evolutionary dialogue between the hand and the brain.

There is, however, a problem about grips, especially important to people who develop an advanced hand technique. This is how to let go. In music, for instance, one can play rapidly and cleanly only by learning how to come off a piano key or how to release the finger on a string or on a valve. In the same way, mentally, we need to let go of a problem, usually temporarily, in order to see better what it's about, then take hold of it afresh. Neuropsychologists now believe that the physical and cognitive capacity to release underlies the ability of people to let go of a fear or an obsession. Release is also full of ethical implication, as when we surrender control—our grip—over others.

One of the myths that surround technique is that people who develop it to a high level must have unusual bodies to begin with. As concerns the hand, this is not quite true. For instance, the ability to move one's fingers very rapidly is lodged in all human bodies, in the pyramidal tract in the brain. All hands can be stretched out through training so that the thumb forms a right angle to the first finger. A necessity for cellists, pianists with small hands can likewise develop ways to overcome this limit.[8] Other demanding physical activities like surgery do not require special hands to begin with—Darwin long ago observed that physical endowment is a starting point, not an end, in any organism's behavior. This is certainly true of human hand technique. Grips develop in individuals just as they have developed in our species.

Touch poses different issues about the intelligent hand. In the history of medicine, as in philosophy, there has been a long-standing debate about whether touch furnishes the brain a different kind of sensate information than the eye. It has seemed that touch delivers invasive, "unbounded" data, whereas the eye supplies images that are contained in a frame. If you touch a hot stove, your whole body goes into sudden trauma, whereas a painful sight can be instantly diminished by shutting your eyes. A century ago, the biologist Charles Sherrington reformatted this discussion. He explored what he called "active touch," which names the conscious intent guiding the fingertip; touch appeared to him proactive as well as reactive.[9]

A century on, Sherrington's research has taken a further turn. The fingers can engage in proactive, probing touch without conscious intent, as when the fingers search for some particular spot on an object that stimulates the brain to start thinking; this is called "localized" touch. We've already seen an instance of it, for this is how the medieval goldsmith made an assay; his judgments were made by the fingertips rolling and pressing the metallic "earth" until a particular spot that seemed impure was found. From this localized sensate evidence, the goldsmith reasoned backward to the nature of the material.

The calluses developed by people who use their hands profession-ally constitute a particular case of localized touch. In principle the thickened layer of skin should deaden touch; in practice, the reverse occurs. By protecting the nerve endings in the hand, the callus makes the act of probing less hesitant. Although the physiology of this process is not yet well understood, the result is: the callus both sensitizes the hand to minute physical spaces and stimulates the sensation at the fin-gertips. We could imagine the callus doing the same thing for the hand as the zoom lens does for the camera.

About the hand's animal powers, Charles Bell believed that dif-ferent sense limbs or organs had separate neural channels to the brain and thus that the senses could be isolated from one another. Today's neural science shows his belief to be false; instead, a neural network of eye-brain-hand allows touching, gripping, and seeing to work in con-cert. Stored information about holding a ball, for instance, helps the brain make sense of a two-dimensional photograph of a ball: the curve of the hand and the hand's sense of the ball's weight help the brain think in three dimensions, seeing a flat object on paper in the round.

Prehension
To Grasp Something

To say that we "grasp something" implies physically that we reach for it. In the familiar physical gesture of grasping a glass, the hand will assume a rounded shape, suitable for cupping the glass, before it actu-ally touches the surface. The body is ready to hold before it knows whether what it will hold is freezing cold or boiling hot. The technical name for movements in which the body anticipates and acts in advance of sense data is *prehension*.

Mentally, we "grasp something" when we understand the concept, say, of an equation like $a / d = b + c$ rather than simply perform the operations. Prehension gives a particular cast to mental understanding as well as physical action: you don't wait to think until all information is in hand, you anticipate the meaning. Prehension signals alertness, engagement, and risk-taking all in the act of looking ahead; it is in spirit the very opposite of the prudent accountant who does not exert a mental muscle until he or she has all the numbers.

Human newborns begin to practice prehension as early as their second week by reaching for baubles held in front of them. Since the eye and the hand act in concert, prehension increases when the baby can hold up its head; with the neck more under control, an infant can better see what it is reaching for. In the first five months of life, the baby's arm develops the neuromuscular capacity to move independently toward what the eye sees. In the next five months, the baby's hand develops the neuromuscular capacity to shape itself into different grasping positions. Both skills are tied to the development of the pyramidal tract in the brain, a pathway between the primary motor region of the cortex and the spinal cord. By the end of the first year, in Frank Wilson's words, "the hand is ready for a lifetime of physical exploration."[10]

The verbal results of prehension are illustrated by an experiment the philosopher Thomas Hobbes conducted in tutoring the young children of the Cavendish family. Hobbes sent the young Cavendishes into a darkened room into which he'd placed all sorts of unfamiliar objects. After they'd groped about, he asked them to leave the room and describe to him what they "saw" with their hands. He noted than the children used sharper, more precise language than the words they used when they could see in a lit space. He explained this in part as a matter of them "grasping for sense" in the dark, a stimulus that served them to speak well later, in the light, when the immediate sensations had "decayed."[11]

Reaching for something, in the prehensive way, establishes facts on the ground. For instance, when a conductor gives directive hand gestures a moment ahead of the sound. If the hand gesture for a down-beat came exactly in time, the conductor would not be leading, since the sound would already have happened. Batsmen in cricket get the same advice: "get ahead of the swing." Beryl Markham's remarkable memoir *West through the Night* provides yet another example. In the days when pilots lacked much guidance from instruments, she flew through the African night by imagining that she had already made the lift or turn she was about to make.[12] All these technical feats are based on what anyone does in reaching for a glass.

Raymond Tallis has given the fullest account we now have of pre-hension. He organizes this phenomenon into four dimensions: antic-ipation, of the sort that shapes the hand reaching for the glass; contact, when the brain acquires sense data through touch; language cognition, in naming what one holds; and last, reflection on what one has done.[13] Tallis does not insist that these must add up to self-consciousness. One's orientation can remain focused on the object; what the hand knows is what the hand does. To Tallis's four I'll add a fifth element: the values developed by highly skilled hands.

Hand Virtues
At the Fingertip
Truthfulness

In learning to play a string instrument, young children do not know at first where to place their fingers on the fingerboard to produce an accurate pitch. The Suzuki method, named after the Japanese music educator Suzuki Shin'ichi, solves this problem instantly by taping thin plastic strips onto the fingerboard. The child violinist places a finger on a color strip to sound a note perfectly in tune. This method emphasizes beauty of tone, which Suzuki called "tonalization," from the start, without focusing on the complexities of producing a beautiful tone. The hand motion is determined by a fixed destination for the fingertip.[14]

This user-friendly method inspires instant confidence. By the fourth lesson, a child can become a virtuoso of the nursery tune "Twinkle, Twinkle, Little Star." And the Suzuki method breeds a sociable confidence; an entire orchestra of seven-year-olds can belt out "Twinkle, Twinkle, Little Star" because the hand of each knows exactly what to do. These happy certainties erode, however, the moment the strips are removed.

In principle, habit should have ingrained accuracy. One might imagine that the fingers would simply go down on the unmarked fingerboard exactly where the tape had been. In fact, habit of this mechanical sort fails—and for a physical reason. The Suzuki method has stretched small hands laterally at the knuckle ridge but has not sensitized the fingertip that actually presses down on the string. Because the fingertip doesn't know the fingerboard, sour notes appear as soon as the tapes come off. As in love, so in technique; innocent confidence is weak. A further complication ensues if the player looks at the fingerboard, trying to see where the fingertip should go. The eye will find no answer on this smooth, black surface. Thus, a child orchestra when first untaped sounds like a howling mob.

Here is a problem of false security. The musical child's problem recalls Victor Weisskopf's caution to adult scientific technicians that "the computer understands the answer but I don't think you understand the answer." Another adult analogy to taping would be the "grammar-check" functions of word-processing programs; these give the button-pusher no insight into why one grammatical construction is preferable to others.

Suzuki well understood the problem of false security. He counseled removing the tapes as soon as the child feels the pleasure of making music. A self-taught musician (his interest in the late 1940s began when he heard a recording by Mischa Elman of Franz Schubert's "Ave Maria"), Suzuki knew from his experiments that truthfulness lies at the fingertips: touch is the arbiter of tone. There is a parallel here also to the goldsmith's assay, the slow, probing touch of materials at the fingertips that eschewed instant, false security.

We want to know what sort of truth is this, which casts off false security.

In music, the ear works in concert with the fingertip to probe. Put rather dryly, the musician touches the string in different ways, hears a variety of effects, then searches for the means to repeat and reproduce the tone he or she wants. In reality, this can be difficult and agonizing struggle to answer the questions "What exactly did I do? How can I do it again?" Instead of the fingertip acting as a mere servant, this kind of touching moves backward from sensation to procedure. The principle here is reasoning backward from consequence to cause.

What follows for someone acting on this principle? Imagine an untaped boy struggling to play in tune. He seems to get one note exactly right, but then the ear tells him that the next note he plays in that position sounds sour. There's a physical reason for this trouble: in all stringed instruments, when the pressed string becomes shorter in length, the width between the fingers must also diminish; feedback from the ear sends the signal that lateral adjustment is needed at the knuckle ridge (a famous exercise in Jean-Pierre Duport's *Études* explores the interplay between diminishing lateral width and maintaining the rounded hand as the cellist moves across all strings for their entire two-foot length). Through trial and error the untaped neophyte might learn how contract at the ridge, yet still no solution will be in sight. He may have held his hand at a right angle to the fingerboard. Perhaps now he should try sloping the palm to one side, up toward the pegs; this helps. He can produce an accurate sound because the slope equalizes the relations between the first and second fingers, which are unequal in length. (Moreover, a perfectly right-angle address to the string strains the second, longer finger.) But this new position makes a hash of the lateral ridge problem he thought he had solved. And on it goes. Every new issue of playing in tune causing him to rethink solutions arrived at before.

What could motivate a child to pursue such a demanding path? One school of psychology says that the motivation is lodged in an experience fundamental to all human development: the primal event of separation can teach the young human to become curious. This research is associated with, in the mid-twentieth century, D. W. Winnicott and John Bowlby, psychologists interested in humans' earliest experiences of attachment and separation, beginning with the infant's disconnection from its mother's breast.[15] In pop-psychology, the loss of that connection begets anxiety and mourning; the British psychologists sought to show just why it is a much richer event.

Winnicott posited that once no longer one with the maternal body, the infant is newly stimulated, directed outward. Bowlby went into the nursery to study the difference separation makes in the ways young children touch, weigh, and turn around inanimate objects. He observed with care daily activities that before him had been taken to be of little consequence. For us, one aspect of this research is particularly valuable.

Both psychologists emphasized the energies children come to invest in "transitional objects"—technical jargon for the human capacity to care about those people or material things that themselves change. As psychotherapists, this school of psychologists sought to aid adult patients who seemed fixated in infantile traumas of security to dwell more easily in the realm of shifting human relationships. But the idea of the "transitional object" more largely names what can truly engage curiosity: an uncertain or unstable experience. Still, the child submitting to the uncertainties of tone production, or indeed any highly demanding hand activity, is a special case: he or she seems confronted by what might seem an unending, mushy process yielding only provisional solutions that give the musician no sense of increasing control and no emotional experience of security.

Matters don't quite become so dire because the musician has an objective standard to meet: playing in tune. Like the policy wonks described in Chapter 1, it might be argued that high levels of technical skill can be reached only by people with fixed objective standards of truth. Musically we need simply observe that *believing* in correctness drives technical improvement; curiosity about transitional objects evolves into definitions of what they should be. The quality of sound is such a standard of correctness—even for Suzuki. This is why he begins with tonalization. The belief in and search for correctness in technique breeds expression. In music, this passage occurs when standards modulate from physical events liking playing with a good tone to more aesthetic measures of, for instance, a well-shaped phrase. Of course, spontaneous discoveries and happy accident inform what a musical piece should sound like. Still the composer and the performer must have a criterion to make sense of happy accidents, to select some as happier than others. In developing technique, we resolve transitional objects into definitions, and we make decisions based on such definitions.

Both composers and performers are said to hear with the "inner ear," but that immaterial metaphor is misleading—famously for composers like Arnold Schoenberg, shocked by the actual sounds of what they've written on the page, equally for the performer whose study of scores is necessary but not sufficient preparation for putting bow to string or lips to reed. The sound itself is the moment of truth.

This is therefore also the moment when error becomes clear to the musician. As a performer, at my fingertips I experience error—error that I will seek to correct. I have a standard for what should be, but my truthfulness resides in the simple recognition that I make mistakes. Sometimes in discussions of science this recognition is reduced to the cliché of "learning from one's mistakes." Musical technique shows that the matter is not so simple. I have to be willing to commit error, to play wrong notes, in order eventually to get them right. This is the commitment to truthfulness that the young musician makes by removing the Suzuki tapes.

In making music, the backward relationship between fingertip and palm has a curious consequence: it provides a solid foundation for developing physical security. Practicing that attends to momentary error at the fingertips actually increases confidence: once the musician can do something correctly more than once, he or she is no longer terrorized by that error. In turn, by making something happen more than once, we have an object to ponder; variations in that conjuring act permit exploration of sameness and difference; practicing becomes a narrative rather than mere digital repetition; hard-won movements become ever more deeply ingrained in the body; the player inches forward to greater skill. In the taped state, by contrast, musical practice becoming boring, the same thing repeated over and over. Here handwork, not surprisingly, tends to degrade.

Diminishing the fear of making mistakes is all-important in our art, since the musician on stage can't stop, paralyzed, if she or he makes a mistake. In performance, the confidence to recover from error is not a personality trait; it is a learned skill. Technique develops, then, by a dialectic between the correct way to do something and the willingness to experiment through error. The two sides cannot be separated. If the young musician is simply given the correct way, he or she will suffer from a false sense of security. If the budding musician luxuriates in curiosity, simply going with the flow of the transitional object, she or he will never improve.

This dialogue addresses one of the shibboleths in craftsmanship, the employment of "fit-for-purpose" procedures or tools. Fit-for-purpose seeks to eliminate all procedures that do not serve a predetermined end. The idea was embodied in Diderot's plates of L'Anglée, which showed no litter or wasted paper; programmers now speak of systems without "hiccups"; the Suzuki tape is a fit-for-purpose contrivance. We should think of fit-for-purpose as an achievement rather than a starting point. To arrive at that goal, the work process has to do something distasteful to the tidy mind, which is to dwell temporarily in mess—wrong moves, false starts, dead ends. Indeed, in technology, as in art, the probing craftsman does more than encounter mess; he or she creates it as a means of understanding working procedures.

Fit-for-purpose action sets the context for prehension. Prehension seems to prepare the hand to be fit and ready, but this is an incomplete story. In making music we certainly prepare yet cannot recoil when our hand does not then fit its aim or purpose; to correct, we have to be willing—more, to desire—to dwell in error a bit longer in order to understand fully what was wrong about the initial preparation. The full scenario of practice sessions that improve skill is thus: prepare, dwell in mistakes, recover form. In this narrative, fit-for-purpose is achieved rather than preconceived.

The Two Thumbs
From Coordination, Cooperation

An abiding virtue of craftsmen appears in the social imagery of the workshop. Diderot idealized cooperation in the images of papermaking at L'Anglée, its employees laboring together in harmony. Is there some bodily basis for working cooperatively? In the social sciences, that question has been most recently and most often addressed in discussions about altruism. Debate has focused on whether altruism is programmed into human genes. I want to tack in a different direction: What might experiences of physical coordination suggest about social cooperation? This is a question that can be made concrete in exploring how the two hands coordinate and cooperate with each other.

The digits of the hands are of unequal strength and flexibility, impeding equal coordination. This is true even of the two thumbs, whose capabilities depend on whether one is right- or left-handed. When hand skills develop to a high level, these inequalities can be compensated; fingers and thumbs will do work that other digits cannot perform for themselves. The colloquial English usages of "lending a hand" or the "helping hand" reflect such visceral experience. The compensatory work of the hands suggests—perhaps it is no more than a suggestion—that fraternal cooperation does not depend on sharing equally a skill. I'm going to use music again as a medium for exploring coordination and cooperation among unequal members, but I'll shift instruments from strings to the piano.

Independence of the hands is a big issue in piano playing, as is independence of the fingers. Simple piano music often assigns the starring melodic role to the fourth and fifth fingers, the weakest in the right hand, and the rock-bottom harmonic role to the equally weakest two fingers in the left hand. These digits must strengthen, and the thumb, the strongest finger in each hand, has to learn to work with them by holding back power. The music vouchsafed beginners will most likely give the right hand a more important role than the left. So, at the outset, the player's hand coordination encounters the problems of reconciling inequalities.

In jazz piano, this physical challenge becomes even more difficult. Modern jazz piano today seldom separates melody and harmony between the two hands, as they were in barrelhouse blues. In modern jazz piano, rhythms are often set by the right hand rather than, as they once were, by the left. When he first began playing jazz, the pianist and philosopher David Sudnow discovered just how difficult the resulting problems of coordination could be. In his remarkable book *Ways of the Hand*, Sudnow, classically trained, recounts how he began to transform himself into a jazz pianist. He began by taking a logical but wrong path.[16]

In jazz piano playing, the left hand more often has to execute wide lateral palm stretches or scrunch up its fingers into bundles to achieve the harmonies peculiar to this art. Sudnow began logically enough by sequencing the movements from stretch to scrunch. Correspondingly, he worked separately on the rapid lateral movement of his right hand across wide spaces on the keyboard, the hopping hand that in traditional jazz "strides"; in more modern jazz, getting quickly to the piano's upper registers keeps the rhythmic pulse flowing at the top.

Breaking his technical problems into parts proved counterproductive. The separation did little to help him scrunch on the left and stride on the right together. Worse, he overprepared the separate practices, which can be fatal for improvisation. More subtly, working with the two hands separately created a problem for his thumbs. These are the jazz pianist's most valuable fingers, the anchors on the keyboard. But now, anchoring as it were different-sized ships, each traveling its own course, the thumbs couldn't work together.

A eureka moment came to him when he discovered that "a single note would perfectly well suffice" to orientate him. "One note could be played during one chord's duration and another right next to it for another's, and melodies could be done that way."[17] In terms of technique, this means that all the fingers begin to work like thumbs, and the two thumbs begin to interact, taking on each other's roles when needed.

Once Sudnow had his eureka moment, he changed his practice procedure. He used all the fingers as true partners. If physically one of these partners was too weak or too strong, he asked another to do the job. Photographs that show Sudnow at work horrify conventional piano teachers; he looks contorted. But hearing him, one senses how easily he plays. He does so because he had at a certain point made coordination his goal whenever he practiced.

There is a biological reason why coordination between unequal members works. The corpus callosum in the brain is a gateway connecting the brain's right motor cortex to its left motor cortex. The gateway passes information about the control of bodily movement from one side to the other. Practice that divides handwork into parts weakens this neural transfer.[18]

Compensation also has a biological foundation. *Homo sapiens* has been described as the "lopsided ape."[19] Physical prehension is lopsided. We reach for things with one hand more than the other—in most humans, with the right hand. In the cupping grip described by Mary Marzke, the weaker hand cups the object on which the stronger hand works. The French psychologist Yves Guiard has studied how to counter lopsidedness—with some surprising results.[20] Strengthening the weaker limb is, as we might expect, part of the story, but exercises aimed at achieving this alone will not make the weaker hand more dexterous. The stronger hand has to recalibrate its strength to permit dexterity to develop in the weaker partner. The same thing is true of fingers. The index finger has to think, as it were, like a fourth finger to "help out." So, too, with the two thumbs: we hear Sudnow's two thumbs working together as one, but physiologically, his stronger thumb is holding back tensile force. This is even more necessary when the thumb helps the weak fourth finger; it needs to behave like a fourth finger. Playing an arpeggio in which the strong left thumb reaches out to assist the weaker right little finger is perhaps the most demanding physical task in cooperative coordination.

Hand coordination confronts a great delusion about how people become skilled. That is to imagine that one builds up technical control by proceeding from the part to the whole, perfecting the work of each part separately, then putting the parts together—as though technical competence resembles industrial production on an assembly line. Hand coordination works poorly if organized in this way. Rather than the combined result of discrete, separate, individualized activities, coordination works much better if the two hands work together from the start.

The arpeggio also provides a hint about the sort of fraternity idealized by Diderot, and after him Saint-Simon, Fourier, and Robert Owen, the fraternity of people who share the same skill. The real test of their bond comes when they recognize that they share it in unequal degree. The "fraternal hand" represents finger restraint among stronger digits that Yves Guiard sees as the crux of physical coordination; has this a social reflection? This hint can be taken further by understanding better the role of minimum force in developing hand skills.

Hand-Wrist-Forearm
The Lesson of Minimum Force

To make sense of minimum force, let's look into another kind of skilled handwork, the chef's hand.

Archaeologists have found sharpened stones used for cutting that are 2.5 million years old; bronze knives date back at least six thousand years, and hammered iron at least 3,500.[21] Raw iron was simpler than bronze to cast and an improvement in knives because it could be more easily sharpened. Today's tempered-steel knives consummate that rude quest for sharpness. The knife, notes sociologist Norbert Elias, has always represented "a dangerous instrument . . . a weapon of attack," which all cultures must surround with taboos in peaceable times, especially when knives are used for domestic purposes.[22] Thus, in setting a table, we place the knife with its sharp edge inward rather than facing outward and so threatening our neighbor.

Because of its potential danger, the knife and its use have long been associated symbolically with self-control. For instance, C. Calviac, in his treatise Civilité of 1560, counsels a young person to "cut his meat into very small pieces on his cutting board," then lift the meat to his mouth "with his right hand . . . with three fingers only." This behavior replaced a prior use of the knife as a spear to hold up great chunks of food so that the mouth could gnaw on them. Calviac criticized that way of eating not only because juices were likely to dribble down one's chin or that one ran the risk of inhaling snot and fluids from the nose but also because it sent no signal of self-restraint.[23]

At the Chinese table, chopsticks have for thousands of years replaced the knife as a peaceable symbol; its use enables small pieces of food to be eaten in the hygenic, disciplined way recommended a mere five hundred years ago by Calviac. The Chinese craftsman's problem was how to deliver food that could be consumed with the peaceable chopsticks rather than the barbaric knife. Part of the solution lies in the fact that, as a killing instrument, the sharpened tip of a knife matters; as a cooking instrument, the side of the blade counts for more. When China emerged into the hammered-iron age in the Chou dynasty, specialized knives meant only for cooking appeared, notably the cleaver, with its razor-sharp edge and squared-off tip.

The cleaver chef in China, from the Chou dynasty up to recent times, prided himself on using the cleaver as an all-purpose tool, cutting meat into parts, slices, or mince (*hsiao, tsu,* or *hui*), whereas less skillful cooks resorted to several knives. The *Chuang-tzu,* an early Taoist text, celebrated the cook Ting, who used the cleaver to find "the gaps in the joints," a fine dissection that will ensure that human teeth can get to all the edible meat in an animal.[24] The cleaver chef sought precision in slicing fish and dicing vegetables, increasing edible yield; the knife created regular sizes in animal and vegetable pieces so that they could be cooked more equally in a single pot. The secret enabling these aims is the calculation of minimum force, through the technique of fall and release.

Ancient cleaver technique derived from the same kind of choice a home carpenter faces today in deciding how to hammer a nail into wood. One option is to put one's thumb on the side of the hammer's shank in order to guide the tool; all the strength of the blow will then come from the wrist. The alternative wraps the thumb around the shank; now one's whole forearm can provide the force. If the home carpenter chooses the second, he or she will increase the raw power of the blow but will also risk losing accuracy in aiming it. The ancient Chinese cleaver chef opted for the second position but worked out a different way to use the combined forearm, hand, and cleaver in order to cut food finely. Instead of hammering a blow, he or she guided from the elbow joint the fused forearm, hand, and cleaver so that the knife edge *fell* into the food; the moment the blade made contact, the forearm muscles contracted to *relieve* further pressure.

Recall that the chef holds the cleaver with the thumb around the shank; the forearm serves as an extension of the shank, the elbow as its pivot. At the minimum, the weight of the falling cleaver would provide the only force, which would cleave soft food so that it is not crushed—rather as though the chef is playing pianissimo. But raw food can be harder, and the cook must play, as it were, louder, applying more pressure from the elbow to create a culinary forte. Still, in chopping food, as in sounding chords, the base line of physical control, the starting point, is the calculation and application of minimum force. The cook turns the pressure down rather than scales it up; the chef's very care not to damage the materials has trained him or her to do so. A crushed vegetable cannot be recovered, but a piece of meat that has not been severed can be salvaged by a repeated, slightly harder blow.

The idea of minimum force as the base line of self-control is expressed in the apocryphal if perfectly logical advice given in ancient Chinese cooking: the good cook must learn first to cleave a grain of boiled rice.

Before teasing out the implications of this craft rule, we need to understand better a physical corollary of minimum force. This is the release. If the cook, like a carpenter, holds the cleaver or hammer down after striking a blow, it works against the tool's rebound. Strain will occur all along the forearm. For physiological reasons that are still not well understood, the ability to withdraw force in the microsecond after it is applied also makes the gesture itself more precise; one's aim improves. So in playing the piano, where the ability to release a key is an integral motion with pressing it down, finger pressure must cease at the moment of contact for the fingers to move easily and swiftly to other keys. In playing stringed instruments, as we go to a new tone, our hand can make the move cleanly only by letting go, a microsecond before, of the string it has pressed before. In the musical hand, for this reason, it is harder to produce a clear, soft sound than to belt out loud notes. Batting in cricket or baseball requires that same prowess in release.

In hand-wrist-forearm movement, prehension plays a significant role in the release. The arm assemblage must do the same sort of anticipation as in reaching for a cup but in reverse. Even as the blow is about to occur, the arm assemblage is preparing for the next step, in the microsecond before contact—reaching for release, as it were. The accounting of objects that Raymond Tallis describes proceeds in this step, as the arm assemblage now undoes the tension involved in gripping, and the hammer or cleaver is held more loosely.

"Cleave a grain of rice" thus stands for two bodily rules intimately connected: establish a base line of minimum necessary power, and learn to let go. Technically the point of this connection is control of movement, but it is indeed full of human implication—to which ancient Chinese cookery writers themselves were attuned. The *Chuang-tzu* advises, do not behave like a warrior in the kitchen, from which Taoism derives a broader ethics for *Homo faber:* an aggressive, adversarial address to natural materials is counterproductive. Zen Buddhism in Japan later drew on this heritage to explore the ethics of letting go, embodied in archery. Physically this sport focuses on release of tension in letting go of the bowstring. The Zen writers evoke the lack of physical aggression, the tranquil spirit, which should attend that moment; this frame of mind is necessary for the archer to hit the target accurately.[25]

In Western societies, knife use has also served as a cultural symbol of minimal aggression. Norbert Elias found that Europeans in the early Middle Ages viewed the dangers of the knife rather pragmatically. What Elias calls "the civilizing process" began as the knife took on a more symbolic importance, summoning to collective mind both the evils and the remedies for spontaneous violence. "Society, which was beginning at this time . . . to limit the real dangers threatening people . . . placed a barrier around the symbols as well," Elias observes. "Thus the restrictions and the prohibitions on the knife increased, along with the restraints on individuals."[26] He means by this, for instance, that in 1400 knife fights might have been a normal event at a supper party but that by 1600 these eruptions were frowned on. Or again, that in 1600 a man encountering a stranger on the street did not automatically put his hand to his hilt.

A "well-bred" person disciplined the body in the most elementary of biological necessities—unlike boors, bumpkins, peasants taken to be, in American slang, "slobs" who farted freely or wiped runny noses on their sleeves. One consequence of such self-control was to relieve people of aggressive tension. The chef's chopping makes this quixotic proposition more comprehensible: self-control pairs with ease.

In examining the emergence of court society in the seventeenth century, Elias was struck by how this coupling had come to define the gracious aristocrat, easy with others and in control of himself; eating properly was one of the aristocrat's social skills. This mark of good manners at table was possible only because the dangers of physical violence were retreating in polite society, the dangerous skills associated with the knife ebbing. In the surging of bourgeois life in the eighteenth century, the code passed downward a grade in social class and changed again in character; easy self-restraint became a mark of the "naturalness" celebrated by the philosophes. The table and its manners still made for social distinction. For instance, the middle class observed the rule that one should cut, with a knife, only the food that one cannot slice or pierce with the more delicate but blunter edge of a fork, and snooted the lower orders for using the knife as a spear.

Elias is an admirable historian, but he errs, I think, as an analyst of the social life he so vividly describes. He treats civility as a veneer beneath which lies a more the solid, more personal experience: shame—the real catalyst of self-discipline. His histories of nose blowing, farting, or pissing in public, like the evolution of table manners, all originate in shame over natural bodily functions, shame over their spontaneous expression; the "civilizing process" inhibits spontaneity. Shame appears to Elias as an inward-turning emotion: "The anxiety that we call 'shame' is heavily veiled to the sight of others . . . never directly expressed in noisy gestures. . . . It is a conflict within his own personality; he recognizes himself as an inferior."[27]

This strikes a false note applied to aristocrats but rings truer about middle-class mores. Still, this is not an explanation that could in any way apply to the ease or self-control the craftsman seeks; shame does not motivate the craftsman learning minimum force and release. Just considered physically, he or she cannot be so driven. There is indeed a physiology of shame, which can be measured by muscular tension in the stomach as well as in the arms—shame, anxiety, and muscular tension form an unholy trinity in the human organism. The physiology of shame would disable the freedom of physical movement that an artisan needs to work. Muscular tension is fatal to physical self-control. Put positively, as muscles develop in bulk and definition, the reflexes that cause them to tense become less pronounced; physical activity becomes smoother, less jerky. This is why people whose bodies are physically strong are more capable of calibrating minimum force than people whose bodies are weak; a gradient of muscle force has developed. Well-developed muscles in the body are equally more capable of release. They maintain shape even when they let go. Mentally, the craftsman of words could no more explore and use them well if he or she were full of anxiety.

To be just to Elias, we might imagine that self-control has two dimensions: one a social surface beneath which there lies personal distress, the other a reality at ease in itself both physically and mentally, a reality that serves the craftsman's development of skill. This second dimension carries its own social implication.

Military and diplomatic strategy must constantly judge degrees of brute force. The strategists who used the atomic bomb decided that overwhelming force was needed to achieve Japanese surrender. In current American military strategy the "Powell doctrine" proposes an intimidating number of soldiers massed on the ground, while the doctrine of "shock and awe" substitutes technology for men—a massive amount of robot missiles and laser-guided bombs thrown hard against an enemy all at once.[28] A contrary approach has been proposed by the political scientist and diplomat Joseph Nye, dubbed by him "soft power"; it is more the way a skilled craftsman would work. In hand coordination the issue turns on inequalities of strength; the unequal hands working together rectify weakness. Restrained power of the craftsman's sort, coupled with release, takes a further step. The combination provides the craftsman's body self-control and enables accuracy of action; blind, brute force is counterproductive in handwork. All these ingredients— cooperation with the weak, restrained force, release after attack—are present in "soft power"; this doctrine, too, seeks to transcend counterproductive blind force. Here is the craft contained in "state-craft."

Hand and Eye
The Rhythm of Concentration

"Attention deficit disorder" currently worries many teachers and parents, focused on whether children can pay attention for sustained periods rather than attend to short moments. Hormonal imbalances account for some of the causes of attention deficit, cultural factors for others. About the latter, the sociologist Neil Postman spawned a large body of research on the negative effects watching television produces in children.[29] Students of expertise often define attention span, however, in terms that may not seem entirely useful in responding to such adult worry.

As mentioned at the outset of this book, ten thousand hours is a common touchstone for how long it takes to become an expert. In studies of "composers, basketball players, fiction writers, ice skaters, . . . and master criminals," the psychologist Daniel Levitin remarks, "this number comes up again and again."[30] This seemingly huge time span represents how long researchers estimate it takes for complex skills to become so deeply ingrained that these have become readily available, tacit knowledge. Putting the master criminal aside, this number is not really an enormity. The ten-thousand-hour rule translates into practicing three hours a day for ten years, which is indeed a common training span for young people in sports. The seven years of apprentice work in a medieval goldsmithy represents just under five hours of bench work each day, which accords with what is known of the workshops. The grueling conditions of a doctor's internship and residency can compress the ten thousand hours into three years or less.

The adult worry about attention deficits, by contrast, is much smaller in scale: how a child will manage to concentrate even for one hour at a time. Educators frequently seek to interest children mentally and emotionally in subjects in order to develop their skills of concentration. The theory on which this is based is that substantive engagement breeds concentration. The long-term development of hand skills shows the reverse of this theory. The ability to concentrate for long periods comes first; only when a person can do so will he or she get involved emotionally or intellectually. The skill of physical concentration follows rules of its own, based on how people learn to practice, to repeat what they do, and to learn from repetition. Concentration, that is, has an inner logic; this logic can, I believe, be applied to working steadily for an hour as well as for several years.

To fathom the logic we might explore further the relations between the hand and the eye. The relations between these two organs can organize the process of practicing in sustainable ways. We could find no better guide than Erin O'Connor about how the hand and eye together learn to how to concentrate.[31] A philosophical glassblower, she has explored the development of long-term attention through her own struggles to fashion a particular kind of wineglass. She reports in the pages of an august scholarly journal that she has long enjoyed the Barolo wines of Italy and therefore sought to fashion a goblet big and rounded enough to support the fragrant "nose" of the wine. To accomplish this, she had to expand her powers of concentration from the short- to the long-term.

The frame for this learning was the critical moment in the craft of glassblowing when molten glass is gathered at the end of an extended narrow pipe. The viscous glass will sag unless the pipe is constantly turned. In order to get a straight bead, the hands have to do something akin to twirling a teaspoon into a pot of honey. All the body is involved in this handwork. To avoid strain when twirling the pipe, the glassblower's back must incline forward from the lower rather than upper torso, like a rower reaching for the beginning of a stroke. This posture also steadies the craftsman in drawing back molten glass out of the furnace. But critically important is the relation of hand and eye.

In learning to make a Barolo goblet O'Connor passed through stages that resemble those we've explored among musicians and cooks. She had to "untape" habits she'd learnt in blowing simpler pieces in order to explore why she was failing, discovering, for instance, that the easy way that had become her habit meant that she scooped too little molten glass at the tip. She had to develop a better awareness of her body in relation to the viscous liquid, as though there were continuity between flesh and glass. This sounds poetic, though poetry was perhaps dispelled by the shouted comments of her mentor, "Slow it down there, cowgirl, keep it steady!" O'Connor happens to be small and demure; wisely, she took no offense. Her coordination thereby increased.

Now she was better positioned to make use of the triad of the "intelligent hand"—coordination of hand, eye, and brain. Her coach urged, "Don't take your eyes off the glass! It [the molten gob at the blow-tip] is starting to hang!" This had the effect of her loosening her grip on the tube. Holding it more lightly, as a cleaver chef would his knife, she increased her control. But she still had to learn how to lengthen her concentration.

This stretch-out occurred in two phases. First, she lost awareness of her body making contact *with* the hot glass and became all-absorbed in the physical material as the end in itself: "My awareness of the blowpipe's weight in my palm receded and in its stead advanced the sensation of the ledge's edge at the blowpipe's mid-point followed by the weight of the gathering glass on the blowpipe's tip, and finally the gather towards a goblet."[32] The philosopher Maurice Merleau-Ponty describes what she experienced as "being as a thing."[33] The philosopher Michael Polanyi calls it "focal awareness" and recurs to the act of hammering a nail: "When we bring down the hammer we do not feel that its handle has struck our palm but that its head has struck the nail. . . . I have a subsidiary awareness of the feeling in the palm of my hand which is merged into my focal awareness of my driving in the nail."[34] If I may put this yet another way, we are now absorbed *in* something, no longer self-aware, even of our bodily self. We have become the thing on which we are working.

This absorbed concentration now had to be stretched out. The challenge O'Connor met was the result of a further failure. Though her well-positioned, relaxed, absorbed self had succeeded in gathering the glass into a bubble and forming it into the desired Barolo-friendly shape, the glass, when left to cool, turned out "lopsided and stout," a thing now dubbed by the master craftsman a "globlet."

The problem, she came to understand, lay in dwelling in that moment of "being in a thing." To work better, she discovered, she needed to anticipate what the material should next become in its next, as-yet nonexistent, stage of evolution. Her instructor called this simply "staying on track"; she, rather more philosophically minded, understood that she was engaged in a process of "corporeal anticipation," always one step ahead of the material as molten liquid, then bubble, then bubble with a stem, then stem with a foot. She had to make such prehension a permanent state of mind, and she learned to do so, whether she succeeded or failed, by blowing the goblet again and again. Even had she succeeded the first time by chance, she would have practiced it, in order to ensure the acts of gathering, blowing, and turning in her hands. This is repetition for its own sake: like a swimmer's strokes, sheer movement repeated becomes a pleasure in itself.

· We might think, as did Adam Smith describing industrial labor, of routine as mindless, that a person doing something over and over goes missing mentally; we might equate routine and boredom. For people who develop sophisticated hand skills, it's nothing like this. Doing something over and over is stimulating when organized as looking ahead. The substance of the routine may change, metamorphose, improve, but the emotional payoff is one's experience of doing it again. There's nothing strange about this experience. We all know it; it is *rhythm*. Built into the contractions of the human heart, the skilled craftsman has extended rhythm to the hand and the eye.

Rhythm has two components: stress on a beat and tempo, the speed of an action. In music, changing the tempo of a piece is a means of looking forward and anticipating. The markings *ritardando* and *accelerando* oblige the musician to prepare a change; these large shifts in tempo keep him or her alert. The same is true of rhythm in miniature. If you play a waltz strictly in time using a metronome, you will find it increasingly hard to focus; the act of regularly stressing a beat requires micropauses and microspurts. To recur to the discussion in the previous chapter, repeated stress on a beat establishes the type-form. Tempo shifts are like the varied species that emerge within this generic rubric. Prehension is focused on the tempo; the musician concentrates productively.

The rhythm that kept O'Connor specifically alert lay in her eye disciplining her hand, the eye constantly scanning and judging, adjusting the hand, the eye establishing the tempo. The complexity here is that she was no longer conscious of her hands, she no longer thought about what they were doing: her consciousness focused on what she saw; ingrained hand motions became part of the act of seeing ahead. For the musician, the conductor appers visually just slightly ahead, indicating the sound, the executant registering that signal again just in the microsecond before making the sound happen.

I fear that my descriptive powers have reached their limit in describing the rhythm involved in concentration, and I have certainly made this experience seem more abstract than it is. The signs of a person who concentrates in practicing are concrete enough. A person who has learned to concentrate well will not count the number of times he or she repeats a motion at the command of the ear or the eye. When I am deep into practicing the cello, I want to do a physical gesture again and again to make it better but also do it better so that I can do it again. So too with Erin O'Connor. She is not counting how often; she wants to repeat breathing down the blowpipe, holding and turning it in her hands. Her eye, however, sets the tempo. When the the two elements of rhythm combine in practicing, a person can stay alert for long periods, and improve.

What then of the substance one practices? Does one practice a three-part invention by J. S. Bach better than an exercise by Ignaz Moscheles just because the music is better? My own experience is, no; the rhythm of practicing, balancing repetition and anticipation, is itself engaging. Anyone who has learned Latin or Greek as a child might reach the same conclusion. Much of this language learning was "rote," its substance remote. Only gradually did the routines that enabled us to learn the Greek language help us gain interest in a long-vanished, foreign culture. As for other apprentices who have not yet fathomed the content of a subject, learning to concentrate has to come first. Practicing has its own structure and an inherent interest.

The practical value of this advanced handwork to people dealing with attention deficit disorder consists in focusing attention on how practice sessions are organized. Rote learning is not in itself the enemy. Practice sessions can be made interesting through creating an internal rhythm for them, no matter how short; the complicated actions performed by an advanced glassblower or cellist can be simplified while preserving the same structuring of time. We do a disservice to those who suffer from attention deficit disorder by asking that they understand before they engage.

※　※　※

The view of good practicing may seem to slight the importance of commitment, but commitments themselves come in two forms, as decisions and as obligations. In the one, we judge whether a particular action is worth doing or a particular person is worth spending time with; in the other, we submit to a duty, a custom, or to another person's need, not of our own making. Rhythm organizes the second kind of commitment; we learn how to perform a duty again and again. As theologians have long pointed out, religious rituals need to be repeated to become persuasive, day after day, month after month, year upon year. The repeats are steadying, but in religious practice they are not stale; the celebrant anticipates each time that something important is about to happen.

I moot this large point in part because the practicing that occurs in repeating a musical phrase, chopping meat, or blowing a glass goblet has something of the character of a ritual. We have trained our hands in repetition; we are alert rather than bored because we have developed the skill of anticipation. But equally, the person able to perform a duty again and again has acquired a technical skill, the rhythmic skill of a craftsman, whatever the god or gods to which he or she subscribes.

※　※　※

This chapter has pursued in detail the idea of the unity of head and hand. Such unity shaped the ideals of the eighteenth-century Enlightenment; it grounded Ruskin's nineteenth-century defense of manual labor. We haven't followed quite in their path, for we've charted forms of mental understanding that emerge from developing specialized and rarified hand skills, whether these be playing perfectly in tune, cleaving a grain of rice, or blowing a difficult goblet. But even such virtuoso skills are based on fundamentals of the human body.

 Concentration consummates a certain line of technical development in the hand. The hands have had before to experiment through touch, but according to an objective standard; they have learned to coordinate inequality; they have learned the application of minimum force and release. The hands thus establish a repertoire of learned gestures. The gestures can be further refined or revised within the rhythmic process that occurs in, and sustains, practicing. Prehension presides over each technical step, and each step is full of ethical implication.

CHAPTER SIX

Expressive Instructions

The Principle of Instruction
Show, Don't Tell

This is a short chapter on a vexing subject. Diderot found printers and typesetters inarticulate in explaining what they did; I found myself unable to put clearly into words how hand and eye coordinate. Language struggles with depicting physical action, and nowhere is this struggle more evident than in language that tells us what to do. Whoever has tried to assemble a do-it-yourself bookcase following written instructions knows the problem. As one's temper rises, one realizes how great a gap can exist between instructive language and the body.

In the workshop or laboratory, the spoken word seems more effective than written instructions. Whenever a procedure becomes difficult, you can immediately ask someone else about it, discussing back and forth, whereas when reading a printed page you can discuss with yourself what you read but you cannot get another's feedback. Yet simply privileging the speaking voice, face-to-face, is an incomplete solution. You both have to be in the same spot; learning becomes local. Unscripted dialogue, moreover, is often very messy and wandering. Rather than getting rid of print, the challenge is to make written instructions communicate—to create expressive instructions.

This vexed problem has a biological side, revealed by studies that relate the activities of the hands to the uses of language. The most useful to us of these studies focus on coordination of instructions in words and hand gestures. Researchers have probed this tie by studying connections between apraxia and aphasia. Apraxia (loss of skilled movement) concerns the difficulties people may suffer in performing a task like buttoning a shirt. Correspondingly, aphasia (loss of the ability to use or comprehend words) can take the form of a person's not understanding the verbal instruction to button one's shirt. The neurologist Frank Wilson has worked with patients who suffer from both disorders. He proposes that treating apraxia first will aid in then coping with aphasia; that is, recovering a physical skill helps people then to understand language, particularly the language of instructions.[1] Aphasia itself can, as Sheila Hale has shown in her moving memoir *The Man Who Lost His Language,* take many varied forms, but in all forms aphasia becomes especially stressful when the aphasiac is told to do something physical.[2]

Wilson's therapeutic insight has suggested more broadly that bodily movement is the foundation of language. The suggestion appeals to many of the researchers who collaborated on the influential volume *Gesture and the Nature of Language.*[3] Their guiding idea is that the very categories of language are created by intentional hand actions, so that verbs derive from hand movements, nouns "hold" things as names, and adverbs and adjectives, like hand tools, modify movements and objects. The focus here is particularly on how experiences of touch and grip, such as were presented in our previous chapter, give language its directive power.

The neurologist Oliver Sacks has followed a different route in understanding the instructions given by hand gestures. His fascinating study *Seeing Voices* explores the work of "signers" to the deaf.[4] He is struck by how the signers' hand movements often illustrate a verbal concept in gestures, rather than making an abstract sign, as when the sign "watch out for" is signaled by the right first finger pointing forward, the other fingers curled back into the palm. The procedures he describes for the deaf recall the art of mime, as developed in *commedia dell'arte* in the Renaissance, or the use of mime in nineteenth-century ballet. Like mimes, signers to the deaf are engaged in the physical activity of display.

※　※　※

Display translates into a craft command frequently given young writers: "Show, don't tell!" In developing a novel this means avoiding such declarations as "She was depressed," writing instead something like "She moved slowly to the coffee pot, the cup heavy in her hand." Now we are shown what depression is. The physical display conveys more than the label. Show, don't tell occurs in workshops when the master demonstrates proper procedure through action; his or her display becomes the guide. Yet this kind of miming contains a wrinkle.

The apprentice is often expected to absorb the master's lesson by osmosis; the master's demonstration shows an act successfully performed, and the apprentice has to figure out what turned the key in the lock. Learning by demonstration puts the burden on the apprentice; it further assumes that direct imitation can occur. To be sure, the process often works, but equally often it fails. In music conservatories, for instance, the master often has trouble putting him- or herself back into the rude state of the pupil, unable to show the mistake, only the right way. Sacks observes that deaf people learning signage have to work hard to figure exactly what they should be absorbing what the instructor has actually done.

Written, directive language can make the process of osmosis more concrete and definite. Specific tools in the writer's workshop enable instructive expression. In this chapter I will show how these can be effectively used, and their lessons concretely absorbed, by probing a written direction that every reader has tried to follow: the cooking recipe. The recipe I've chosen is demanding—how to prepare a boned, stuffed chicken—but this arcane challenge opens the gates to the large, difficult subject of the role of imagination in craftsmanship.

The Written Recipe

During the Napoleonic Wars, General Suchet won an important victory over the English at the Spanish lake of Albufera in Valencia. A grateful Napoleon transformed General Suchet into the duc d'Albufera, and the eminent chef Carême invented a series of dishes in his honor, notably *Poulet à la d'Albufera*. This boned chicken, stuffed with rice, truffles, and foie gras and coated with a sauce of sweet peppers, veal stock, and cream, is one of the glories of nineteenth-century haute cuisine—and undoubtedly a relentless source of heart attack in that era. As is true of much French cooking, high art eventually made its way into more ordinary practice. How in that practical realm would one go about preparing it?

Dead Denotation
The Misfortunes of a Chicken

Let's start with the fact that the chicken is to be boned. The Provençal-American cook Richard Olney tells precisely how to do so, using a seven-inch, thin-bladed knife rather than the Chinese chef's cleaver: "Sever the attachment of each shoulder blade at the wing joint and, holding it firmly between the thumb and fore-finger of the left hand, pull it out of the flesh with the other hand. Force the flesh loose from the breastbone, working along the crest with the point of the knife and forcing that at the sides loose with fingertips. With fingertips, loosen all the way around the rib case, and finally at the highest point of the breastbone, cut through the cartilage connecting the skin being careful not to pierce the skin."[5] Olney tells rather than shows. If the reader already knows how to bone, this description might be a useful review; for the neophyte it is no guide. Many unfortunate chickens will be hacked to bits if a beginner follows it.

The language itself harbors a particular cause for this looming disaster. Each verb in Olney's instruction issues a command: sever, pull, loosen. These verbs *name* acts rather than explain the process of acting; this is why they tell rather than show. For instance, when Olney counsels, "Force the flesh loose from the breastbone, working along the crest," he cannot convey the dangers of tearing the chicken's flesh just below the bone crest. In their sheer number and density the verbs cast an illusory spell; in reality, the verbs are at once specific and inoperative. The problem they represent is dead denotation. The problem has a visual parallel in do-it-yourself illustrations—the twisting arrows, pictures of different-sized screws, and the like are all accurate but serviceable only to someone who has already put the piece together.

One remedy for dead denotation is to "write what you know," a piece of advice frequently given to young writers. The idea is that a person can unpack instructive meaning in experiences he or she has lived through. However, this remedy is no remedy; what you know may be so familiar to you that you might take for granted its touchstone references, assuming that others have identical touchstones. Thus you might write of an architect, "McGuppy's slick mall resembles a Bon Jovi song." A reader in Borneo might not be able to summon up the image of a slick shopping mall and I have never heard a Bon Jovi tune. Much contemporary writing is stuffed with casual references to consumer products; in two generations, this writing will be incomprehensible. Familiarity risks producing only more dead denotation. The challenge posed by dead denotation is precisely to take apart tacit knowledge, which requires bringing to the surface of consciousness that knowledge which has become so self-evident and habitual that it seems just natural.

When I've taught writing, I've thus asked my students to rewrite the printed instructions that accompany new software. Perfectly accurate, these nefarious publications are often unintelligible. They take dead denotation to an extreme. Not only do engineer-writers leave out "dumb things" that "everyone knows"; they repress simile, metaphor, and adverbial color. The act of unpacking what's buried in the vault of tacit knowledge can make use of these imaginative tools. By invoking the signals birds send by twittering or bees by dancing, the person rewriting software instructions can make comprehensible what hypertext does and how economically it should be used. (Hypertext calls across documents; if there's too much calling, too much twittering, too much marking of hypertext, the procedure loses value.)

The twittering birds of hypertext is an image based on analogy. The culinary recipe takes the task I set my writing students a step further. The imaginative trope becomes itself the explanation. I'll show how this happens, and how unpacked tacit knowledge can become expressive instruction, via the challenges faced by three modern cooks in contriving recipes based on Poulet à la d'Albufera. Two of these cooks became famous; the third died in obscurity. All admired Richard Olney; none wrote like him. Their chicken recipes stressed, variously, language's powers of sympathetic illustration, narrative, and metaphor.

Sympathetic Illustration
Julia Child's Poularde à la d'Albufera

Americans in the 1950s suffered the first onslaught of industrialized food; the shops generally favored fruits and vegetables that packed and shipped well rather than tasted good; meat and poultry processing became standardized; everything fresh was wrapped in protective cellophane. Of course some forms of American cooking had great finesse, particularly cuisine from the Old South, but the suburban chef in those sterilized years was more likely to look for inspiration abroad. Child led them to France.

To expand her readers' horizons, Julia Child wrote down procedures she learned professionally in Paris as a young woman. She re-imagined these procedures for the foreign novice; crossing that cultural divide prompted her to transform the denotative recipe. Child's recipes, I think, are meant to be read twice, once before cooking begins, for overall sense, then again in stages during the process, as the cook puts hand to bird.

Child's Poularde à la d'Albufera uses a bird, the poulard, which in Brittany runs free for most of its life, then is confined and fattened for cooking. Stretching over four printed pages, her recipe divides into six detailed steps. (Her version makes use of a half-boned chicken [*demi-désossée*], the breast meat and breast cage removed so that the chicken can be stuffed and trussed for cooking.) In each stage she expresses forebodings. For instance, she imagines the neophyte picking up the knife and counsels: "Always angle the cutting edge of knife against bone and not against flesh."[6] In cooking on television, Child pioneered the use of the close-up to make sense of the hands moving from one task to the next. The drawings that accompany her book text similarly focus on the hardest procedure the hand will have to work with.

Child's recipe reads quite differently than Olney's precise direction because her story is structured around empathy for the cook; she focuses on the human protagonist rather than on the bird. The resulting language is indeed full of analogies, but these analogies are loose rather than exact, and for a reason. Cutting a chicken's sinew is technically like cutting a piece of string, but it doesn't feel quite the same. This is an instructional moment for her reader; "like" but not "exactly like" focuses the brain and the hand on the act of sinew cutting in itself. There's also an emotional point to loose analogies; the suggestion that a new gesture or act is roughly like something you have done before aims specifically to inspire confidence.

In the eighteenth century, as we have seen, sympathy was thought to bind people together, as for Adam Smith, who asked his readers to enter into the misfortunes and limits of other human beings. Sympathy in his view instructs ethically—but not because we are supposed to imitate the misfortunes and difficulties of other people; understanding them better, we will be more responsive to their needs. The writer of instructional language who makes the effort of sympathy has to re-trace, step by step, backward knowledge that has bedded in to routine, and only then can take the reader step by step forward. But as an expert, he or she knows what comes next and where danger lies; the expert guides by anticipating difficulties for the novice; sympathy and prehension combine. This is Julia Child's method.

Child is occasionally criticized by chefs for being a fuzzy writer and in the same breath for being too detailed. Each of these six steps is necessary, however, because there are so many danger points in cook-ing this particular dish. Supporting the reader at such moments places a burden on any writer who aims to instruct expressively. He or she has to recover the sentiment of insecurity. The paralyzing tone of authority and certainty in much instructional language betrays a writer's inability to re-imagine vulnerability. In craftwork done for ourselves, we of course seek for closure. Child, as I've observed her in televised presen-tations, adopts a particular, not to say peculiar, way of holding the boning knife. Practice has led her to arrive at that decision; the practice has given her confidence; she bones without hesitation. When we wish to instruct, however, particularly in the fixed medium of print, we have to return emotionally just to the point before such habits were formed, in order to provide guidance. So for a moment Child will imagine holding the knife awkwardly; the cello master will return to playing wrong notes. This return to vulnerability is the sign of sympathy the instructor gives.

Scene Narrative
Elizabeth David's Poulet à la Berrichonne

Like Julia Child, Elizabeth David sought to improve the quality of cooking by teaching her readers how to cook foreign food. After the Second World War, there was much less food to be had in Britain than in America; what there was, was massacred. The domestic cook's address to vegetables, for instance, treated them as adversaries who had to be boiled into submission. David sought to remedy this miserable state of affairs by teaching her readers not only about foreign foods but how to cook in a foreign way.

David is most often a writer of clear, simple recipes, but she prefers another kind of writing when she has to take her readers far abroad. Her recipe for a country cousin dish to Carême's masterpiece sets the example. David describes the making of Poulet à la Berrichonne as though it were a tale from Ovid, the transforming journey from a tough old hen flopped on the butcher's cutting board to the tender poached dish nestling inside its cushion of parsleyed rice. Unlike Child, she seeks to impart technique through evoking the cultural context of this journey. Her recipe for poached, demi-désossée chicken first evokes a chef in Berry pondering what to do with old hens that by Easter are no longer fit for laying. David notices the local cook touching and prodding the bird, like a musician who has removed Suzuki tapes from a violin. The cook's education in touch will continue by assessing the texture of the solid ingredients that will fill the bird's cavity—the ground pork and veal one would use for a pâté, how light do they feel? These ingredients, laced with brandy, wine, and veal stock, are sown beneath the skin. The story moves forward as David describes how a cook in Berry achieves lightness in poaching; it is slow, very slow, a bird cooking at low heat, bathed in a thyme, parsley, and bay leaf–scented stock.

The long recipe works as a once-read procedure: it is an orienting short story one would read *before* cooking; one might then go to work without referring again to the book. It's a safe bet that even now not one in a thousand of David's readers had ever visited the province of Berry, where her recipe originates. But like her mentor the travel writer Norman Douglas, David believed you need to imagine first and foremost what it's like to be somewhere else in order to do the sorts of things people do there.

This particular recipe embodies a phenomenon we previously explored in the chapter on consciousness of materials: the domain shift. In David's account, the state of the bird's flesh governs the story throughout, just as the tight right angle of the weaver's loom served as a guide in other ancient crafts. With the fleshy reference as a guide, the neophyte chef is ready to travel. In all production processes, change of positions frequently serves us: the sculptor walks around the statue, the carpenter turns a cabinet upside-down, just to get a fresh perspective; the cut-and-paste function in word-processing programs helps the writer quickly move a paragraph into the foreign territory of a different chapter. The sustained point of reference in a domain shift, be it right angle or flesh, keeps these shifts from dissipating into fragments. A specific kind of writing issues the passport for such guided travel.

This is the scene narrative, in which "where" sets the scene for "how." If you have the estimable privilege of a Middle Eastern uncle (Jewish or Muslim, it makes no difference), you will immediately understand the instructional point of the scene narrative. Words of advice are introduced with the phrase, "Let me tell you a story." The uncle wants to grab your attention, get you outside of yourself, rivet you in an arresting scene. Journalists have, unfortunately, written scene narratives almost to death; accounts of political negotiations in the Middle East or advances in chemotherapy inevitably begin with a vignette of personal history in order to take the reader "there," even if "there" is a diplomatic document. Effective scene narratives are not perfect encapsulations of a point; rather, as in the great travel writer Robert Byron's

Road to Oxiana, we are taken to a place, and there shown a scene that is clear in detail but puzzling in import.

So it is will your instructional uncle: the more he wants to drive home an indelible message, the less direct will be the connection between the scene he sets and the moral; you'll work that out for yourself once the frame is set. This is the provocative function of any parable. In Elizabeth David's writing, too, the scene narratives frequently skirt making specific instructional points. It has been indeed been objected that this way of writing ducks coming to terms with technique. For instance, in David's recipe for boned bird she tells the reader that if the boning task seems too daunting, "The poulterer or butcher must be persuaded to bone the bird for you; there are still many competent ones who will do this and you never know until you ask."[7]

In her defense it could be said that David's purpose is to jolt the reader into thinking gastronomically. Gastronomy is a narrative, with a beginning (raw ingredients), a middle (their combination and cooking), and an end (eating). To get at the "secret" of preparing unfamiliar food, the reader has to move through this narrative rather than focus on just the middle term; it is by imagining the whole process that you get outside yourself. The scene narrative has a specific role—like a passport, you use it to gain entry to a foreign place. Because she wants this entry to be a jolt, David's prose has few of the reassuring, sympathetic supports that figure in Child's pages. Instead, she has applied uncle-logic to the culinary recipe.

Instruction through Metaphors
Madame Benshaw's Recipe for Poulet à la d'Albufera

A third way of writing expressive instructions was furnished me by Madame Benshaw, who taught me to cook Poulet à la d'Albufera. Madame Benshaw had come to Boston, a refugee from Iran, in 1970.

Her name she could scarcely pronounce herself, since an immigration official had simplified a more complicated Persian moniker, and she spoke English haltingly. She was an amazing cook, somehow mastering French and Italian cuisine as well as Persian. I became her student at a night-school course and, until she died, her friend. (So imposing was she that I never called her by her first name, Fatima, and she will remain Madame Benshaw here.)

Because her English was poor, she taught cooking mostly by hands-on example, coupled with slight smiles and emphatic, frowning contradictions of her thick eyebrows. I nearly cut off my left hand trying to bone my second chicken, and she frowned not at my pain but because there was human blood on the chopping board. (Cleanliness and kitchen order were indeed to her godly virtues.) To explain the stuffing ingredients, she could only hold up what she'd found in the market; she didn't know their names in English, and neither did we, her students. Hands-on learning didn't work very well for us; the problem was that her hands were too quick, and once she started working she never paused or hesitated.

So I asked her to write down the recipe; I'd correct the language and then give it to the three other students (we were all at an advanced level, so it wasn't a question of the basics). I've kept what she wrote, because it was a monthlong struggle for her to produce this formula and because the result was quite surprising from such a technical virtuoso.

Here's the unadulterated text: "Your dead child. Prepare him for new life. Fill him with the earth. Be careful! He should not over-eat. Put on his golden coat. You bathe him. Warm him but be careful! A child dies from too much sun. Put on his jewels. This is my recipe." To make sense of it, I've inserted my own crude references: "Your dead child. [the chicken] Prepare him for new life. [bone] Fill him with the earth. [stuff] Be careful! He should not over-eat. [stuff lightly] Put on his golden coat. [brown before baking] You bathe him. [prepare the poaching liquor] Warm him but be careful! A child dies from too much sun. [cooking temperature: 130 Celsius] Put on his jewels. [once cooked, pour the sweet-pepper sauce] This is my recipe." Many Persian recipes, I've since learned, are couched in such poetic language. And they are meant to be recipes: how could they possibly work?

This is a recipe conceived entirely in metaphors. "Your dead child" stands for a chicken straight from the butcher, but making this simple substitution takes away the gravity Madame Benshaw evidently wishes to convey about slaughtered animals; in classic Persian cuisine, animals have an inner being, an anima, no less than human beings. Certainly the command "Prepare him for new life" is a charged image. An ancient Egyptian mummifier or an especially devout Christian undertaker might find the phrase unremarkable; to the cook, the command alerts the hand. Madame Benshaw's image of preparing for a new life magnifies the mundane task of scraping away flesh from the bird's breastbone, the technical trick of not breaking the skin in boning now seeming an act of child protection. The two cautions are also arousing. An error beginning cooks make is to stuff birds too tightly. Madame Benshaw's caution, "He should not over-eat" arouses the cook's own physical revulsion so as to prevent that error. "A child dies from too much sun" clarifies the logic of slow cooking; the bird-child should feel warm to the touch but not burning. My Celsius number of 130 derives the sensation of touching my own son's skin in and out of fever. (Some cooks would reduce the temperature, indeed, to just above the human fever level.)

Fanciful? Not if you are Persian. The metaphors that figure in material consciousness of brick as "honest" or "chaste" are no more fanciful. The issue is the purposes such acts of imagination serve.

Analysts of metaphor treat it in two ways.[8] The physicist Max Black thought that metaphors like "the rosy-fingered dawn" create a whole greater than the sum of its parts, complete in itself, a stable compound. The philosopher Donald Davidson is somewhat unhappy about this way of understanding metaphors. To him metaphors are more like processes fashioned from words. The point about metaphors as processes is that they roll forward and sideways, allowing one to touch on further meanings—whereas to Black the metaphor, complete in itself, has come to rest. Davidson's view derives in part from empirical work the linguist Roman Jakobson did on aphasia. What aphasics can't do well is use metaphorical language as a tool to generate more understanding; instead, the metaphors seem inert nonsense. If and when aphasics recover, they are shocked with what they can do with metaphoric language. (I am sensible of Sheila Hale's caution that many aphasics are fully capable mentally, even if they cannot speak or write down what they are thinking. As far as is possible to determine, Jakobson's sample was of people who had suffered more invasive internal damage.)

Madame Benshaw is firmly in the Davidson-Jakobson camp. Each of her metaphors is a tool to contemplate consciously and intensely the processes involved in stuffing, browning, or setting the oven. The metaphors do not prompt us to retrace and reverse, step by step, the manner in which a repeated action has already become tacit knowledge. Instead, they add symbolic value; boning, cooking, and stuffing create together a new metaphor of reincarnation. They do so for a point: they clarify the essential objective the cook should strive for at each stage of the work.

We three students found "your dead son" a metaphor too over the top for our American taste but found the cautions useful and the metaphor of dressing even more so. "Put on his golden coat" is an excellent guide to judging how much browning to do of vegetables as well as meats; "put on his jewels" makes clear the purpose of saucing and is a better guide to how little sauce to pour than any cup measure—a sauce should adorn rather than conceal the food beneath. Our cooking visibly improved. Madame Benshaw was at last content. "This is my recipe."

※   ※   ※

In these three ways expressive imaginative language can serve the practical end of guidance. We might compare the three chefs as follows.

Julia Child has identified with the cook, Madame Benshaw with the food. The scene narratives employed by Elizabeth David are meant to decenter the reader, while the story Madame Benshaw tells is meant to induct him or her into a sacred performance. Julia Child's language makes instructive use of moments of difficulty; these she is able to foresee. The scene narratives devised by Elizabeth David make productive use of lateral data; she brings in facts, anecdotes, and observations that have nothing directly to do with cooking. Madame Benshaw's language sticks strictly to metaphor, in order to give each physical action heavy symbolic weight. All these ways of writing culinary recipes guide by showing rather than telling; they all transcend dead denotation.

The three kinds of guidance are not limited to cooking recipes. Expressive directions connect technical craft to the imagination. These language tools can be applied to musical instruction, to writing computer manuals, or to philosophy. But what about physical tools? We need now to delve deeper into the issue that lurked in the historical discussions of machinery in Part One, that of how tools might be used imaginatively.

CHAPTER SEVEN

Arousing Tools

An old photograph of an American piano factory shows a cabinet that a piano maker has carved for his tools, the mahogany cabinet beautifully inlaid with ivory and mother-of-pearl, a sign of this craftsman's love for his tools.[1] Each tool in this cabinet is fit-for-purpose—the tuning wrench for tightening the string pins, the pick for softening the striking hammers, the felt knife for the dampers—each has its job to do. These tools send the message of clarity, of knowing which act should be done with which thing, a message more precise than Madam Benshaw's written recipe. And yet the cabinet of tools is not a seat of learning.

Getting better at using tools comes to us, in part, when the tools challenge us, and this challenge often occurs just because the tools are not fit-for-purpose. They may not be good enough, or it's hard to figure out how to use them. The challenge becomes greater when we are obliged to use these tools to repair or undo mistakes. In both creation and repair, the challenge can be met by adapting the form of a tool, or improvising with it as it is, using it in ways it was not meant for. However we come to use it, the very incompleteness of the tool has taught us something.

The all-purpose tool seems a special case. In the piano maker's cabinet, the flat-edged screwdriver comes close to being such a tool, since it can gouge, lift, and line as well as screw. But in its sheer variety this all-purpose tool admits all manner of unfathomed possibilities; it, too, can expand our skills if only our imagination rises to the occasion. Without hesitation, the flat-edged screwdriver can be described as sublime—the word *sublime* standing, as it does in philosophy and the arts, for the potently strange. In craftwork, that sentiment focuses especially on objects very simple in form that seemingly can do anything.

Both the limited, frustrating tool and the all-purpose sublime tool have already appeared in these pages, the frustrating tool in the medieval alchemist's retorts that yielded no precise information, the sublime tool in the shuttle of Vaucanson's loom, its elegantly simple action suggesting many other industrial applications, each with potentially terrifying consequences for workers. We want to understand how the craftsman might gain control, and indeed improve his or her skill, in using either of these kinds of instruments—which means better understanding our own powers of imagination.

Difficult Tools
Telescopes, Microscopes, and Scalpels

As the modern scientific era took shape in the late sixteenth and seventeenth centuries, scientists used new tools and old tools in novel ways to gain a new understanding of the natural world. Three tools— the telescope, the microscope, and the scalpel—challenged the medieval view of humanity's place in the world and the understanding of the body. The telescope helped dethrone human beings' former place at the center of the universe; the microscope revealed teeming life invisible to the naked eye; the scalpel allowed anatomists a new understanding of organic structure. These scientific instruments stimulated scientific thinking as much by their flaws and limitations as by their revelatory powers.

As early as the eleventh century, the Islamic writer Alhazen wished to search the heavens beyond what the naked eye could see. The glass available to him defeated him. As we've learned, ancient recipes for glass produced a blue-green hue; medieval glassworkers could clear some of the color by adding fern ash, potash, limestone, and manganese, but still the glass was of poor quality. Alhazen's dream was also frustrated by the molding of glass, because the glass distorted when poured into curved shapes rather than flat panes.

The distortion cleared somewhat in the early sixteenth century when hotter ovens were contrived to heat the sand-bed for glass. Two Dutch lens grinders, Johann and Zacharias Janssen, probably invented the first compound microscope in 1590, with a convex lens at one end of a tube and a concave eyepiece at the other. The astronomer Johannes Kepler proposed in 1611 an instrument that truly compounded sight, employing two convex lenses, thus greatly magnifying objects. With the lenses switched around in the tube, this more powerful instrument became what Galileo called an "inverted telescope"; the modern term *microscope* came into being in 1625.[2]

Speaking for his contemporaries about the new cosmology revealed by the telescope, Blaise Pascal declared, "The eternal silence of these infinite spaces frightens me."[3] The microscope seemed at first more marvel than menace. In the *Novum Organum* Francis Bacon was astounded at the precisions of nature revealed under the microscope, "the latent and invisible fine details of bodies . . . the precise shape and features of the body of a flea." Bernard de Fontenelle in the 1680s marveled at the profusion of life revealed under the lens: "We see from the elephant down to the mite; there our sight ends. But beyond the mite an infinite multitude of animals begins for which the mite is an elephant, and which can't be perceived with ordinary eyesight."[4] These two tools of the seventeenth century led the historian Herbert Butterfield to say science in this era was like "putting on a new pair of spectacles."[5]

Yet the glass for telescopes and microscopes still produced imprecise data because glass lenses remained difficult to polish; the feldspar-impregnated polishing cloth lay a century in the future. And though widening and lengthening the tube could increase magnification, magnification enlarged the minute irregularities on the lens's surface. Looking through the telescopes used in the time of Galileo, the modern viewer strains to distinguish a distant star from a pit in the glass.

These lens tools exemplified the generic problem of a difficult tool that simply is not good enough. An equal problem resides in the tool that works well but which people have trouble inferring how best to use. The seventeenth-century scalpel raised this problem.

Medieval doctors used cooking knives for dissection. Ordinary surgery famously made use of the barber's razor; these razors were made of primitive iron and thus difficult to keep sharp. In the late 1400s knives appeared made of better-tempered iron, an iron now mixed with the same silica used for glass; these knives could be finely sharpened thanks to blocks of composite stone that replaced the traditional leather strap.

The modern scalpel was a product of this technology. Its blade was smaller, its shanks shorter than the cooking knife. Scalpels came in varieties fit for the particular purposes of dissection and surgery, some sharpened only at the tip for cutting membranes, others hooked but dulled around the curve to lift up blood vessels. The bone saw and bone scissors became practical tools in the early sixteenth century; though these devices had existed before in crudely tempered iron, their edges were so dull that they must have mashed as many bones as they separated.

These finer tools, however, proved harder to use; the very precision of the scalpel challenged the hand technique required of the doctor or dissector. Andreas Vesalius, a Brussels doctor, published his *De humani corporis fabrica* (On the fabric of the human body) in 1543. The work marked an event in handcraft as well as in the understanding of the body, for Vesalius drew on "repeated observation of cadavers that he had dissected with his own hands."[6] Before his time, the expert would stand over the corpse, explaining to others what was revealed, as a barber or student hacked away. The Renaissance anatomist still followed the ancient Galenic principle for dissecting bodies, peeling away layers of skin and muscle, then removing organs, to get finally at the skeleton.[7] By taking matters literally into his own hands, Vesalius sought more exact information, such as precisely how blood vessels were marbled into the fabric of muscles and organs.

To get at this data, Vesalius's investigation required virtuoso hand technique in using the scalpel. Emphasis had to shift to the fingertips, as less shoulder and upper-arm effort was required to get inside the body. The application of minimum force, discussed in our chapter on the hand, became an urgent necessity; the very sharpness of the scalpel meant that the slightest misstep of the hand would ruin the dissection or cause disaster in operations on living bodies.

In the first generations of the scalpel's use, surgeons had to deduce by trial and error how they could best control it. The very simplicity and lightness of the scalpel was a challenge. The Chinese cleaver chef had a heavy instrument that in its very weight dramatized the problem of brute force and the necessity of controlling it, as does a heavy hammer alert us, whereas a light, simply shaped instrument offers fewer clues about how the user might practice self-control.

Simple tools often raise this problem; the possibilities of using simple tools in many ways increases the puzzle of how they are best employed in a particular application. A modern analogy lies in the contrast between the Phillips head screwdriver and the flat-edge screwdriver. With the Phillips head, a fit-for-purpose instrument, the hand motion is clear to infer; rotation of the wrist tightens or loosens the screw. The straight edge screwdriver can also be used as a gouge, an awl, or a cutter, but the wrist grips that will accomplish these actions are harder to deduce from the instrument's form.

The scalpel resembled, in function and in form, the flat-edge screwdriver. Perplexity about how best to deploy it entwined with the problem of replication. Vesalius's demonstrations were visual rather than visceral. A small vein could be lifted from its marbling of tissue, for instance, the vein then analyzed and discussed as a distinct object. What was hard to show others, at first, was how to handle the scalpel to replicate the motion. In 1543, knowledge of muscular action was too primitive for the master to explain that the muscles controlling the fourth and fifth fingers have to be contracted in order to steady the thumb and first finger in lifting the vein with the flat side of the scalpel; as in all craftwork, understanding of what one was doing appeared only slowly, after the fact of doing it. Three generations lapsed before this procedure bedded in, to become common knowledge by the late 1600s. As the medical historian Roy Porter observes, the instant appeal of the dissecting tools was metaphysical rather than technical—"dissection of the soul," as it appeared, for instance, in Philip Stubbs's *Anatomy of the Soul* (1589).[8] Faced with perplexity in how to use this all-purpose tool, our medical ancestors resorted to grandiose language to convey a technical mystery.

These brief descriptions should, however, be astonishing: a great advance in science occurred by using imperfect or puzzling tools.

Making Repairs
Fixing and Exploring

Repair is a neglected, poorly understood, but all-important aspect of technical craftsmanship. The sociologist Douglas Harper believes that making and repairing form a single whole; he writes of those who do both that they possess the "knowledge that allows them to see beyond the elements of a technique to its overall purpose and coherence. This knowledge is the 'live intelligence, fallibly attuned to the actual circumstances' of life. It is the knowledge in which making and fixing are parts of a continuum."[9] Put simply, it is by fixing things that we often get to understand how they work.

The simplest way to make a repair is to take something apart, find and fix what's wrong, then restore the object to its former state. This could be called a static repair; it occurs, for instance, when the blown fuse in a toaster is replaced. A dynamic repair will change the object's current form or function once it is reassembled—if a broken heating filament in the toaster is replaced by a more powerful filament, the device might be able to toast bagels as well as sliced bread. At a more complex technical level, the dynamic repair may involve a jump of domains, as when a mathematical formula corrects defects in observed data. Or the dynamic repair may invite new tools for working with objects; sometime in the sixteenth century someone discovered that damaged nails are better removed with the curved double claw on a hammer than with the single-edged wedge.

Acts of repair are a proving ground for all tools. More, the experience of making dynamic repairs establishes a fine but definite line between the fixed and the all-purpose tool. The tool that simply restores is likely to be put mentally in the toolbox of fit-for-purpose-only, whereas the all-purpose tool allows us to explore deeper the act of making a repair. The difference matters because it signals two sorts of emotional responses we make to an object that doesn't work. We can want simply to relieve its frustration and will employ fit-for-purpose tools to do so. Or we can tolerate the frustration because we are now also curious; the possibility of making a dynamic repair will stimulate, and the multipurpose tool will serve as curiosity's instrument.

So it proved during the scientific turn of the seventeenth century. Dynamic repairs occurred both through domain shifts and through the development of corrective skills. About the domain shift, the historian Peter Dear remarks, "Nicolaus Copernicus' reputation as an astronomer rested on his mathematical ability, not his presumed competence as an observer; astronomers were *mathematicians*," a declaration that applied also to Galileo and later to Newton.[10] Given the pitted images available to them, they could only get somewhere by thinking beyond what they could see. Bacon had declared in the *Novum Organum* that "vision clearly holds the first place for providing information."[11] Yet the visual tools of that time held up, in the words of the philosopher Richard Rorty, no clear "mirror of Nature"; the poor-quality visual data could not be itself fixed physically.[12] Physics reached for mathematical tools that led them beyond vision; repair occurred in another domain.

Dynamic repairs of a more physical sort marked the lifework of an exemplary figure of the seventeenth century, Christopher Wren. The son of an English High Churchman, Wren and his family were put to flight by the advent of revolutionary Puritans in the 1640s; Wren came to manhood in this political trauma with science as his safe haven. As a child Wren toyed with telescopes and microscopes. at thirteen, Wren gave his father a pasteboard telescope of his own devising; three years later he was studying astronomy at Oxford; in 1665 he attempted to construct an eighty-foot telescope. He was equally fascinated by the revelations of the microscope, thanks in large part to his friendship with Robert Hooke, the virtuoso of this instrument in the seventeenth century.

Though a fine mathematician, Wren sought to repair the defects in lenses by remaining within the field of vision. A famous drawing of the eye of a gray drone fly, published in Robert Hooke's *Micrographia* of 1665, is an image modern scholars now think was probably drawn by Wren. The drawing is a much clearer image than what Hooke or Wren could have seen under the microscope's lens.[13] The image was also shaded as it could not appear under any microscope, Wren borrowing chiaroscuro conventions used by artists of his time to emphasize the contrasts between light and dark. Here "repair" produced a new kind of image, combining science and art rather than employing a mathematical formula. The pen became a corrective tool to deal with defects in glass.

In early adolescence Wren learned his third craft, dissection of animals. He had developed his physical dexterity largely by trial and error, since Vesalius's hand-mastery had not yet become school learning. His motive for gaining hand technique was intellectual; in 1656, by cutting into the veins of dogs and then pouring in an emetic, *crocus metallorum*, he meant to test William Harvey's thesis, first published in 1628, about the circulation of the blood. If Harvey's idea was correct violent results should ensue, and did: "Thus injected," Wren wrote, "the dog immediately fell a vomiting and so vomited till he died."[14] Some contemporaries objected that torturing experiments like these had no place in medicine and that surely no repair of the body could issue from them. The objection unsettled Wren's age; it feared unbounded curiosity and the Pandoric consequences of its own science.

Wren was, I think, as sensible as Milton to the potentially destructive impact of new knowledge. But the particular tools and techniques of dissection enabled him to address a giant disaster that occurred in his lifetime, London's Great Fire of 1666. In response to this event Wren sought to apply the principle of dynamic repair he had learned scientifically to the healing of a wounded city.

Wren had added architecture to his scientific interests beginning with Pembroke Chapel in Cambridge, then the Sheldonian Theater in Oxford in the early 1660s. With the return of Charles II to the English throne in 1660, Wren reentered the public stage as an architect. In that capacity, he was asked to make a new plan for London after the fire. The fire displaced two hundred thousand Londoners and destroyed more than thirteen thousand buildings in four days, the worst being the second and third days of the fire.[15] The fire spread rapidly because most of London's buildings were made of wood. Natural disaster was made worse by looting, an easy crime since most people had fled the wall of flame with few possessions on the second and third days. Flight itself was anarchic; London's growth in the three centuries before the fire obeyed no overall plan, and movement through the city's twisted streets was difficult.

Simply restoring the old city in form as it had been, merely substituting brick for wood in its buildings, might have been an option but was not what Wren chose. Rather, the prospect of repairing the city stimulated him to think about urban design in innovative ways.[16] Wren's scientific background guided him, though he couldn't mechanically apply what he and his contemporaries knew about lenses or the human body to shaping streets and buildings; the tools at his disposal were not fit for that purpose.

Five competing proposals were put forward to rebuild the ravaged city. Wren's, like John Evelyn's, transposed something like the view of the heavens seen through a telescope to the form of streets. The straight street receding to a vanishing point had been a planning aspiration since Pope Sixtus had devised in the 1590s corridor streets leading off Rome's Piazza del Popolo. In Sixtine Rome the urbanite finds a guide in "caps"—giant obelisks strategically planted at the ends of street corridors to invite and focus the pedestrian on the street's termination. Wren's design was uncapped, like the channeling of space as seen through a telescope, a channel lacking the determinacy of Sixtine planning. The great east-west street Wren imagined punctuated by Saint Paul's would be irregularly pitted with markets. Saint Paul's would itself be irregularly placed, the street passing by it rather than terminating coherently at this great structure. To the west the boulevard would cross the Fleet River and then go on without a full stop. To the east it would go around the Customs House and then end in pure space.

To Wren, as to many of his contemporaries, the microscope also suggested a new way to investigate the density of the city. Except when plague attacked a city, the density of its population had not attracted much analysis from the authorities. Wren now put under a microscope the blocks of urban fabric contained within the major streets. He did this in a quite specific way. By reckoning as minutely as possible the density of population in the city's parishes, he recalculated the number of churches needed to serve a uniform number of congregants. In his plan, these density calculations suggested nineteen churches rather than the pre-fire eighty-six. In this, the urban plan was a little like his drawing of the fly's eye; it imposed more clarity than existed in reality.

Finally, Wren's drunk dogs helped him to think about repairing London. The scalpel had permitted anatomists to study the circulation of the blood; that knowledge, applied to circulation of movement in streets, suggested that streets worked like arteries and veins; this was thus the era in which planners began to incorporate one-way streets in their designs. Wren's circulatory city was commercial in intent, aiming to deal efficiently in particular to create streets that moved goods to and from the necklace of warehouses draped along the Thames. But this design lacked the equivalent of a human heart, one central, coordinating square.

Roger Pratt, an old enemy, argued that Wren's plan should be defeated just because it was exploratory surgery, raising more problems than it answered. The city fathers could not move forward, Pratt said, "being that no man can tell how to offer any acceptable design till they [the results] be determined" in advance. To this bureaucratic objection, Wren's riposte lay in the virtue of experimentation; his was, in the words of a contemporary, a "fertile power of imagination" whose very fertility incorporated incompleteness and ambiguity.[17]

I've dwelt on this monumental event in part because disasters of a kindred sort appear today when cities like New Orleans or Gloucester are flooded; global warming may well bring further, sudden destruction. The issues Wren's age faced are still ours: whether to restore what existed in form before or to make a more dynamic, innovative repair. The second option may seem too technically demanding; no adequate, fit-for-purpose tools lie to hand. Wren's story might strengthen the desire to pursue the second option; it reveals how limited and uncertain tools can play a play a positive role in change, by stimulating imagination and so expanding competence. We are all familiar with the saying of Heraclitus that "no man ever steps in the same river twice, because it is not the same river and not the same man." The craftsman will not construe this dictum as suggesting that life is purely flux and flow. He or she may simply rethink how to do things when repairing them; limited or difficult tools may prove useful tools in that work of renewal.

Sublime Tools
Luigi Galvani's Miraculous Wires

"Galvanism" names the movement and the moment in material culture when the study of electricity seemed to offer intimations of the sublime. Galvanism drew on both good science and spiritual hocus-pocus—the latter evidenced by séances where people gathered in darkened salons, connected to mysterious wires and bottles, hoping the sudden passing of electrical current through their bodies would cure them instantly of disease or restore their sexual powers. The good science of galvanism in the eighteenth century had been ripening since ancient times.

Thales of Miletus in the sixth century BCE pondered why rubbing fur on amber made the fur stand up; some kind of energy transfer must have occurred. (The modern word *electricity* derives from *elektron*, Greek for amber.) *Electricity* appeared as an English word first in Sir Thomas Browne's *Pseudodoxia Epidemica* of 1646; though Girolamo Cardano, Otto von Guericke, and Robert Boyle made important contributions to the study of electricity, this field came into its own in the eighteenth century thanks to the invention of new experimental tools.

Probably the most consequential of these was contrived in 1745 by Pieter van Musschenbroek. The Leyden jar was a glass bottle containing water with a metal wire immersed in the water. This device stored electricity when by various means an electrostatic charge was sent through the wire; coating the outside glass with metal foil seemed to improve storage. How this storage occurred was a mystery at the time; Benjamin Franklin believed, incorrectly, that the glass itself stored the charge. We now know that the outer and inner surfaces of the Leyden jar store equal, opposite charges; van Musschenbroek did not. Nor was it well understood why the energy stored in the Leyden jar could cause so powerful a shock to a living organism, especially when these jars were wired up in parallel—but just these shocks became the Bolognese physician Luigi Galvani's passion.

Galvani experimented with passing electric currents through the bodies of frogs and other animals. Their jerking reactions seemed to him evidence that a juice containing "animal electric fluid" animated the muscles—that is, that living bodies somehow resembled a Leyden jar. His colleague Alessandro Volta believed that the jerking reaction came instead from the chemical reaction of metallic elements in the muscles responding to the charge. For both, the twitching frog muscles intimated something sublime; here were potential explanations for the energy, and so the life, of all living things.

In her study of eighteenth-century English materialism, *The Lunar Men,* Jenny Uglow shows how galvanism became a scientific sublime even to the most practical-minded people. It was a wonder to Stephen Gray in the 1730s simply that electricity could be transmitted long distances over a wire. By the end of the century Erasmus Darwin, the grandfather of Charles Darwin, had glimpsed much more. "Was the whole body an electrical circuit?" he asked in *The Temple of Nature.* "Would it be too bold to imagine that all warm-blood animals have arisen from one living filament, which the first great cause endowed with animality, with the power of acquiring new parts, attended with new propensities . . . thus possessing the faculty of continuing to improve by its own inherent activity?"[18] Uglow notes that the theory of evolution is foreshadowed in these words; we might note just the one word, *filament.* The electric wire, so prosaic to us, so potent to them.

The "sublime": for Hegel, "symbolic art with its yearning, its fermentation, its mystery, and sublimity."[19] These terms could be translated into the practice of a craft. The Leyden jar and the electric filament were enrolled in a project in the effort to reanimate fresh corpses electrically. Galvani's nephew Giovanni Aldini had tried exactly this on the bodies of criminals who had just been executed, publishing the results in 1803 to a large, credulous British public who believed that the electrified, twitching muscles of the freshly dead were signs, as Aldini put it, of "imperfect resurrection." And yet the project promised to penetrate the mystery of life.

The "sublime": for Edmund Burke, "founded upon pain . . . no pleasure from a positive cause belongs to it."[20] These would be the consequences if the craft were rigorously pursued; the quest for the scientific sublime would create man-made Pandoric suffering—or so it appeared to Mary Shelley in contemplating galvanism: the jars and wires liberating imagination in pursuit of the Ultimate Mystery, pain caused in the effort to induce life.

Frankenstein was written in 1816 as the result of a party game. Mary Shelley, her husband, Percy Shelley, and Lord Byron traveled together that summer; to pass the time, Byron suggested that they each write a ghost story. Mary Shelley, an untried writer of nineteen, instead wrote a horror story. She describes a flesh-and-blood Creature (never further named) created by her Dr. Victor Frankenstein, larger and stronger and tougher than any human, its thin yellow skin stretched tight over huge muscles, its eyes all cornea.

Her Creature wants to be loved by the people it encounters; it is a robot who wants to be a replicant. But ordinary people shrink from the Creature in horror, and in anguished revenge it becomes a killer, murdering Frankenstein's little brother, his best friend, and his wife. In a dream she recorded, just when she started writing, she imagined a Creature standing over his sleeping creator, watching the maker with "yellow, watery, but speculative eyes."[21]

Percy Shelley had dabbled in experiments with "life electricity" at university. Mary Shelley leaves clues in the novel that her readers would have understood from the popularity of galvanism and that would have made the story creditable to them; the young Dr. Franken-stein follows these clues for fabrication. He assembles body parts from dead corpses and distills the fluids, wires, and cranking machinery necessary for gluing and electrifying flesh. "The subject of electricity and galvanism," Frankenstein tells us, "was at once new and astonish-ing to me."[22] Shelley does not explain how the gluing happens or how the body parts have become larger and stronger. In her introduction to the story she invokes simply a "powerful engine" that makes Dr. Fran-kenstein's work possible, which would refer to some kind of voltaic battery then used in galvanic experiments.[23]

Readers of Shelley's tale have been struck by Dr. Frankenstein's obsession with death as much as with life. "To examine the causes of life, we must first have recourse to death," he succinctly declares, a statement that echoes Aldini's stage experiments.[24] This same liminal zone between life and death appears in much science fiction, in Alfred Jarry's *Supermale* later in the nineteenth century, in Isaac Asimov's twentieth-century robots dwelling in outer space. But a particular imaginative act enabled Mary Shelley to open the doors to the scien-tific sublime.

This lay in her imagining what it would be like to be someone else's tool, brought to life. An intuitive leap was required to envision what it would be like to be a living machine. Galvani believed he provided the means for making this intuitive leap, in speaking about the Leyden jar and the electrically charged filament as "the instruments for life," but he did not, as it were, follow the arc of this intuitive leap himself. The mumbo jumbo of the séances intervened, and profitably so; Galvani became rich from them. Whether patients ultimately died or lived, whether their sperm counts rose or not, they paid—before each séance began. Though she lacked a laboratory, Mary Shelley could be said to be a better investigator than Galvani; she wanted to know the conse-quences of his science. She wanted to understand his science better through imagining being its tool.

Today, as in Shelley's fiction, we may make the same intuitive leap, but as a matter of necessity. The more thinking machines become a reality, the more it becomes necessary to intuit what these machines are thinking. Before recent advances in microelectronics, intelligent automation seemed a fantasy. By 2006, the British government's Office of Science and Innovation issued a report on "Robot-rights." Its authors declare that "if artificial intelligence is achieved and widely deployed, or if [robots] can reproduce and improve themselves, calls may be made for human rights to be extended to robots."[25] At what point, though, does the self-organization of a complex machine become self-sustaining? Noel Sharkey, a critic of the "Robot-rights" report, worries instead about military robots that fight intelligently, without reference to human death.[26] Like Shelley's Creature the robots may have a will if not rights of their own.

Even avoiding the thickets of artificial intelligence, we want to understand how tools can more generically engage us in large intuitive leaps into the unknown. Just to make matters more complicated, we want to understand how intuitive leaps relate to the work of dynamic repair.

Arousal
How Intuitive Leaps Happen

The sublime suggests a limitless horizon. Yet a concrete account can be given of how intuitive leaps happen. They occur in four stages.

Hume argued that the mind enlarges its frame of reference by "stumbling" on the unexpected, the unforeseen; imagination happens *to* us. The craftsman's mind works differently than Hume imagined, because specific practices prepare the ground on which people might stumble. Intuition begins with the sense that what isn't yet could be. How do we sense this? In technical craftsmanship, the sense of possibility is grounded in feeling frustrated by a tool's limits or provoked by its untested possibilities. The imperfect telescopes and microscopes of the seventeenth century suggested there could be something beyond the powers of the lens; in the eighteenth-century scientific sublime, Leyden jars and electrically charged filaments suggested hazy applications to the human body.

How does then using a tool organize these possibilities? The first stage occurs when we break the mold of fit-for-purpose. That break occupies a different part of the imaginative realm than retrospection. In Thomas Hobbes's idea of imagination, for instance, people look backward on sensations they've already experienced. "Imagination," he declared, "is nothing but decaying sense." Once an object that has aroused us is removed "or the eye shut, we still retain an image of the thing seen, though more obscure than we [actually] see it." As in the Cavendish family experiment, wrote Hobbes, we begin to reconstitute this experience as language, "the sequel and contexture of the names of things into Affirmations, Negations, and other formes of Speech."[27] Imagination here names a process of reconstruction but is not how dynamic repair operates. When Wren drew the drone fly eye, he was not reconstructing something in his memory "more obscure than we [actually] see it"; on the contrary, he was constructing clarity from obscurity. We can label this first stage one of reformatting. The ground is prepared because reformatting draws on established technical skills— in Wren's case, his capacity to draw using chiaroscuro effects and fine-tipped pens. Reformatting is no more and no less than the willingness to see if a tool or practice can be changed in use.

The next stage in an imaginative leap occurs through establishing adjacency. Two unlike domains are brought close together; the closer they are, the more stimulating seems their twined presence. In the experiments of Galvani and Volta, the Leyden jar and its paraphernalia brought the impalpable domain of energy close to the material substances of water or metal. Two domains, the invisible and the palpable, had been brought nearer by the instruments. So, too, in making a dynamic repair with simpler instruments; the hand or eye senses that this isn't what the tool was meant for—easy and awkward sit side by side. At the most embracing, Mary Shelley sought to make life and death adjacent; her fictional Dr. Frankenstein, like the real nephew of Galvani, sought to understand what these two states intimately share. To refer to an earlier instance in this book: in order to invent the mobile telephone, it was necessary for researchers to shove close together two quite different technologies, those of the radio and the telephone, then to think about what they might, but didn't yet, share.

The actual intuitive leap across domains then occurs in two further stages. Although you were preparing for it you didn't know in advance precisely what you would make of the close comparison. In this third stage, you begin dredging up tacit knowledge into consciousness to do the comparing—and you are surprised. Surprise is a way of telling yourself that something you know can be other than you assumed. Many technology transfers that were meant to be merely rote applications of one procedure to another become illuminating just in this stage; there was something fuller or more manifold in the initial procedure than had been assumed. It's at this point that the maker begins to experience wonder. Ancient Greek embedded wonder in *poiein*, the root word for *making*. In the *Symposium* Plato says, "Whatever passes from not being into being is a poesis," a cause for wonder. The modern writer Walter Benjamin uses another Greek word, *aura*—"bathed in its own light"—to describe the wonder that a thing exists. People can wonder fresh, innocent of any initial complication, about things they have not made; but about the things they make, the ground of surprise and wonder has to be prepared.

The final stage is recognition that a leap does not defy gravity; unresolved problems remain unresolved in the transfer of skills and practices. Imagining that he could analyze the density of a city's population by using microscopic technique, Wren still couldn't count accurately. Roger Pratt spotted the imprecision and reproached Wren for it, but Wren persevered, knowing the technique was burdened; though imperfect it provided a new insight. The recognition that an intuitive leap cannot defy gravity matters more largely because it corrects a frequently held fantasy about technology transfer. This is that importing a procedure will clarify a murky problem; more often, the technical import, like any immigrant, will bring with it its own problems.

These are the four elements, then, involved in making an intuitive leap: reformatting, adjacency, surprise, gravity. The sequence is not strict, at least in its first two stages; sometimes comparing two unlike tools can prompt the realization that each might be used differently. In the piano maker's toolbox, for instance, the pick used to soften piano hammers happens to lie next to a felt knife. Staring at this conjunction, made simply because they are the same size, one might be prompted to think that the awl could also be used to lift felt, though it was not designed for that task.

However the first stages are ordered, why call the cumulative process of an intuitive leap "intuitive"? Isn't what I've described a form of reasoning? It *is* reasoning, but not of a deductive sort, and it constitutes a special form of induction.

Intuitive leaps defy syllogisms. Classical logic provides syllogisms such as the following ancient nostrum: "All men are mortal / Socrates is a man / Therefore Socrates is mortal." The first line is the axiom, or major premise, and is a universal proposition. The flow in the syllogism in the second statement is from the general to the particular. The third statement makes a deduction based on this flow. Induction has shaped the first statement; it declares a general truth that all men are mortal, which we decide to explore by applying the generality to a particular case and finally by drawing a conclusion.

The mentor of the seventeenth-century scientists, Francis Bacon, argued that syllogisms can be misleading; he rejected "induction by enumeration"—that is, piling up a mass of similar cases and ignoring examples that don't fit. Moreover, he pointed out, the fact that a number of cases are similar doesn't itself explain their nature: you can't understand how wine is made simply by drinking lots of it. Syllogistic thinking, Bacon declared, is not much good for "inquiring into truth" of the first principles.[28]

The intuitive leap does not fit well into the pattern of deductive, syllogistic thinking. Reformatting and close comparison decant a familiar practice or tool from an established container; the stress in the first three stages of an intuitive leap is on *if*, on what if? instead of *then*. That final, conscious reckoning carries a burden—in technology transfer as in the arts, the burdened carryover of problems—rather than the clarifying finality of a syllogistic conclusion.

Without detracting from the experience, I have sought to take some of the mystery out of intuition. It can be crafted. Tools used in certain ways organize this imaginative experience and with productive results. Both limited and all-purpose instruments can enable us to take the imaginative leaps necessary to repair material reality or guide us toward what we sense is an unknown reality latent with possibility. These tools furnish only a corner of imagination's domain, however. I want now to add more furniture to this corner by exploring resistance and ambiguity. Like intuition, these also shape the craftsman's imagination.

CHAPTER EIGHT

Resistance and Ambiguity

Don't try to hit the target!" This bit of Zen advice seems so baffling that the young archer may be tempted to aim the arrow at the master. The master is not perverse: the author of *The Art of Archery* means "Don't try so hard," and he's offering practical advice: if you try too hard, are too assertive, you will aim badly and hit the target erratically.[1] The advice goes beyond counseling minimum force. The young archer is urged to work with resistance in the bow, to explore different ways of pointing the arrow, as though the procedure were ambiguous. In the end the archer will aim better.

The Zen master's advice could be applied to urbanism. Much twentieth-century urban planning proceeded on the principle: demolish all you can, grade it flat, and then build from scratch. The existing environment has been seen as standing in the way of the planner's will. This aggressive recipe has frequently proved disastrous, destroying many viable buildings as well as ways of life bedded into urban fabric. The replacements for these destroyed buildings have also, too often, proved worse; big projects suffer from overdetermined, fit-for-purpose form; when history moves on, as it always does, tightly defined buildings can soon become obsolete. So the good urban craftsman wants to take the Zen master's advice, work less aggressively, befriending ambi-guity. These are attitudes—but how do they become skills?

How the Craftsman Can Work with Resistance

We want to start with resistances, those facts that stand in the way of the will. Resistances themselves come in two sorts: found and made. Just as a carpenter discovers unexpected knots in a piece of wood, a builder will find unforeseen mud beneath a housing site. These found resistances contrast to what a painter does who scrapes off a perfectly serviceable portrait, deciding to start over again; here the artist has put an obstacle in his or her own path. The two sorts of resistance would seem entirely unlike: in the first something blocks us, in the second we make our own difficulties. Yet certain techniques are shared in learning to work well with both.

The Path of Least Resistance
Boxes and Tubes

To explore what people do when they find resistance, we might consider one of the shibboleths of engineering: follow the "path of least resistance." This dictum is rooted in the human hand, based on the precept of combining minimum force with release. The history of ur-ban engineering offers an illuminating experiment in its environmental dimensions.

Modern capitalism began, Lewis Mumford has argued, in the act of systematically colonizing the ground. Networks of mines provided the coal that fueled the steam engine; the steam engine in turn begat mass transport and mass manufacturing.[2] The technology of tunneling enabled modern sanitation systems, underground pipes diminishing the scourge of plague, and so helping to increase the population. The underground realm below cities remains today as important as in the past; tunnels now house the fiber-optic cables that exploit the resources of digital communication.

Modern mining technology derived originally from the bodily revelations of the scalpel. Andreas Vesalius, the doctor in Brussels who founded modern dissection, published *De humani corporis fabrica* in 1533. In 1540 modern technology for working belowground was codified in Vannoccio Biringuccio's *Pirotechnia*, a treatise that urged its readers to think like Vesalius, using mining techniques that lifted plates of stone or stripped back strata of earth rather than simply chopping through them.[3] Working in this way, Biringuccio argued, would follow the path of least resistance in going underground.

The end of the eighteenth century marks the time when planners felt it imperative to apply these mining principles to the realm under urban ground. The expansion of cities made it clear that transporting clean water and removing excrement required tunnels of a size that exceeded those of the ancient Roman city. More, the planners intuited that people might be moved around the city more rapidly underground than was possible on the tangle of surface streets. In London, though, the earth was an unstable mud mass; eighteenth-century techniques used to mine coal would not quite serve. Moreover, tidal pressure on the London mud mass meant that the timber supports used in hard rock or coalmines could not stabilize even relatively solid sectors of the earth. Renaissance Venice offered to eighteenth-century builders in London some insight into how pilings could float warehouses above mud—but not how to inhabit the mud itself.

Could these underground resistances be overcome? The engineer Marc Isambard Brunel had an answer. He had at age twenty-four left France for Britain in 1793 and sired the even more illustrious engineer Isambard Kingdom Brunel. The Brunels treated natural resistance as their enemy, and tried to defeat it, when in 1826 father and son sought to construct a road tunnel under the Thames River, east of the Tower of London.[4]

The elder Brunel concocted a mobile metal house that allowed workers to build a brick-lined tunnel as the metal house moved forward. The house consisted of three linked iron chambers, each roughly a yard wide and seven yards tall, each pushed forward by a large screw-turn at its base. Within each compartment, men laid the brick sides, bottoms, and tops of the tunnel as the house advanced; behind the men in the front room came a larger army of masons to thicken and reinforce the new walls. On the advancing wall of the house, small slits in the metal allowed mud to seep through, relieving forward pressure; more men carried this mud away.

Struggling against, rather than working with mud and water, they worked poorly. In a day, the underground house could advance only about ten inches along the tunnel's four-hundred-yard path. As well as slow, the shield was fragile; it lay about five yards below the bed of the Thames, so that unusual tidal pressures could crack the first layer of walling, and indeed many workers died in the compartments when this occurred. Work stopped temporarily in 1835. The Brunels were, however, nothing if not determined. In 1836 Brunel père reconfigured the screw mechanism pushing the shield forward, and the tunnel was completed in 1841 (it opened officially in 1843). Fifteen years had been required to advance the four hundred yards underground.[5]

We owe to the younger Brunel everything from the invention of pneumatic caissons for bridges to iron-cage ships to the creation of efficient railroad carriages. The picture many people know of him is a photograph in which he poses, cigar in hand, top hat tipped back, slightly crouching as if ready to spring, against a background of massive chains handing from the great iron-sided ship he created. It is the image of a heroic fighter, a conqueror, overcoming whatever stands in his path. But in his case, aggressive combat proved inefficient.

In the wake of the Brunels, others succeeded by working with water and mud pressure rather than fighting against it. This happened in a tunnel under the Thames built in 1869, safely and in little more than eleven months. In place of the Brunels' flat wall, Peter Barlow and James Greathead designed a snub-nosed structure, its rounded surface more easily pushing into the mud. The tunnel was also smaller, a yard wide and only two and a half yards high, the size calculated in terms of tidal pressures—a reckoning lacking in the Brunels' giant underground fortress. The new ovoid construction made use of cast-iron tubing rather than bricks for the tunnel structure. The rings of cast-iron were bolted together as excavation proceeded, the tube shape diffusing surface pressure. Practical results followed quickly; by magnifying the same ovoid tube-shape, new engineering made possible the beginnings of the Underground transport network in London.

The tubular form may seem self-evident technically, yet the Victorians didn't grasp its human implications. They labeled the new solution the "Greathead shield," generously crediting the junior partner; the moniker misleads because a shield still suggests a weapon in battle. It is certainly true, as defenders of the Brunels said in the 1870s, that without their initial example the alternative of Barlow and Greathead would never have come into being. Which is the point. Seeing that arbitrary imposition worked poorly, the engineers who came after the Brunels reimagined the task. The Brunels fought, Greathead worked with, resistance underground.

✳   ✳   ✳

This passage in engineering history raises first of all a problem in psychology that, like a cobweb, needs to be swept away. A classic proposition in psychology has been that resistance begets frustration and, taken a step further, that frustration begets anger. Here is the impulse to smash to bits the pieces in a do-it-yourself kit that don't fit together. In the jargon of the social sciences, this is the "frustration-aggression syndrome." Mary Shelley's Creature embodies the syndrome even more violently; her Creature is driven to kill by frustrated love. The connection ultimately linking frustration to violent behavior seems good common sense; it is common sense, but it does not make good sense.

The frustration-aggression syndrome derives from the reflections of nineteenth-century observers, notably Gustave Le Bon, on revolutionary crowds.[6] Le Bon set aside the specifics of political grievance and emphasized the fact that pent-up frustrations swell the numbers of people in crowds. Unable to discharge its anger through formal political channels, the crowd's growing frustration becomes like charging a battery; at a certain moment, the crowd releases this energy through violence.

Our engineering example makes clear why the behavior Le Bon observed in crowds is not an apt model for labor. The Brunels, Barlow, and Gateshead all had a high tolerance for frustration in their work. The psychologist Lionel Festinger explored such toleration of frustration, under laboratory conditions, by observing animals exposed to prolonged frustration; he found that rats and pigeons, just like engineers, often became adept at sustaining frustration rather than going berserk; the animals organized their behavior to make do, that is, at least temporarily, without gratification. Festinger's observations drew on earlier researches by Gregory Bateson on the toleration of "double-binds," frustrations from which there is no exit.[7] And a recent experiment with young people who are shown true answers to questions they have first answered falsely presents another side of tolerating frustration; they will sometimes continue to probe and poke at alternative methods or solutions even though they are now presented with the correct answer. Not surprising: they want in these instances to understand *why* they got the answer wrong.

Certainly the mental machine can grind to a halt when faced with too much resistance, or for too long, or resistance that admits of no investigation. Any of these conditions might well induce a person to give up. Are there then skills that allow people to dwell, and productively dwell, in frustration? Three skills stand out.

The first draws on the reformatting that can inaugurate a leap of imagination. Barlow records that he imagined himself swimming across the Thames (a revolting thought in that age of untreated sewage). He then imagined what inanimate shape would most resemble his body: his body was more like a tube than a box. This is an anthropomorphic assist to reformatting, and it resembles the human investment we noted in honest bricks—but with the difference that the assist here aims at problem solving. The problem is recast with, as it were, different protagonists, a swimmer instead of a channel in water. Henry Petroski makes Barlow's point much more largely: without recasting resistance, many strictly defined problems remained impossible for the engineer.[8]

This skill differs from the detective work of tracing an error back to its source. Recasting a problem with different protagonist is a technique to be employed when that detective work reaches a dead end. At the piano we do something akin physically to what Barlow did mentally when, faced with an intractably difficult chord in one hand, we play it with the other; a change in the fingers used to make the chord, a different hand-protagonist, often provides insight into the problem; frustration is then relieved. Again, this productive address to resistance could be likened to making a literary translation; though much can be lost in moving from one language to another, meanings can also be found in translation.

The second response to resistance concerns patience. The frequently noted patience of good craftsmen signals a capacity to stay with frustrating work, and patience in the form of sustained concentration, we have seen in Chapter 5, is a learned skill that can expand in time. But Brunel was also patient, or at least determined, over many years. Here a rule can be formulated, opposite in character to the frustration-aggression syndrome: when something takes longer than you expect, stop fighting it. This rule operated in the pigeon maze Festinger contrived in his laboratory. At first the disoriented pigeons banged against the plastic walls of the maze, but as the birds proceeded further, they stopped attacking the walls even though they remained confused; they trudged more composedly forward, still not knowing where they were going. But this rule is not quite as simple as it seems.

The difficulty lies in judging time. If a difficulty lasts, one alternative to giving up is to reorient one's expectations. In most work we estimate how long it will take; resistance obliges us to revise. The error might seem that of imagining we could accomplish a task quickly, but the wrinkle is that we have to fail consistently to make this revision—or so it seemed to the author of *The Art of Archery*. The Zen master offers his counsel to stop fighting specifically to that neophyte who fails again and again to hit the target. The patience of a craftsman can thus be defined as: the temporary suspension of the desire for closure.

From which follows a third skill in working with resistance that I am somewhat embarrassed to state baldly: identify with the resistance. This might seem a vacuous principle, suggesting that to cope with a dog that wants to bite, think like a dog. But in craftwork, identification has a sharp point. Imagining himself swimming in the filthy Thames, Barlow responded more to the flow of water than to its pressure, whereas Brunel focused on the least forgiving element—water pressure—and fought against that bigger challenge. The identification a good craftsman practices is selective, that of finding the most forgiving element in a difficult situation. Often this element is smaller, and so seems less important, than the larger challenge. It is an error in technical as in artistic work to deal first with the big difficulties and then clean up the details; good work often proceeds in just the opposite fashion. Thus, at the piano, when faced with a complicated chord, the tilt of the palm is a less difficult point of entry than finger-stretch; the pianist is more like to improve by responding positively to this detail.

To be sure, focus on small, yielding elements is a matter of attitude as much as procedure. The attitude derives, I think, from that power of sympathy described in Chapter 3—sympathy not as touchy-feely love but just the disposition to turn outward. Thus, Barlow did not approach his engineering difficulty hoping to find something like a fault in an enemy's defenses, a weak point to exploit. He dealt with the resistance by selecting an aspect of it that he could work with. Faced with a barking dog, you do better to hold your open hand in front of it than to bite back.

The skills of working well with resistance are in sum, those of reconfiguring the problem into other terms, readjusting one's behavior if the problem lasts longer than expected, and identifying with the problem's most forgiving element.

Making Things Difficult
Skin Work

At the opposite pole of encountering resistance, we may make things difficult for ourselves. We do so because easy and lean solutions often conceal complexity. The young musician who strips off the Suzuki tapes from a string instrument makes things hard for himself or herself for just this reason. Modern urbanism offers a kindred, and richer, instance of making things difficult. This case concerns a building familiar to many readers, Frank Gehry's Guggenheim Museum in Bilbao. The work of building it contains a story not evident to the visitor's eye.

When the leaders of Bilbao commissioned an art museum in the 1980s, they hoped to stimulate investment in a tired port. Shipping had declined in Bilbao, and the city had darkened and decayed through generations of environmental abuse. Gehry, whose impulses are those of a sculptor, was in part chosen because Bilbao's leaders realized that yet another tasteful glass-and-steel box of a museum would not send a distinctive signal of change. Yet the site they had chosen made this

signal difficult to send: though next to water, the location was en-
meshed in a spaghetti of roads cooked up by past, poor urban planning.

Gehry has long sculpted buildings of metal, a pliant material suited
to the challenge of bending over and around the tangle of streets. Here,
he wanted to roll out his metal in a quilted pattern, to crinkle the light
bouncing off the building and so soften its enormous mass. Lead copper was the material that would have most easily and cheaply suited
Gehry's design; its fabrication in large sheets is fairly straightforward.
But this metal is outlawed in Spain as a toxic material.

The path of least resistance would have been corruption. The
powerful patrons of the project might have bribed government officials
to permit lead copper or changed the law or obtained an exemption for
the star architect. The officials and the architect accepted, however,
that lead copper poses environmental hazards. So Gehry searched for
another material. "It took," he has written, with a certain restraint, "a
long time."[9]

At first his office experimented with stainless steel, which didn't
reflect, as Gehry wanted, the play of light on the curved surfaces. In
frustration he turned to titanium, which had "warmth and character"
but might prove too expensive and had rarely before the 1980s been
used to sheath buildings. The titanium produced for military purposes,
principally airplane parts, would have cost a fortune and was never
meant for architectural work on the ground.

Gehry visited a factory in Pittsburgh where such titanium was
rolled out, seeking to alter the way the metal was made. Gehry says, a
little misleadingly, "We asked the fabricator to continue to search for
the right mix of oil, acids, rollers, and heat to arrive at the material we
wanted"; the phrase "right mix" is deceptive because he and the other
designers did not know exactly what they wanted at the start.

Moreover—and here was the harder technical challenge—new machinery had to be created. Gehry had at hand rollers designed to press
molten steel into sheets, but these rollers were too crude and too heavy,

especially when he decided he wanted a fabric imprinted with a quilt-like surface to break up reflected light. In order to roll precisely, the cushions that held the rollers had to be rethought; the new cushioning mechanism was imported and adapted from hydraulic shock absorbers in automobiles.

This domain shift only raised more difficulties. The composition of the metal now had to be explored in concert with the rolling tools, Gehry and his team at each stage judging both aesthetic and structural qualities. This took a year. Eventually the fabricators produced titanium alloy sheets, rolled out in the quilted pattern, a third of a millimeter thick. These sheets are both thinner than stainless-steel plates and less rigid, giving a bit in the wind. Light does indeed crinkle and flutter on the quilted surface; the ribbed sheets also proved immensely strong.

The spirit of craftsmanship steering this material investigation was more flexible than that of mere problem solving. The fabricators had to rethink a tool—the rollers, which were imported from another machine and reimagined as a metal-weaving loom. Investigating the composition of the titanium itself was more straightforward, proceeding by controlled variation of its elements. It's hard to know what the technicians thought and felt in staying with this demanding task, but we do know something about Gehry's mental processes. He found this experience—and I use the word advisedly—enlightening.

Once he could make and use quilted titanium, Gehry writes, he began to rethink his assumptions about stability, the most fundamental aspect of building design. He realized that "the stability given by stone is false, because stone deteriorates in the pollution of our cities whereas a third of a millimeter of titanium is a hundred-year guarantee." He concluded, "We have to rethink what represents stability." Stability can mean—counter-intuitively—thin rather than thick, or undulating rather than rigid.

Perhaps the most interesting aspect of this museum's backstory is what the architect gained by making all these difficulties for himself about the building's skin. By working on a surface he came to question a basic aspect of structure. Certainly, simplicity represents a goal in craftwork—it's part of the measure of what David Pye calls "soundness" in a practice. But to make difficulties where none need be is a way to think about the nature of soundness. "It's too easy" is a test of "there's more here than meets the eye."

This rather general observation has today a practical application. Urban planning, like other technical practices, often zeroes in on needless complexity, trying to strip away tangles in a street system or in public space. Functional simplicity carries a price; urbanites tend to react neutrally to stripped-down spaces, not caring about much about where they are. The designer-planner seeking to bring these dead public spaces to life can succeed by introducing what may seem unnecessary elements, such as indirect approaches to the front entrances or bollards arbitrarily to mark out territory, or, as Mies van der Rohe did with the Seagram Building in New York, by contriving complicated side entrances to his elegantly simple tower. Complexity can serve as a design tool to counter neutrality. Additions of complexity can prompt people to engage more with their surroundings. This is the rationale for making the judgment about a public space that it's too simple, it's too easy.

In the production process, introducing complexity is a procedure that addresses the suspicion that things are not what they seem; here, making things more complex is a technique of investigation. In this regard we might note that for Gehry's industrial crew, the result of their efforts was a new understanding of the sheet roller rather than aesthetic enrichment; introducing complexity led had them back to that simple tool. Sometimes, in planning that embraces complexity, the result is also that people focus on simple elements in the built environment—a single bench, a clump of trees that have been inserted into a spatial void.

Resistances, then, can be either found or made. Both cases require toleration of frustration, and both require imagination. In found difficulties, to cope we will identify with the obstacle, seeing the problem, as it were, from the problem's point of view. Made difficulties embody the suspicion that matters might be or should be more complex than they seem; to investigate, we can make them even more difficult.

The philosopher John Dewey embraced positive learning from resistance, in part due to his embattled position at the turn of the twentieth century. His contemporaries the social Darwinists had magnified Brunel's attitude. They supposed that all living creatures aim to defeat the obstacles posed by all other contending creatures. The natural world appeared to these faulty disciples of Charles Darwin as a place of strife only; society, they argued, was ruled by self-interest, absent any altruistic cooperation. To Dewey this seemed a macho fantasy that missed the real issue: working with resistance is the key to survival.

Dewey was an heir to the Enlightenment. Like Madame d'Épinay, he believed in the necessity of learning one's limits. He was also a pragmatist, believing that to get things done you need to understand the resistances you encounter rather than aggressively conduct war against them. Dewey was a philosopher of cooperation; he declares, "Only when an organism shares in the ordered relations of its environment does it secure the stability essential to living."[10] As will appear at the end of this book, he derived from these straightforward principles an entire philosophy of action. But most of all, he was interested in resistance as an environmental problem. Dewey's use of the word *environment* is rather general and abstract; sometimes he refers to the ecology of a forest, sometimes to factories, as "the environment." He meant to convey that resistance always has a context, be that natural or social, that the experience of resistance is never an isolated event. In his spirit, but with a bit more focus, we want to specify where resistances occur.

Sites of Resistance
Walls and Membranes

All living things contain two sites of resistance. These are cell walls and cell membranes. Both resist external pressures to keep intact the internal elements of the cell, but they do so in different ways. The cell wall is more purely exclusionary; the membrane permits more fluid and solid exchange. The filter function of these two structures differs in degree, but for the sake of clarity let's exaggerate it: a membrane is a container both resistant and porous.

A homology between cell wall and cell membrane can be found in natural ecologies. An ecological boundary resembles the cell wall, an ecological border the cell membrane. A boundary can be a guarded territory, like those established by prides of lions or packs of wolves, a "no-go" zone for others. Or the boundary can be simply an edge where things end, like the tree line on a mountain that marks the boundary above which trees cannot grow. An ecological border, by contrast, is a site of exchange where organisms become more interactive. The shoreline of a lake is such a border; at the edge of water and land organisms can find and feed off many other organisms. The same is true of temperature layers within a lake: where layer meets layer constitutes a watery zone of intense biological exchange. An ecological border, like a cell membrane, resists indiscriminate mixture; it contains differences but is porous. The border is an active edge.

These natural distinctions are reflected in the built human environment. The wall Israel is building through the West Bank territories, for instance, is meant to function like a cell wall or ecological boundary; for the sake of security, not incidentally, the wall is made of metal, the least porous of materials. The plate glass window walls used in modern architecture are another version of the boundary; though these windows permit sight within, they exclude smell and sound and prohibit touch. The gated community is yet another modern variant, life sealed within its walls, policed by surveillance cameras. Most pervasive in the modern city is the inert boundary established by highway traffic, cutting off parts of the city from each other. In all these spaces, resistance to the outside is meant to become absolute, the boundary fending off human interaction.

Walls themselves are worth a little more thought, because in the history of cities, walls meant to be inert boundaries have occasionally morphed into more active borders.

Until the invention of artillery, people sheltered behind walls when attacked; in medieval cities, gates set into walls regulated commerce coming into cities; the lack of wall porosity meant that taxes could be effectively collected at these few checkpoints. Some massive medieval walls, however, such as those surviving in Avignon, modulated in time; inside Avignon's walls there grew up by the sixteenth century uncontrolled, unregulated housing; outside, informal markets selling black-market or untaxed goods nestled against the stones; foreign exiles and other misfits gravitated toward the walls, far from the controls of the center. Though they certainly don't appear to, such walls functioned more like cell membranes, both porous and resistant.

The first ghettoes in Europe also morphed into places with walls like this. Intended to contain supposedly impure or alien presences in the city, such as Jewish or Muslim traders, the walls of the early ghettoes soon, as it were, began to leak. In Venice, for instance, the islands reserved for Jews and the buildings called *fundacos* where Germans, Greeks, and Armenians lodged were defined by walls near which economic activity continually increased. The ghettoes were in form more complicated than prisons, reflecting Venice's complexity as an international city.[11]

Most urbanists now want to foster growth in a form that echoes the transformation of medieval walls. Working *with* resistance means, in urbanism, converting boundaries into borders. Economics as well as liberal values drive this strategy. A city needs constantly to absorb new elements. In healthy cities, economic energy pushes outward from the center to the periphery. The problem is that we are better at building boundaries than borders, and this for a deep reason.

From its origins, the center of the European city has been more important than its periphery; courts, political assemblies, markets, and the most important religious shrines have been located in the city center. That geographical stress translated into a social value: the center as a place where people are most likely to share. In modern planning this has meant that efforts to strengthen community life seek to intensify life at the center. But is the center, as a space and as a social value, a good place in which to mix the cocktail of cultural diversity?

It is not, as I discovered some years ago in helping create a market to serve Spanish Harlem in New York. This community, then one of the poorest in the city, lay above 96th Street on Manhattan's Upper East Side. To the south, in an abrupt shift, was one of the richest communities in the world, comparable to Mayfair in London or the Seventh Arrondissement in Paris. We chose to locate La Marqueta in the center of Spanish Harlem and to regard 96th Street as a dead edge where little would happen. We chose wrongly. We should have treated this street itself as an important border; locating the market here would have encouraged activity that brought rich and poor into daily commercial contact. (Wiser planners have learned from this mistake; at the southwestern edge of Afro-American Harlem, they have sought to locate new community resources at the borders between communities.)

※   ※   ※

In all craftwork, we want to follow the urbanist's impulse to work *with* resistance in borderline conditions. We develop skill at the live edge. The planning mistake made in Spanish Harlem embodies, though, a danger facing labor. Many managers harbor a mental map of the work done in their organizations: boxes containing specialized activities, arrows and flow charts connecting them. On this mental map—so beloved of personnel experts—the important work usually occupies a prominent, central position, the more minor or self-contained tasks pushed to the bottom or sides of the chart; the work environment is visualized in the same way as a city or a community. The map frequently misleads, because real issues can be missed, having been pushed to the periphery. Moreover, the arrows and flow diagrams in this mental map often misrepresent the kind of work that can only be done in a border zone. That's where repair occurs as technicians, nurses, or salespeople deal with difficult and ambiguous problems; the arrows from box to box are most likely to depict only who reports to whom.

If only such organizational charts were the office furnishings of the capitalist dogs. Unfortunately, most people at work make similar mental maps, charting the parts of their labor rather than its processes. A more accurate if rather more complex process of visualization is required particularly at the edge, the zone in which people have to deal with difficulty; we need to visualize what is difficult in order to address it. This is probably the greatest challenge facing any good craftsman: to see in the mind's eye where the difficulties lie.

Thus, the tilt of the palm seems peripheral to the mental map a musician makes for a chord stretch yet turns out to be a zone for productive work with finger resistance; the palm becomes a working space. So too, in hammering a nail, we have to establish that border zone on the hammer shaft in which secure grip interacts with freedom of the elbow; this fulcrum point is our working space. In evaluating the fleshy firmness of a slaughtered chicken, the fingertip becomes a sensate border. In goldsmithy, the moment of truth in the assay is a border zone both physically and mentally, the fingertips probing the texture of a problematic substance, seeking to name it. These are ways to *see* work, especially work that is difficult.

This challenge forms a fitting cap to the problem with which we begin, trying to pin down the "site of resistance." The phrase has two meanings: it denotes either a boundary, resisting contamination, excluding, deadening, or a border, a site of exchange as well as of separation. Walls in cities have embodied both meanings. In the context of a multicultural city, the second kind of site is both more challenging and more necessary. In labor, too, the boundary is a space of containment; the more productive environment for working with resistance is a border.

Ambiguity

The literary critic William Empson wrote a famous study about seven types of ambiguity in language, spanning the gamut from blatant contradiction to sheer fuzziness. Any skilled writer doles out any sort of ambiguity like very good wine—that is, sparingly. We can make an expressive point about hanging stories or unresolved characters if we do not leave them hanging or resolved too often. How should we then set about making matters imprecise?

Anticipating Ambiguity
Making an Edge

This is first of all making a move that we know will produce an ambiguous result. That event occurred, for instance, when the young violinist first removed the Suzuki tapes; he or she didn't quite know what would come next, but still, it was a decisive step. Ambiguity can also be mechanically created, as in the "fuzzy logic" built into many computational programs; in them the organizing principle is delay. A fuzzy logic program is sophisticated enough to delay resolving one set of problems until it works in another realm, searching for useful inputs; the modern computer is able to hold in its memory a huge number of these provisional solutions. Though in terms of human time the wait in fuzzy logic may be imperceptible, as little a few microseconds, still, within the computer's time-scale the machinery is pausing, the application momentarily unresolved.

In urban design, too, we can decisively plan for ambiguity by contriving places where people don't know quite where they are, places where they feel lost. The maze is such a space. Planned ambiguity acquires more value if the designer intends that others learn something from momentary disorientation, become skilled in dealing with ambiguity. Amsterdam offers a graphic instance of such instructive ambiguity made by design, in a particular kind of live edge.

In the years immediately after the Second World War, the architect Aldo van Eyck began filling up Amsterdam's empty spaces with playgrounds—in trash-filled backyards, at traffic circles, on forlorn corners and the edges of streets. Van Eyck cleaned out the trash and graded the ground; his team sometimes painted the walls of adjoining buildings; the architect himself designed playground equipment, sandpits, and wading pools. Unlike school playgrounds, these street pocket-parks invited adults in as well. Many had comfortable benches or were located next to cafés and bars, allowing adult child-minders to nip inside for a quick drink to steady their nerves. Van Eyck built many urban playgrounds of this sort by the mid-1970s; the urban historian Liane Lefaivre puts their total number in the hundreds, as other Dutch cities imitated Amsterdam.[12] Few, unfortunately, have survived.

The designer's aim for these small parks was to teach children how to anticipate and manage ambiguous transitions in urban space. Infants taken to the Hendrikplantsoen playground, in its 1948 form, could for instance wallow in sandpits that had no neat separation from grassy areas.[13] The lack of a clear boundary between sand and grass was by design, providing the toddler an opportunity to puzzle through this tactile difference. Next to the sandpits were places for older children to climb and adults to sit. The architect enabled the passage from toddling to climbing by putting stones of different heights close together—but not in a straight-line sequence; rather, the young child had to test a kind of forest of stepping-stones against his or her body. The lack of clear physical definition again provided a challenge; there were edges, but not sharp separations; probing that condition was meant to stimulate inquiry.

Van Eyck intuited that such spatial ambiguities would also provoke children to engage with one another, toddlers tending to help each other crawl and totter about. This intuition was elaborated in the making of the Buskenblaserstraat park.[14] Here a park was contrived from empty space at a street corner, with cars flowing past. While the sandpit here is well marked and set well back from the streets; equipment for children to climb on has not been so protected. Cooperative activity—looking out for cars, shouting, lots of shouting—becomes a matter of keeping safe; from its inception, this has been a noisy park. If when playing around these tubular frames kids need to watch out for each other as cars approach, they moreover need to define rules about how to use the play furniture itself. Like the anatomist with his scalpel, Van Eyck favored simple forms of play furniture that give few directions for use. And just because in the Buskenblaserstraat there is enough room for tossing and kicking balls around, kids have had to come up with game rules that permit play without their being hit by cars. The architect, then, designed a park using the simplest, clearest elements that invite its young users to develop the skill of anticipating danger and managing it; he did not seek to protect them through isolation.

Van Eyck's park at Van Boetzelaerstraat is his most ambitious.[15] Another found space at a corner in a densely built section of Amsterdam, here the architect put in his climbing stones and tubular equipment, but also tried to include buildings fronting one side and shops across the street in the design—a risky idea because traffic flows here could be intense. Moreover, teenagers took over the corner at night, hanging around and hoping something would happen, when adults sitting on benches hoped nothing would.

What's interesting about the park at Van Boetzelaerstraat is how its children, adolescents, and adults learned to use it together. The design provides subtle guidance; the benches are placed so that parents can supervise small children playing near the edge of the street. Once the park was finished, knots of adolescents colonized the sidewalk across the street; resting shoppers tended to watch but not interfere with children cavorting on the edge of traffic; active shoppers cut across the space to pass from store to store, violating the turf of those dwelling in the playground. In this public realm, people physically mingled rather than verbally interacted. Yet the public realm was not neutral or indifferent; it drew young and old in the neighborhood.

Here, then, were projects that realized concretely the goal of making a live edge, a porous membrane. Van Eyck found simple, clear ways to make the users of his parks, young and old, more skilled in anticipating and managing ambiguity at the edge. Of course, there is a paradox. Van Eyck thought through clearly how best visually to achieve this; his visual logic is hardly "fuzzy" in the ordinary sense of that word. And the children who learned how to deal well with the ambiguity built into his park designs emerged with rules of behavior for themselves. These parks make a point about security opposed to the health-and-safety regulation of most park design today, which cocoons and isolates children.

The practitioner's skill in these designs can be likened to the "uncle logic" that lay in Elizabeth David's recipe, a conclusion left intentionally unstated, or, more concretely, to the use in writing of the ellipsis (. . .). As in writing, the designer uses such a device best by following the modernist principle that less is more. That is, effectively using an ambiguity forces its maker to think about economy. Ambiguity and economy seem unlikely bedfellows, but they take their place in the larger family of craft practices if we think of creating ambiguity as a special instance of applying minimum force. Van Eyck was thus quite selective about where he placed blurred edges in his playgrounds; usually the relation of playground space to the doorways of buildings is by contrast sharp, highly defined. So too would I have misled if conveying that David's recipes have no sharp edges. They are filled with do's and don'ts about bird flesh; the gaps that occur in the scene narrative stand out against these commands. In writing, the strategic economy of the ellipsis should be located precisely where the reader wants the release from tension that an explicit conclusion might provide but where the writer wants to hold the reader . . . to keep the reader going.

Van Eyck's great antagonist was Le Corbusier—Le Corbusier as urbanist rather than as the architect of individual buildings. Le Corbusier was the enemy of street life; he thought it was at best clutter, at worst irrational confusion on the ground plane. His Plan Voisin for Paris, conceived in the 1920s for the Marais district, sweeps its streets empty of human beings, leaving the arteries and veins as a purified space of traffic flows. Van Eyck expressed the contrast between Le Corbusier and himself as that between making space and making place—in a memorable essay called "Whatever Space and Time Mean, Place and Occasion Mean More."[16] Whereas Corbusier relegated streets to traffic functions, the ground plane represented to Van Eyck the realm in which people "learn" cities. The placement of benches and bollards, the height of stepping-stones, the ill-defined separations of sand, grass, and water are all tools in that learning, an education in ambiguity.

Improvising
Steps

The tenements of New York's Lower East Side furnish an example of how people can become skilled in ambiguity without benefit of instructive designs like Aldo van Eyck's. Here people have improvised. The buildings in this poor part of New York took on a uniform look in three generations of tenement acts, from 1867 to 1879 to 1901, the building codes designed to provide light and fresh air to new, dense housing for the poor. Immigrant dwellers ignored the laws' promptings. The raised front stoops of the tenements, usually made of brownstone, were designed to be functional passages in and out of the buildings. Tenement dwellers early on began to use the stair treads as seats; the side walls to the stairs became armatures on which goods for sale were displayed and clothes were dried. Rather than a passage, the stoop became an inhabited public space, people hanging around, gossiping and selling, a street life that relieved the crowding within the tenement interiors.

The architect Bernard Rudofsky was inspired by the example of these steps. In *Architecture without Architects* he documented the ways in which most cities were mostly built by improvisation, following no consistent formal design. Building was added to building, street to street, their forms adapting to different site conditions in the process of extension: this is how central cities like Cairo, or the vast peripheries of Mexico City, have developed.

Improvisation is a user's craft. It draws on the metamorphoses of type-form over time. In the microenvironment of the New York tenement stoop, from block to block on the Lower East Side, changes occurred in what goods were displayed and how they were displayed on clotheslines. The ethnic shadings of different neighborhoods also worked changes in type-form. One can still see this today; the chairs in Asian neighborhoods tend to face the street in parallel, whereas the chairs in old Italian neighborhoods are placed at right angles to the street so that people can see their neighbors on other stoops.

The making of these territories would be misunderstood if called spontaneous, if "spontaneous" represents a mindless occurrence. On the steps of the tenements, the improvisers observe and experiment with stoops in relation to their own bodies. Like a jazz musician, tenement dweller who improvises follows rules. The physical materials at hand in the street are givens, like the written melody and fundamental harmonies spelled out for each number in a jazz musician's "cheat book" (cheating because many of these songs are lifted illegally out of copyright). Good jazz improvisation follows rules of economy; variations pick out an element to explore, otherwise they lose focus; the harmonic reversals are disciplined by what came before. Above all, the jazz musician has to select elements for his or her own instrument than someone playing a different instrument can respond to. A successful improvisation will avoid sounding like the equivalent of a visual maze.

So too for people who improvise street use. In the surviving street cultures of the Lower East Side, booksellers clump together but display wares that separate themselves from their neighbors, like a musical theme and variations; hawkers using the steps choreograph themselves so that browsers can move from stoop to stoop; tenants hang out laundry from house to house so that key windows are not blocked. To the casual visitor it may look a mess, but in fact the street dweller has improvised a coherent, economical form. Rudofsky thought that this hidden order is how most settlements of poor people develop and that the work of improvising street order attaches people to their communities, whereas "renewal" projects, which may provide a cleaner street, pretty houses, and large shops, give the inhabitants no way to mark their presence on the space.

Improvisation occurs in workshops, offices, and laboratories as much as on streets. As in jazz, other forms of improvisation involve skills that can be developed and improved. Anticipation can be strengthened; people can become better at negotiating borders and edges; they can become more selective about the elements they choose to vary. In the next chapter we shall explore just how organizations could become like good streets, but at this point we might want to summarize the path we have so far traveled.

A Summary of Part Two

The thread through all the twists and turns of subject in Part Two is *progress* in the development of skill—a word that needs no apology. In craftwork, people can and do improve. The twists and turns in Part Two have occurred because progress is not linear. Skill builds by moving irregularly, and sometimes by taking detours.

Development of an intelligent hand does show something like a linear progression. The hand needs to be sensitized at the fingertip, enabling it to reason about touch. Once this is achieved, problems of coordination can be addressed. Integration of hand, wrist, and forearm then teaches lessons of minimum force. Once these are learned, the hand can work with the eye to look ahead physically, to anticipate and so to sustain concentration. Each stage, though challenging, grounds moving on to the next; but each is also an independent challenge.

Taking guidance from expressive directions aids this process in ways that more denotative directions would not. Expressive directions provide guidance about the sense of a practice whole. I've described, among many possibilities, three expressive tools that can provide this guidance: sympathetic illustration, which identifies with the difficulties a neophyte encounters; scene narrative, which places the learner in a strange situation; and instruction through metaphor, which encourages the apprentice to reframe imaginatively what he or she is doing.

The necessity of imagination appears in the use of tools. If these tools prove limited or difficult to use, still inventiveness enables a certain kind of repair work, one that I've called a dynamic repair. And imagination is required to make sense of potent tools, or all-purpose tools, full of untapped and perhaps dangerous possibilities. I have tried to take some of the mystery out of the imaginative use of tools by explaining the structure of an intuitive leap.

No one draws on all these resources all the time, and in labor as in love, progress occurs in fits and starts. But people can and do get better. We might wish to simplify and rationalize skills, as teaching manuals often do, but this is not possible because we are complex organisms. The more a person draws on these techniques, the more he or she plumbs them, the more will that person gain the craftsman's emotional reward, the sentiment of competence.

PART THREE   Craftsmanship

Quality-Driven Work

I n this and the next chapter, I address two large issues that consummate craftsmanship. The first is the craftsman's desire to do good work; the second lies in the abilities required to do good work. As appeared at the beginning of Part One, some groups, like the Linux programmers, are quality-driven, while others, like the Soviet construction workers, are not. We want to look more closely at the human factors that stimulate this ambition.

Our Enlightenment ancestors believed that Nature furnished humanity at large with the intelligence to do good work; they saw the human being as a capable animal; demands for greater equality depended on this conviction. Modern society tends to emphasize differences in ability; the "skills economy" constantly seeks to separate smart from stupid people. Our Enlightenment forebears had it right, at least as concerns craftsmanship. We share in common and in roughly equal measure the raw abilities that allow us to become good craftsmen; it is the motivation and aspiration for quality that takes people along different paths in their lives. Social conditions shape these motivations.

When W. Edwards Deming first put forward in the 1960s his views on "total quality control" for organizations, the pursuit of quality seemed a frill to many profit-driven corporation executives. Deming put forward such nostrums as "The most important things cannot be measured" and "You can expect what you inspect"; the Deming-Shewhart cycle for quality control is a four-step process that investigates and discusses before setting to work.[1] Hardheaded managers preferred the practical experiments on worker motivation by Elton Mayo and his colleagues at the Western Electric Company in the 1920s. What most stimulated workers to achieve higher productivity, Mayo found, was simply being noticed as human beings. But Mayo did not focus on the quality of the objects these workers produced or on their critical faculties. Mayo's business clients were more interested in obedience than quality; happy workers keep at their tasks and do not go on strike.[2]

The successes of the Japanese economy after the Second World War, and of the *Wirtschaftswunder* in Germany in the same years, changed the discussion. By the mid-1970s these two economies had carved out a market niche with high-quality products, some inexpensive but good, such as Japanese automobiles, others both expensive and good, such as German machine tools. As these market niches expanded, and the quality standards of American and British firms sank, alarm bells began to ring, and Deming was "rediscovered" as a prophet in the late 1980s. Today both managers and business schools sing the praises of the "search for excellence," in the words of the business gurus Tom Peters and Robert Waterman.[3]

Much of this rhetoric is mere hype, but Deming's story is complex and cautionary. The complexity is that to arouse the aspiration for quality and make good on it, the organization itself has to be well crafted in form. It needs, like Nokia, open information networks; it has to be willing to wait, as Apple is, to bring its products to market until they are really good. Deming knew that these aspects of organization seldom appear on management charts of who reports to whom. Deming was not, however, a simple salesman, a booster of quality; he recognized that quality-driven work, focused on achieving good concrete results, does not necessarily unify or sustain organizations.

As we saw in Britain's National Health Service, higher standards can be pursued in ways that create a great deal of internal conflict. This is because people may harbor different versions of higher standards; in the NHS, correct form versus practices that can bed in. Who demands quality can also divisive. Insistence from the top of the NHS on correct procedure indeed improved treatment of cancer and heart disease, while the same command from the top drove down quality in treating less grave chronic medical conditions. The pursuit of excellence can create problems for the longevity of organizations, as in Stradivari's workshop. Here the experience of doing high-quality work was contained in the master's own tacit knowledge, which meant his excellence could not be passed on to the next generation.

Most of all quality becomes an issue, rather than an advertisement, in a way signaled by the second word in the phrase "quality-driven." *Driven* means the obsessional energy invested in making a concrete object or forming a skill. Obsessional energy marks the characters of great workmen like Christopher Wren but is also and more elementally a trait of actions small as well as large. Rewriting a sentence again and again to get its imagery or rhythm just right requires a certain obsessional energy. In love, obsession risks deforming the character; in action, obsession risks fixation and rigidity. These dangers the individual craftsman also has to address, as so does the well-crafted organization. The pursuit of quality entails learning how to use obsessional energy well.

"Quality-driven" work came home to me in all its obsessional energy in a sushi bar in New York, a small place in Greenwich Village that caters to Japanese working abroad. In part the bar caters by printing its menu only in Japanese, thus repelling American diners, and in part by connecting via satellite to television in Tokyo, the television on always but only as loud as a living person's voice. As well as viewing, people talk back to the tube. I usually come here with the Japanese friend who keeps my cello in order.

One night we watched *Project X,* a television series about product engineers in the mother country. This week's episode described the invention of the handheld calculator, and the story was indeed riveting to the regulars; *Project X* enthralled my bar mates just at the moment when an engineer pressed the "on" button of his new handheld calculator and suddenly exclaimed, "It works!" But almost instantly, running commentary in the bar contrasted those postwar glory days to a spate of recent well-publicized product failures in which Japanese-made batteries and photocopiers have shown a risk of catching fire. Quite a lot of comment evidently, as people gestured at the images of handheld calculators, applauded their on-screen fabricators, in order to discuss the nation's current, fallen state, occasionally out of politeness furnishing me the synopsis consisting of "bad . . ." "shameful . . ." while I toyed with a mysterious bit of fish.

This is the crux of obsession: good and not-good-enough had become inseparable. In the bar, once we switched into near-English, I pointed out that only the occasional battery exploded or photocopier caught on fire, but my companions were not having it. Something in them was offended by the very idea of sort-of-safe. Obsession applies to the quality of every single one of the handheld calculators and computer batteries in their millions. Obsession expresses a passion for the generic, which is why Deming spoke of *total* quality control. The cognomen of obsession, relentlessness, has that same character—attending to all cases, letting no exceptions slip by through carelessness or indifference. The coupling of good and not-good-enough results works as a relentless monitor.

Why would someone be gripped by such an obsession? The artisans in the sushi bar were mostly people who had fallen by the wayside in Japan's viciously competitive educational system and, at some point in their youth or young adulthood, had opted to leave a tough, unforgiving culture; via varied personal routes, that fork in the road had eventually led them to this quiet corner of New York. Over the years I have come to learn that a fair number of these craftsmen are at best semilegal migrants (lacking green cards but often possessing fake social security cards that enable them to find employment for those who don't check too carefully); if pride in the quality of their work keeps them connected to "Japanese values," they use that pride as an icon to set themselves apart from other ethnic and racial minorities in the city. The people in the sushi bar are racists of a special sort; to the laziness they believe is rife among American blacks and Hispanics they contrast their own striving for quality.

They thus evince a second hallmark of obsession: the relentless pursuit of excellence as a badge of distinction. The sociologist Pierre Bourdieu has argued that the rhetoric of quality serves people within organizations, as in ethnic groups, as a tool for claiming status: I/we are more motivated, driven harder, more aspirational than the others.[4] The badge of distinction can lead toward increasing social isolation and disconnection as well as to claims of superiority. These immigrant Japanese are not like medieval goldsmiths. Rather than integrating them into a larger society, their passion for good-quality work has become part of an internalized history, an icon of their foreignness. As we shall see, other quality-driven workers can behave more largely as isolates in an organization.

Obsessing about quality is a way of subjecting the work itself to relentless generic pressure; workers given over to this passion can dominate or detach themselves from others less driven. Both are dangers; let's explore the latter first.

Expertise
The Sociable and the Antisocial Expert

The danger to others posed by people driven by excellence crystal-lizes in the figure of the expert. He or she appears in two guises, socia-ble or antisocial. A well-crafted institution will favor the sociable ex-pert; the isolated expert sends a warning signal that the organization is in trouble.

The expert's provenance and prestige is ancient, beginning with the civic honor of the demioergoi. The expert has since the Middle Ages figured as a master craftsman who is perforce a sociable expert. The civic and religious rituals that organized the guilds forged a social bond in which it was the master's duty to participate; the internal orga-nization of each workshop, based on face-to-face authority and exer-cised within a small community, further cemented sociability. Closer to modern times, the amateur gradually lost ground, especially with the dawn of the Industrial Age—the amateur's foraging curiosity seeming of lesser value than specialized knowledge. Yet the modern expert has few strong rituals to bind him or her to the larger community or indeed to colleagues.

So argues the sociologist Elliott Krause in *The Death of the Guilds*. His studies of engineers, lawyers, physicians, and academics show how the power of professional associations weakened in the last century under the pressures of an impersonal market and bureaucratic state even as the professions themselves became stricter, more expert dis-ciplines. National or international professional organizations are of course far larger than were the urban guilds of the past, but their meetings have had, Krause believes, some of the same bonding, ritual character. The first modern usage of the term *professional* referred to people who saw themselves as something other than just employees. On balance, government and legal regulation has done more to con-strict the professions than did the market; the law bureaucratized the very content what professionals know. What went missing was community—a point also and first made by Robert Perrucci and Joel Gerstl in their pioneering study *Profession without Community.*[5]

The scholarly study of expertise has gone through three phases. [6] At first, "the expert" was studied as a person who had developed analytic powers that could be applied to any field; a consultant roaming from corporate turf to turf figures as such an expert. Analysts of expertise then "discovered" that content mattered; the expert had to know a great deal about something in particular (the ten-thousand-hour rule derived from this discovery). Today, both concerns combine with the social explorations made by Perrucci, Gerstl, and Krause to frame a problem: How can an expert act sociably if he or she lacks a strong professional community, a strong guild? Can good work itself turn the expert outward?

Vimla Patel and Guy Groen have explored the sociable expert by comparing the clinical skills of brilliant but novice medical students to doctors with several years of experience behind them.[7] The experienced doctor, as one would expect, is a more accurate diagnostician. This is due in large part to the fact that he or she tends to be more open to oddity and particularity in patients, whereas the medical student is more likely to be a formalist, working by the book, rather rigidly applying general rules to particular cases. Moreover, the experienced doctor thinks in larger units of time, not just backward to cases in the past but, more interestingly, forward, trying to see into the patient's indeterminate future. The novice, lacking a storehouse of clinical histories, has trouble imagining what might be an individual patient's fate. The experienced doctor focuses on a patient's becoming; raw talent thinks strictly in terms of immediate cause and effect. The craftsman's capacity of prehension, discussed in our chapter on the hand, is thus elaborated in long-term medical practice. Treating others as whole persons in time is one mark of sociable expertise.

Craft experience of imperfect tools has also found its way into the understanding of sociable expertise. These tools obliged their users, as we have seen among seventeenth-century scientists, to be minded to fixing as well as making; repair is a fundamental category of craftsmanship; today again, an expert is seen as someone who can equally make and repair. We may recall the sociologist Douglas Harper's words: an expert is someone "with knowledge that allows them to see beyond the elements of a technique to its overall purpose and coherence. . . . It is the knowledge in which making and fixing are parts of a continuum."[8] In Harper's study of small machine shops, the sociable experts tend to be good at explaining and giving advice to their customers. The sociable expert, that is, is comfortable with mentoring, the modern echo of medieval in loco parentis.

Finally, the sociable side of expertise addresses the issue of knowledge transfer posed in Stradivari's workshop. He could not pass on his experience, which had been become his own tacit knowledge. Too many modern experts imagine themselves in the Stradivari trap—indeed, we could call Stradivari Syndrome the conviction that one's expertise is ineffable. This syndrome appears among British doctors who have failed to discuss treatment options, to expose themselves to criticism, to unpack their tacit understandings with colleagues. As a result, their skills degrade over time in comparison with doctors who turn outward professionally.[9] Local family doctors—those reassuring figures in medical romance—seem particularly to suffer from Stradivari Syndrome.

The GoodWork Project at Harvard University, led by Howard Gardner, has investigated various ways to surmount the problem of hoarding expertise. Researchers in the GoodWork Project have studied, for instance, a famous breakdown in standards at the New York Times at a moment when a few reporters became spectacularly corrupt.[10] In the GoodWork Project's view, the fault lay with the institution. "We are the New York Times," ineffable, the Stradivari of news organizations. As a result, the paper didn't communicate its standards explicitly; this silence opened a gap for unscrupulous reporters to colonize the organization. To Gardner, transparency can counter this danger, but transparency of a certain sort: the standards of good work must be clear to people who are not themselves experts. For Gardner and his colleagues, the effort to devise such a language jolts experts into working better as well as more honestly. Matthew Gill makes a similar analysis of accounting practices in London: the standard that makes sense to nonexperts—rather than self-referential rules and regulations—is what keeps accountants honest. Turning outward, they hold themselves to account and can also see what the work means to others.[11] Standards comprehensible to nonexperts raise quality in the organization as a whole.

Sociable expertise doesn't create community in any self-conscious or ideological sense; it consists simply of good practices. The well-crafted organization will focus on whole human beings in time, it will encourage mentoring, and it will demand standards framed in language that any person in the organization might understand.

Antisocial expertise has a more complicated side. There is an inherent inequality of knowledge and skill between expert and nonexpert. Antisocial expertise emphasizes the sheer fact of invidious comparison. One obvious consequence of emphasizing inequality is the humiliation and resentment this expert can arouse in others; a more subtle consequence is to make the expert himself or herself feel embattled.

The baking industry in Boston has shown both aspects of invidious comparison. In the 1970s Boston bakeries operated in ways a medieval goldsmith could make sense of; the craft of baking was directed face-to-face by masters who passed on their skills to apprentices. By the year 2000, automation had taken the place of master bakers on site. When the programmers and managers of the machines did appear in the workshops, relations between the experts and "the boys" were tense. The experts spoke about the machines and gave directions that emphasized their knowledge; the boys reacted sullenly. Though they had to obey the masters, they mocked the experts in private. The people who programmed the complicated baking machinery picked up these not-so-subtle signals and, rather than confront the problem, withdrew into themselves. Site visits lessened; rule by e-mail ensued. If the workers felt sullen, the people ruling them also felt, curiously, less connected. They had little loyalty to their bakeries in comparison to the master bakers of the earlier time. The organizations were afflicted by "revolving-door" changes of technical personnel at the top.[12]

Invidious comparison drives competition, and of course a well-run organization like Nokia wants to combine competition and cooperation, but this happy, productive state requires friendly competitors. To become friendly, the competitors have to focus less on better and worse, for in labor these standards carry implications of control. The contempt that bosses so often harbor for their employees arises exactly from dwelling on that distinction, and the wrinkle is that such contempt can also alienate the boss from feeling good about the organization itself, stuffed as it appears to him or her with drones and incompetents.

In the relations among experts themselves, invidious comparison can blind experts to the very meaning of quality. In the scientific realm, this large truth has a particular and painful application. "Racing the clock"—that is, publishing results first—rules scientific laboratories in ways that may trivialize the work itself.

An egregious instance is the controversy about who first discovered HIV, human immunodeficiency virus, as the retrovirus that can prompt AIDS. The discovery occurred separately in the 1980s in two laboratories, one directed by Luc Montagnier at the Pasteur Institute in France, the other directed by Robert Gallo in the United States. A bitter quarrel broke out between these two labs (resolved ultimately by an agreement between French president François Mitterand and American president Ronald Reagan).

The debate focused on who got there first. Montagnier's laboratory published its findings in 1983, Gallo's in 1984, but the Gallo group claimed precedence of a sort based on prior work on retroviruses in 1974. Montagnier's group claimed that Gallo used improperly a sample of HIV first produced by the Pasteur Institute. Gallo claimed that his lab was the first to grow the virus in an "immortalized" cell line, making possible the blood tests for HIV; further, he claimed that he had first developed the techniques for growing T cells in a laboratory. The two labs also squabbled about how the discovery should be named: Montagnier used the acronym LAV, Gallo HTLV-III—the two presidents confirmed the one name HIV. A tiresome dispute vital to the careers of scientists: with an eye to future patents the scientists argued in effect about who "owned" the virus.

Running beneath these questions of dates and names was a bitter quarrel about which lab had done the better work, and here we should be puzzled. There's no reason why people who do the same verifiable work more slowly should be judged inferior just because they are slower. There's no logic to likening the lab that gets there first to a prize thoroughbred, as a better-quality lab; the obsession about who got there first is irrelevant to the discovery itself. Invidious comparison of speed has distorted the measure of quality. Yet the passion to race drives science; those in the grip of this competitive obsession easily lose sight of the value and purpose of what they are doing. They are not thinking in craftsman-time, the slow time that enables reflection.

In sum, there are sociable ways and antisocial ways of being an expert. Sociable expertise addresses other people in their unfolding prospects just as the artisan explores material change; one's skill of repair is exercised as a mentor; one's guiding standards are transparent, that is, comprehensible to nonexperts. Antisocial expertise shames others, embattles or isolates the expert. Invidious comparison can result in losing of the content of quality. Of course inequality is built into all expertise, in carpentry and in cooking as much as in science. The question is what to make of that difference. Whereas invidious comparison has a strongly personal character, the sociable expert is less obsessed with vindicating himself or herself.

To further understand this difference, we need to know more about the phenomenon of obsession itself. Is it inherently destructive, or are there good forms of obsession?

The Janus Face of Obsession
A Story of Two Houses

The negative side of obsession is, in the current state of knowledge, better understood. In academic psychology, "perfectionism" names one of these negatives; it refers to people who compete against themselves. Nothing ever feels good enough to the person measuring who he or she is against who he or she should be. Miriam Adderholdt links perfectionism to anorexic behavior in young girls who believe they are never thin enough; Thomas Hurka sees the inability to release oneself from feelings of inadequacy as a psychosomatic cause of high blood pressure and ulcers.[13] Clinically, perfectionism is classed as an obsessive-compulsive disorder—that is, people will respond in exactly the same ways again and again to their persistent feelings of inferiority. Perfectionism is a behavior trap.

One school of psychoanalysis has explored the dynamics of perfectionism a step further. To the psychoanalyst Otto Kernberg, driving oneself serves as a shield against exposure to the judgments of others: "I will be my own worst critic rather than let you do the judging."[14] Standing behind that defense, analysts of Kernberg's school argue, is the conviction "Nothing is good enough for me." Life is a stage spectacle and oneself is the critic; nothing ever quite measures up; it is as though one becomes one's own isolated expert. The label psychoanalysis contrives for such a phenomenon is narcissism, and in Kernberg's view it is a borderline personality disorder.[15] Perfectionist standards of quality lie on this borderline.

Sociology has also sought to make sense of perfectionism. Max Weber believed it socially and historically bred. He presents this inner drive, in *The Protestant Ethic and the Spirit of Capitalism*, under another name, as a work ethic he labels "worldly asceticism." According to Weber, it arose when Protestant Christianity combined with capitalism in the following way: "[The religious believer,] at first fleeing from the world into solitude, had already ruled the world which it had renounced from the monastery and through the Church. But it had, on the whole, left the naturally spontaneous character of daily life in the world untouched. Now it strode into the marketplace of life, slammed the door of the monastery behind it, and undertook to penetrate just that daily routine of life with its methodicalness, to fashion it into a life in the world, but neither of nor for this world."[16] This drive to achieve is differs from Catholic self-discipline in that it has an audience of one; in the monastery of the self, you are the only, and the most severe, critic. Translated into ordinary experience, Weber's account seeks to explain what a person might not ever be satisfied with what he or she has, why each achievement may feel empty the moment it is attained. Self-justification, under the flag of the Protestant ethic, admits no satisfaction.

Weber's historical account of "worldly asceticism" now seems to most scholars deeply flawed. In the seventeenth century, for instance, many devout Catholics behaved as driven men in the marketplace, while many devout Protestants did not. The strength of Weber's account lies more in his view of the competitive urge carried to an extreme: proving oneself to oneself is a sure recipe for unhappiness. Oddly, the sociologist—a stern puritan—is more forgiving than the psychoanalyst about perfectionism. Whereas the sincerity of self-doubt is called into question by Kernberg's writings on inverted narcissism, Weber did not question the genuine anguish of the driven man.

These, then, are the negatives of a certain form of obsession. The obsessions of the craftsman do not quite fit, however, into either the psychoanalytic or the Weberian frame. In part this is simply because the routines by which craft proceeds take people out of themselves. Perfectionism entails a high degree of inner turmoil; craft routines relieve stress by providing a steady rhythm for work. This is what the philosopher Adriano Tilgher sought to convey in his invocation of the "calm industry" of the craftsman he saw in the pages of the *Encyclopedia*. The craftsman's focus on concrete objects or procedures runs contrary, moreover, to the narcissist's complaint, "If only I could." Glassblower Erin O'Connor is frustrated but determined. If obsession is a problem for the craftsman, it resides in how the work itself is done. Weber's driven man does appear in the work process, often competing against himself and sometimes suffering from perfectionism, but not in the ways Weber imagined and not always, because craftsmanship also brings out a positive form of obsession. The making of two houses in Vienna in the late 1920s reveals this Janus face of obsession.

✳ ✳ ✳

From 1927 to 1929, the philosopher Ludwig Wittgenstein worked on the design and construction of a house for his sister in the Kundmanngasse, a street in Vienna that at the time had many open parcels of land. Though sometimes Wittgenstein would speak with pride about the house in the Kundmanngasse, he eventually became his own severest critic. In a note of 1940 to himself he wrote that the building "lacks health"; he reflected in this somber mood that although his architecture had "good manners," it lacked "primordial life."[17] He made a trenchant diagnosis of the house's disease: it was his own conviction when he began that "I am not interested in erecting a building, but in . . . presenting to myself the foundations of all possible buildings."[18]

No more grandiose project can be imagined. The young philosopher set himself out to understand the nature of all architecture and to build something exemplary, perfect, the first time out of the box—this would be the only structure Wittgenstein ever built apart from a hut in Norway. It was framed in terms of getting something generically right: "the foundations of all possible buildings." The house in the Kundmanngasse came at the end of a period in Wittgenstein's life when he had sought the philosophical equivalent of "the foundations of all possible buildings;" from about 1910 to 1924 he had driven himself relentlessly to do so. In looking back so critically on his architecture he was, I believe, also reckoning the cost of this larger effort to himself. But the building is what matters here: in his own judgment, Wittgenstein's striving for an ideal perfection rendered the object lifeless. Relentlessness deformed it.

A good way to evaluate this project and the philosopher's later diagnosis of its ills to compare Wittgenstein's house to another constructed in Vienna at the same time, designed by the professional architect Adolf Loos. Wittgenstein's taste in architecture was formed by Loos, and Loos's Villa Moller consummated a long professional career. Born in 1870 in Brunn, Czechoslovakia, Loos briefly trained in a technical college, furthering his studies in America while working as a mason. His own architectural practice began in 1897. Known at first more for his writings and paper projects, he nonetheless kept a strong interest in the material processes of building construction. That connection made possible for him a more positive experience of obsession, one in which the relentless desire to get things right became a dialogue with circumstances beyond his control and the labor of others.

Wittgenstein first met Loos on July 27, 1914, at the Café Imperial in Vienna, drawn to his written prescriptions rather than to his extant buildings. Loos envisioned architecture as a *Neue Sachlichkeit*, a "new objectivity," by which he partly meant structures that showed plainly their purposes and their construction in their forms. The ethos of "honest brick" that we traced in the chapter on material consciousness reappears in Neue Sachlichkeit, materials and form all of a piece, but Loos stripped away the anthropomorphic associations of the eighteenth-century discussion of materials. He equally hated the houses of his parents' era, dripping tassels and cut-glass chandeliers, floors thickened by overlapping Oriental carpets, knickknacks on shelves, and tables clotting interior volumes further obstructed by fake antique columns.

In 1908 Loos railed against all this in his pamphlet *Ornament and Crime*. In place of decorative crime Loos sought to incorporate into architecture the practical beauty he had discovered on his travels in America, in utilitarian objects meant for everyday use: suitcases, printing presses, telephones. He particularly admired the purity of the Brooklyn Bridge and the skeletons of New York railway stations. Foreshadowed by the *Encyclopedia,* against the doctrines of John Ruskin, like his contemporaries in the Bauhaus in Germany, Loos embraced a revolutionary aesthetics spawned by industrialism. Machines that made craft and art one revealed the essential beauty of all built form.

"Purity" and "simplicity" would have a special resonance for a young man of Wittgenstein's background—circumstances we need to account not only in understanding his taste but in accounting the problems he would face "in presenting to myself the foundations of all possible buildings." His father, Karl, had become one of the richest industrialists in Europe. The elder Wittgenstein was much more than a crass capitalist. The musicians Gustav Mahler, Bruno Walter, and Pablo Casals found him at home; they would have seen on its walls paintings by Gustav Klimt and other new artists; the architect Josef Hofmann had worked on one of Karl Wittgensteins's country estates.

But Wittgenstein, like other rich Jews of the prewar era, had to take great care in the display of wealth, since Vienna in the 1890s boiled with anti-Semitism aimed particularly at Jews who had risen to the top. The enormous Palais Wittgenstein in the Alleegasse struck a balance between display and discretion in its division of intimate and formal spaces. Although the bathroom faucets were gold-plated and the boudoirs and little sitting rooms were filled with onyx and jasper, the great salon aimed at relative restraint. Karl Wittgenstein could buy any painting he wanted, and bought the best; he hung only a few choice pieces in this, his most public room. This, then, was the resonance that the slogan "ornament is crime" had for rich Viennese Jews: ornament had to declare wealth quietly, as in those rooms where someone would go to take a pee.

When Wittgenstein met Loos in the Café Imperial, though he had no need to work he had already trained as a mechanical engineer in Berlin and then as an aeronautical engineer at the University of Manchester. Little is known about what the young philosopher said to Loos at the café, but the meeting started a friendship. Wittgenstein's wealth inverted the classic relation between master and apprentice. From this meeting on, the younger man began secretly to give money to the elder.

The fortune of the Wittgenstein family matters in understanding the negative form obsession took in his architectural work. Though Wittgenstein would eventually give away his fortune, he used family wealth without hesitation whenever he needed it in the creation of his sister's house in the Kundmanngasse. Lack of restraint appeared in the notorious story told by his niece Hermine Wittgenstein in her *Family Recollections:* "He had the ceiling of a large room raised by three centimeters, just when it was almost time to start cleaning the completed house."[19] Such a seemingly minute adjustment to a ceiling in fact involves a massive amount of structural rebuilding, possible only for a client willing to spare no expense. Hermine explains the many changes of this sort as due to "Ludwig's relentlessness when it came to getting proportions exactly right."[20] Economic constraint and resistance were not to be his teachers, and this untrammeled freedom contributed to the perfectionism that had "sickened" his house.

In Loos's buildings, lack of money often combined with the aesthetics of simplicity, as in the house he built for himself in Vienna from 1909 to 1911. His imagination was not entirely puritanical; in the Chicago Tribune Tower competition of 1922 he added polished granite columns for a rich client. When he could afford it, Loos bought African statues or Venetian glass and displayed them in his houses. The economy and simplicity that both theory inclined him toward and money imposed upon him did not mean that the Neue Sachlichkeit was an exercise in sensual denial; obsession with form would not dull his feel for materials.

Loos's need to respond positively to the difficulties he encountered appeared in the errors that occurred during the construction of the Villa Moller. When the foundations were not laid as specified, he could not afford to dig them up and start again; instead, Loos thickened the form of one side wall to accommodate the mistake, making the thickened wall an emphatic side frame for the front. The formally pure properties of the Villa Moller were achieved by working with many similar mistakes and impediments Loos had to take as facts on the ground; necessity stimulated his sense of form. Wittgenstein, knowing no financial necessity, had no such creative dialogue between form and error.

Getting things in perfect shape can mean removing the traces, erasing the evidence, of a work in progress. Once this evidence is eliminated, the object appears pristine. Perfection of this cleaned-up sort is a static condition; the object does not hint at the narrative of its making. Following on this basic difference, comparison between the two houses shows the consequences in facade proportion, room volume, and material detail.

In form, the Wittgenstein house is a big shoebox with diverse small boxes attached to each side; the only slanting roof is on top of a box at the back. The surface all over is a smooth, gray lime-slime; there is absolutely no ornament. Its windows are cut, particularly on the front facade, severely. The ranks of three windows each on three floors are exactly spaced as though divided in three equal panels, their proportion 1:1. The Villa Moller is a different kind of box. By the time Loos built it he had left behind an earlier conviction that what's inside a building should show on its outside. On the exterior walls are windows cut in different sizes, dotted about to make a composition in themselves, akin to a Mondrian painting. In Wittgenstein's house, the windows rigidly obey a formal rule, whereas at the Villa Moller they are more playful. One reason for the difference is that Loos spent a lot of time at the site, sketching it in drawings that charted the varying play of light on the surface during the passage of the day, redrawing again and again. Wittgenstein did not sketch easily; his drawings are not playful.

Enter the two houses and the contrasts become more acute. In the vestibule of the Villa Moller the planes of columns, stairs, floors, and walls invite the visitor further into the interior. Loos's genius for lighting these surfaces does most of this work, the shifting light changing, as one proceeds, the appearance of the building's solid forms. The Wittgenstein home's vestibule and entry hallway issue no such invitation. The obsession with exact proportion makes the vestibule seem more like an isolation chamber. The reason lies in how calculation has been applied here: interior glass doors are cut in exact proportion to the proportions of the exterior windows, the floor slabs in exact proportion to the doors. Daylight comes into the hall only indirectly and is uniform; at night light comes from one naked light bulb. As one proceeds into the house, this difference between static and dynamic space grows larger.

Modern designers face a basic challenge in relating the volume of individual rooms to the flow between them. The enfilade of ancien-régime aristocratic architecture—that sequencing of rooms so that one yields gracefully on to another—depended more on the placement of doors than on their size. Modern architects, hoping to enable the free movement of people through space, have in domestic interiors enlarged doors erased walls. But the art of enfilade is more complicated than removing barriers between rooms: wall forms, shifts in floor levels, changes of light have to organize movement, so that you know where to go, how fast you can go, and what eventually will bring you to rest.

Loos masterfully calculated the size of rooms in terms of the rhythm of moving from one to another; Wittgenstein treated each room as a problem in dimension and proportion in itself. Loos's mastery is fully displayed in the living room with its split levels, mix of materials, and complications of light; these continue the invitation issued by the entry hall. The drawing room of the Wittgenstein house is a block of space. Wittgenstein tried to create flow by a crude means, designing a folding wall so that the drawing room opens up entirely on one side to an adjoining library, but the absence of a barrier did not establish a walking, directed rhythm between the two rooms. They are simply two adjacent boxes, each precisely calibrated in terms of itself. (It is the ceiling of this drawing room that Wittgenstein pulled down and then raised an inch.)

Finally, a contrast of material detail. In the Villa Moller ornament is sparing rather than missing. Jugs, flowerpots, and paintings are made integral to wall planes; their size is carefully selected so that they do not overwhelm the volumes of the rooms. In the early 1920s Loos began to break with his own convictions of industrial purity to expand this sensuous simplicity. By the time of the Villa Moller he had given free reign to material sensuality in the grain of woods.

Wittgenstein's materials are in one way—at least in my view—beautiful objects that make good on the claim of Neue Sachlichkeit. Wittgenstein let his flair for engineering flourish on objects like radiators and keys and in places like kitchens that professional architects of his time seldom bothered about. Thanks to his wealth, he could design and fabricate everything specially rather than use common stock components. A particularly beautiful handle opens the kitchen window. This handle is striking because it's one of the few pieces of hardware designed in terms of practical use rather than as a demonstration of form. But door handles in this house are again subject to Wittgenstein's obsession with perfect proportion; in its tall rooms, they are placed exactly halfway up to the ceiling and so are difficult to use. In the Villa Moller, Loos does not draw attention to hardware details at all; radiators and pipes tend to be hidden behind or encased within softer tactile surfaces of wood and stone.

❖ ❖ ❖

Here then is an architectural instance of how the Janus face of obsession comes into being. On one face, in Wittgenstein's house, obsession has been given full reign and has led to disappointment; on the other, an architect with the same aesthetic but more constraints, more willing to play and to engage in a dialogue between form and materials, produced a home in which he rightly took great pride. A healthy obsession, we could say, interrogates its own driving convictions. Of course, many architects find Wittgenstein's house a finer piece of work than he himself believed. These admirers of his building dismiss his later judgments as products of the neuroses with which this architect was so abundantly supplied. We'd do better, I think, to take Wittgenstein at his word, as an adult well able to see himself clearly.

The ills he saw in his house reflect, at the time of his self-critique, the destructive effect of perfectionism on philosophy and more largely on mental life as he now conceived it. His early *Tractatus* had aimed to establish the strictest tests for logical thinking; much of the late *Philosophical Investigations*,[21] written about the same time as his reflections on the Kundmanngasse, attempt to free philosophy from the rigidities of that mental building. For a philosopher now interested in the play of language, in color and other sensations, a philosopher now given to writing in paradoxes and parables rather than laying down rules, the pursuit of the ideal, generic form of all building could well seem full of "sickness" and "lacking life."

I've recounted the houses in detail because their Janus faces suggest guides to managing obsession well in more everyday labors.

- The good craftsman understands the importance of the sketch—
  that is, not knowing quite what you are about when you begin.
  Loos wanted the Villa Moller to be good of its kind when he
  began; his experience prepared him for the type-form, but he
  went no further until he got on site. The informal sketch is a
  working procedure for preventing premature closure.
  Wittgenstein's generic drive expressed itself as wanting to
  know what he was doing, what he was going to achieve, before
  work on the site began. In this form of obsession, blueprint
  thinking prevails.
- The good craftsman places positive value on contingency and
  constraint. Loos made use of both. In our chapter on material
  consciousness, we stressed the value of metamorphosis. Loos
  made metamorphosis occur in the objects by looking at
  problems on site as opportunities; Wittgenstein was neither
  minded nor understood the necessity to make use of
  difficulties. Obsession blinded him to possibility.
- The good craftsman needs to avoid pursuing a problem
  relentlessly to the point that it becomes perfectly self-
  contained; then, like the rooms in the Kundmanngasse, it
  loses its relational character. Obsessing about perfect
  proportion was the cause of this loss of relational character in
  Wittgenstein's vestibule. The positive alternative to this drive
  to resolve is allowing the object a measure of incompleteness,
  deciding to leave it unresolved.
- The good craftsman avoids perfectionism that can degrade into
  a self-conscious demonstration—at this point the maker is
  bent on showing more what he or she can do than what the
  object does. This is the problem with the handmade hardware
  like the door handles in the Kundmanngasse house: they
  demonstrate form. The good craftsman's remedy eschews
  self-consciously pointing out that something is important.
- The good craftsman learns when it is time to stop. Further work
  is likely to degrade. Wittgenstein's houses clarifies when
  specifically it is time to stop: just at the moment when one is
  tempted to erase all traces of the work's production in order to
  make it seem a pristine object.

Imagine that building an institution is like building a house. If so, you would want to build it in the manner of Loos rather than of Wittgenstein. Instead of generic perfection all at once you would want to make a particular structure that started as a sketch, capable of evolving. Inside this institution, you would want to solve the problem of enfilade as Loos did, inviting movement from one domain to the next. You would engage with difficulty, accident, and constraint. You would avoid resolving specific duties of people in the institution to the point where the duties, like rooms, became self-contained. You would know when it was time to stop institution building, leaving some issues unresolved, and you would leave intact traces of how the institution grew. You want an institution that is alive. You could not build this institution through the relentless pursuit of perfection; this pursuit, Wittgenstein knew, had rendered his house lifeless. Whereas building a school, a business, or a professional practice in the manner of Loos would make an institution of high social quality.

Vocation
A Sustaining Narrative

Perhaps the greatest difference between Loos and Wittgenstein was that Adolph Loos possessed a work story; each building project was like a chapter in his life. Wittgenstein lacked a narrative of that sort; when his all-or-nothing gamble disappointed, he never built another house. This difference points to a further positive dimension of obsession: how people are driven forward in their work to produce in plenty.

Max Weber called the sustaining narrative a "vocation." Weber's German word for a vocation, *Beruf,* contains two resonances: the gradual accumulation of knowledge and skills and the ever-stronger conviction that one was meant to do this one particular thing in one's life. These marks of vocation Weber advanced in his essay "Science as a

Vocation."[22] An English locution roughly conveys what he meant: your life "adds up." By contrast, "worldly asceticism" provides neither satisfaction in accumulating skill nor the conviction that there is one particular thing in life one is meant to do.

The ideal of vocation is rooted in religion. In early Christianity, a vocation was thought to come *to* the self, as when a priest feels called by God. As in Augustine's conversion, once the call has been answered, in retrospect the believer may believe he or she could do no other; service to God was want he or she was meant to do all along. Unlike Hinduism, Christian vocations cannot be inherited from a previous generation; the individual must respond to the call of his or her own free will. Today, adult "decisions for Christ" in evangelistic Christianity retain this dual character—decision and destiny combine.

Against his own idealization of the scientific vocation, Weber knew well that its religious foundations could be reflected in the secular world. A leader, whether Christ or Napoleon, provides followers with a sudden illumination of the path to be followed; the charismatic leader does the motivating, provides the ambition to others. The scientific vocation is meant instead to arise "from within," drawing on small, disciplined efforts—lab routine or, by extension, practicing music—each with no life-shattering implication. No one needs to be well educated to follow Christ or Napoleon, but in the scientific vocation, formation is all-important. A person's *Bildung*—his or her early training and social indoctrination—prepares the ground for self-motivated, sustained activity through adulthood.

"Relentless" and "obsessive" may seem out of place in this benign version of vocation. But it's rather that time can temper their bite. The sociologist Jeremy Seabrook conducted interviews a few years ago with Len Greenham, an elderly morocco-grainer living in the north of England. Greenham learned as a young man how to prepare the skins of Morocco goats so that the leather could be used in bookbinding and in handbags, a delicate and difficult set of operations to which Green-ham, like his father and grandfather, has given his whole life. The time rhythms of the work organized his family life, and indeed his daily habits. He didn't smoke "because it made a difference to your stamina," and he played sports to keep fit for the job.[23] His work may be driven and obsessive, but not in the same way as the squabbling HIV doctors; he steadily adds value to his life.

Greenham, though, is not at peace with the world. Though he knows he has lived well, in the interviews Greenham expresses much foreboding. Hand bookbinding is simply too expensive for his firm to continue in Britain; the craft now flourishes in India. "My grandfather would have thought it a sad tale that after all those years of this trade and skills, acquired from older people of many years' knowledge, it can't be passed on to anyone else."[24] But still he keeps working with a will; that's the craftsman in him.

In old English a "career" meant a well-laid road, whereas a "job" meant simply a lump of coal or pile of wood that could be moved around at will. The medieval goldsmith within a guild exemplified the roadway of "career" in work. His life path was well laid in time, the stages of his progress were clearly marked, even if the work itself was inexact. His was a linear story. As appeared in Chapter 1, the "skills society" is bulldozing the career path; jobs in the old sense of random movement now prevail; people are meant to deploy a portfolio of skills rather than nurture a single ability in the course of their working histories; this succession of projects or tasks erodes belief that one is meant to do just one thing well. Craftsmanship seems particularly vulnerable to this possibility, since craftsmanship is based on slow learning and on habit. His form of obsession—Len Greenham's—no longer seems to pay.

I'm not convinced that this is the craftsman's fated end. Schools and state institutions, even profit-seeking businesses, can take one concrete step to support vocations. This is to build up skills in sequence, especially through job retraining. Artisanal craftsmen have proved particularly promising subjects for such efforts. The discipline required for good manual labor serves them, as does their focus on concrete problems rather than on the flux of process-based, human relations work. For this very reason it has proved easier to train a plumber to become a computer programmer than to train a salesperson; the plumber has craft habit and material focus, which serve retraining. Employers often don't see this opportunity because they equate manual routine with mindless labor, the *Animal laborens* of Arendt's imagination. But we've seen throughout this book that just the opposite is the case. For good craftsmen, routines are not static; they evolve, the craftsmen improve.

Most people want to believe that their lives add up to more than a random series of disconnected events.[25] The well-crafted institution wants to respond to this desire, once it decides that loyalty matters. Workers who have been retrained by an institution are much more bonded to it than are in-and-out workers. Loyalty especially matters to a business when the business cycle turns down; workers will stay the course, work longer hours, even take pay cuts rather than desert. Strengthening skills is neither an individual nor a collective panacea. In the modern economy, dislocation is a permanent fact. But figuring out how to build on existing skills—to expand them or use them as a base for acquiring other skills—is a strategy that helps orient individuals in time. The well-crafted organization will want to pursue this strategy to keep itself together.

※   ※   ※

In sum, the drive to do good work turns out to be no simple drive. Moreover, this personal motivation is inseparable from social organization. Perhaps in each of us there is a Japanese engineer who wants to do things well consistently and to be distinguished for doing so, but this is only the beginning of the story. Institutions have to socialize that worker; he or she has to come to terms with blind competitiveness. The worker will have to learn how to manage obsession in the very process of working, interrogating and tempering it. The drive to do good work can give people a sense of a vocation; poorly made institutions will ignore their denizens' desire that life add up, while well-crafted organizations will profit from it.

CHAPTER TEN

Ability

I've kept for the end of this book its most controversial proposal: that nearly anyone can become a good craftsman. The proposal is controversial because modern society sorts people along a strict gradient of ability. The better you are at something, the fewer of you there are. This view has been applied not only to innate intelligence but to the subsequent development of abilities: the further you get, the fewer of you there are.

Craftsmanship doesn't fit into this framework. As will appear in this chapter, the rhythm of routine in craftsmanship draws on childhood experience of play, and almost all children can play well. The dialogue with materials in craftsmanship is unlikely to be charted by intelligence tests; again, most people are able to reason well about their physical sensations. Craftwork embodies a great paradox in that a highly refined, complicated activity emerges from simple mental acts like specifying facts and then questioning them.

No one could deny that people are born or become unequal. But inequality is not the most important fact about human beings. Our species' ability to make things reveals more what we share. A political consequence follows from the facts of these shared talents. The pages of Diderot's *Encyclopedia* affirmed the common ground of talents in craftwork, in large principle and in practical detail, because a view of government rested on it. Learning to work well enables people to govern themselves and so become good citizens. The industrious maid is more likely to prove a good citizen than her bored mistress. Thomas Jefferson's democratic celebration of the American farmer-yeoman or skilled artisan stands on the same ground, the practical man being able to judge how well government is built because he understands building—an adage Jefferson unfortunately did not apply to his slaves. The conviction that good work molds good citizenship became distorted and perverted in the course of modern history, ending in the hollow and depressing lies of the Soviet empire. Inequality established by invidious comparison came to the fore as a seemingly more reliable truth about work—but this "truth" undermines democratic participation.

We want to recover something of the spirit of the Enlightenment on terms appropriate for our time. We want the shared ability to work to teach us how to govern ourselves and to connect to other citizens on common ground.

Work and Play
The Thread of Craft

This common ground appears early in human development, in the crafting of play. Work and play appear as opposites if play itself seems just an escape from reality. On the contrary, play teaches children how to be sociable and channels cognitive development; play instills obedience to rules but counters this discipline by allowing children to create and experiment with the rules they obey. These capacities serve people lifelong once they go to work.

Play takes place in two domains. In competitive games, rules are set before the players begin to act; once conventions are established, players become their servants. Games establish the rhythms of repetition. In a more open space of play, as when a child fingers a piece of felt cloth, sensory stimulation dominates; the child plays around with the felt, experiments with it, the dialogue with material objects begins.

The first modern writer on play was Friedrich von Schiller, in *On the Aesthetic Education of Man.* Letter 14 declares, "The sense impulse sways us physically and the form impulse morally . . . both are combined in the play impulse."[1] Play negotiates between pleasure and rigor, in Schiller's view; its rules equilibrate human action. This view disappeared later in the nineteenth century among psychologists who viewed play more akin to dreaming, a spontaneous physical behavior that resembled the floating process of a dream. In the twentieth century, their approach in turn receded and Schiller reappeared, as it were, in the consulting room. Freud showed that dreaming itself follows a certain logic, a logic akin to game playing.[2]

A sharp line between play and work was drawn, a generation after Freud conceived the analogy of dreaming and gaming, in Johan Huizinga's study *Homo Ludens.*[3] This great book showed that in premodern Europe, adults enjoyed the same card games, make-believe charades, and indeed toys as their children. For Huizinga, the rigors of the Industrial Revolution caused adults to put away their toys; modern work is "desperately serious." He argued that, thereby, when utility rules, adults lose something essential in the capacity to think; they lose the free curiosity that occurs in the open, felt-fingering space of play. Still, Huizinga noted the "formal gravity," as he put it, of people in playing games, and he knew this formal gravity was somehow equally important.

Since his time anthropologists have sought to work out this formal gravity in terms of ceremonies. The most notable anthropologist to do so was Clifford Geertz, who coined the phrase "deep play" and applied it to ceremonies as diverse as a Middle Eastern merchant offering customers an obligatory cup of coffee, a cockfight in Indonesia, and a political festival in Bali.[4] Unlike Huizinga, Geertz stressed the ever-open telephone line connecting childhood training in games to adult roles as priests, sales representatives, urban planners, or politicians. Huizinga's regret-stained view of the past had perhaps blinded him, Geertz thought, to the fact that making up and acting out rules endures throughout the human life cycle.

In our studies, Aldo van Eyck's parks in Amsterdam show this open telephone line. The designer sought to distill bodily rituals among the children at play through making borders ambiguous; children are to learn how to choreograph their movements in order to keep safe. Ceremonies of contact and of spectatorship would, Van Eyck hoped, then take form: clumps of toddlers digging in sand, older children playing with balls, adolescents seething and confessing, adults resting from shopping and watching—these compose what Geertz calls the "scenography" of deep play and are everyday rituals that bind people together socially.

But how does the craft of play actually connect play and work? This was a pressing question for Erik Erikson, probably the most eloquent twentieth-century writer on play, a psychoanalyst who devoted much of his life to the serious consequences of what children do with and to their building blocks, stuffed bears, and cards.[5] He connected these experiences to work as early experiments in craftsmanship.

Erikson was a reluctant Freudian in the nursery. When he asked himself why boys built towers of blocks or houses of cards until they toppled over, he could easily draw on the Freudian phallic explanation involving erection and ejaculation. Instead, he noted that the boys were testing the limits of making a viable object by creating a rule for "how high can it go?" Similarly, he wondered why little girls repetitively dressed and undressed their dolls. In the Freudian view this could be explained as hiding and showing the body's sexual parts and erogenous zones. It seemed equally to Erikson that these children were learning how to make a practice work—the girls concentrated on how to make their hands adeptly button and skillfully adjust the clothes. A child of either sex, trying to pull out the sewn-on eyes of a stuffed bear, is not necessarily expressing aggression. The bear is being tested rather than raged against: how strong is it? Play may be a field of infantile sexuality, but in essays such as "Toys and Their Reasons" Erikson asserted that it is also technical work on material objects.[6]

Perhaps his most durable insights concern objectification, the thing valued in itself. The "object-relations" school of D. W. Winnicott and John Bowlby emphasized, we have seen, the infant's experience of things in themselves as a result of separation and loss. Erikson instead emphasized the young child's powers of projection on inanimate objects, the anthropomorphizing power that continues in adult life when, for instance, a brick is described as "honest." But for Erikson this is a two-way connection; material reality talks back, it constantly corrects projection, cautions about material truth. If the toy bear with strong eyes is given a name because a little boy projects himself onto the toy, the bear's unmoving eyes still caution the boy against believing that this bear is really like him. Here, in play, is the origin of the dialogue the craftsman conducts with materials like clay and glass.

What needs to be added to Erikson's approach is an account of the rules that enable this dialogue. There are at least two.

The first concerns the consistency of rule making. Many of the rules children devise for toys or games prove initially dysfunctional, such as a lack of workable rules for keeping score. Consistent rules require collaboration; all children have to agree to abide by them. And consistent rules are inclusive; they have to apply to players of different abilities. At the heart of consistency lies repetition, the invention of rules that permit games to happen more than once. Repetition of games in turn lays the groundwork for experiences of practice, going over a procedure again and again. In childhood play, though, children also learn how to modify the rules they make, and this too has adult consequences, as when in repeating a technical practice we can gradually modify, change, or improve it. To get better at a skill we need to change the rules that repeat—the metamorphosis of rules that helped Erin O'Connor develop as a glassblower. In short, play inaugurates practicing, and practicing is a matter both of repetition and of modulation.

Play is, second, a school for learning to increase complexity. As parents, we may observe that children aged four and five experience boredom in a way they had not before; simple toys no longer interest them. Psychologists explain boredom as a matter of children becoming better critics of their object world. Children certainly can make complex forms out of "impoverished," simple materials—Lego blocks, for instance, or checkers. What counts are objects that permit a child to complicate a structure as his or her cognitive abilities develop.[7] The emerging capacity to read enables the child to create further, more elaborate rules for games.

Making matters complex in one's work derives from these capacities. The scalpel, a simple tool, was put to highly complex purposes in seventeenth-century scientific work, as has from the fifteenth century the flat-sided screwdriver; both began as basic tools. They can perform complex work only because we have, as adults, learned to play with their possibilities rather than treat each tool as fit-for-purpose. Boredom is as important a stimulus to craftsmanship as it is in play; becoming bored, the craftsman looks for what else he can do with the tools at hand.

To be sure, consistency and increasing complexity can conflict, but in resetting the rules for play, children learn how to manage these tensions. In the play of children aged four to six, the psychologist Jérome Bruner observes, complexity has more weight than consistency. In the middle stages of childhood, aged eight to ten, strict rules become more important, and by early adolescence the two can be handled again in balance.[8] Just this balance is what Schiller had in mind by conceiving of play as a fulcrum.

※　※　※

This brief outline of how the craft of play connects to work should be to us literally Enlightening. Craftsmanship draws on what children learn in play's dialogue with physical materials, the discipline of following rules, the advance of complexity in making rules. Play so universal, so full of adult implication—yet modern prejudice clings to the conviction that only a few have the ability to do really good work. Recalling the

political convictions of Jefferson, we might want to recast this prejudice: good citizenship found in play, is lost at work.

Perhaps the way ability itself is understood illuminates the prejudice.

Ability
Localize, Question, Open Up

The Enlightenment thinkers believed that the abilities that nourish
a craft are innate. Modern biology vindicates this conviction; thanks to
advances in neurology, we are gaining a clearer understanding of the
geography of ability in the brain. We can map out neuronally, for instance, where in the brain we hear and how we process that neuronal
information required for musical craft.

Raw response to musical sounds begins in the auditory cortex,
deep in the brain's center. People respond to the physical sounds they
hear principally in the brain's subcortical structures of the brain; here,
rhythm stimulates activity in the cerebellum. The capacity to process
such information also has a neurological geography. The prefrontal
cortex provides feedback on whether the hand has moved correctly;
this is one neurological location for the experience "It works!" Learning
to read music engages the visual cortex. The emotions experienced in
playing and listening to music also have specific regions in the brain.
Simpler responses excite the cerebellar vermis, more complicated responses the amygdala.[9]

Because of its complexity, the brain processes in parallel rather
than in series. Like a group of small computers hooked up and working
all at once, the geographic regions of the brain will simultaneously
process their own information and communicate with other places. In
aural experience, if one of the locales is damaged, thinking in sound
elsewhere will falter. The more neuronal stimulation, transmission,
and feedback occurs throughout the global geography of the brain, the
more we think and feel.[10]

The unease this map of innate ability arouses lies not in its facts—which of course will be revised in time—but in its implications. Is this a map on which indelible inequalities are drawn? Is your prefontal cortex better than mine? We want to note that the worry that human beings are structurally or genetically programmed to be unequal has an ancient root. In Western philosophy it traces back to the idea of predestination.

At the very end of *The Republic* Plato recounts the "Myth of Er," a tale of a man who glimpses the afterlife.[13] Er finds in this netherworld something like the transmigration of souls taking place; the souls choose the body they will next inhabit and the life they will next lead. Some choose badly. Hoping to flee their past sufferings, they enter unsuspected new ones. Some choose wisely because in their earlier life they have gained knowledge about how to do something well, a knowledge that has steadied their judgment. At birth in their new body, however, every person has a destiny, an imprint of what he or she could become.

This view contrasts to predestination as that idea later appeared in Christianity, particularly in Calvinist Protestantism. John Calvin believed that God has predestined some souls for salvation, some for damnation, at birth. Calvin's God is something of a sadist, however, withholding from individuals knowledge of their fate, obliging them to beg for mercy, to prove themselves worthy, in order that their fate be revised. Sadistic but also mystifying: How can an individual have a destiny that can be changed? Without jumping into this theological rabbit hole, we might note simply that this sort of Protestantism yoked the innate and the unequal: some individuals are more worthy of God's mercy because they begin life in better spiritual shape than others; the revisions of fate within a human lifetime still focus on invidious comparison to other people.

Calvinism took a further, malign modern life in the eugenics movement of a century ago, notably in the writings of William Graham

Sumner: do not waste resources on individuals or groups who lack the innate ability to use them. A scarcely less malign version is the educational practice that seeks to determine what an individual is capable of learning before trying to teach him or her. Platonism sought a somewhat more positive view: though you may be innately lesser in capacity than others, make the best of the cards you have been dealt—a consoling view only if others do not make too much of these differences.

Certainly we would be reductionist if we imagined the brain's hard-wiring and parallel processing to be a closed system—one modern, engineering version of predestination—a system laid down at birth and functioning according to its own internal logic thereafter. The alternative engineering model is that of the open system, in which forward developments feed back on the givens of the starting point. Culture functions as an open system in relation to the brain and in a particular way; different sorts of environment stimulate, or fail to stimulate, the brain's work of parallel processing in regions like the prefrontal cortex. Martha Nussbaum and Amartya Sen thus prefer the word *capability* to *ability,* each capability activated or repressed by culture. As appeared in the studies of grips and prehension, a capability is built into the structure of human hand bones; though some hands are larger, some endowed at birth with wide lateral stretch, the real difference between able and clumsy hands lies in how each hand is stimulated and trained.

Even biologists who contest most strongly the image of human nature as a "blank slate" take this view. In part, the focus on inequality effaces an equally powerful issue of oversupply. The researches of the cognitive scientist Steven Pinker on language programming show, for instance, that the human species is capable of manufacturing "too much" meaning—an abundance of contrasting and contradictory meanings in both speaking and writing; culture narrows and sorts out this abundant ability shared by all.[11] Geneticists of a different stripe arrive at the same end by another route. For Richard Lewontin, genetic potentials are unresolved "naturally"; the human body is full of pos-

sibility that requires social and cultural organization in order to become manifest and concrete.[12]

Vaucanson's loom, innately superior to human hands, provides the
most clarifying context for thinking through the consequences of natural inequalities. Smashing the machines—that is, denying their superiority—proved no viable option. The better option was to treat the loom
like a medicine; you wanted to be careful not to take too strong a dose
of it, or so Voltaire came to think about the practical inventions of the
man he had earlier celebrated as the "modern Prometheus." That is,
make use of the innately superior resource but do not dwell on its
superiority. That Enlightened, cool wisdom is a good way, I think, to
understand the import of the map of ability in the brain. Its resources
are apportioned or applied unequally in different individuals; dwelling
on that fact, society can poison itself. Make no judgments of fate;
stimulate the human organism as much as possible.

The narrower realm of craftwork addresses the issue of unequal talents
in a perhaps more focused way. The innate abilities on which craftsmanship is based are not exceptional; they are shared in common by
the large majority of human beings and in roughly equal measure.

Three basic abilities are the foundation of craftsmanship. These
are the ability to localize, to question, and to open up. The first involves
making a matter concrete, the second reflecting on its qualities, the
third expanding its sense. The carpenter establishes the peculiar grain
of a single piece of wood, looking for detail; turns the wood over and
over, pondering how the pattern on the surface might reflect structure
hidden underneath; decides that the grain can be brought out if he or
she uses a metal solvent rather than standard wood varnish. To deploy
these capabilities the brain needs to process in parallel visual, aural,
tactile, and language-symbol information.

The capacity to localize names the power to specify where something important is happening. In the hand, we have seen this localization occurring at the musician's or goldsmith's fingertip; in the eye, localization focuses on the right angle between warp and woof on a loom, or the end of the pipe used in glassblowing. In contriving the mobile phone, there was focus on the switch box, in contriving the handheld calculator, focus on the size of the buttons. The "zoom" function of a computer monitor or a camera performs this same task.

Localizing can result from sensory stimulation, as when in a dissection the scalpel encounters unexpected hard matter; at this moment, the anatomist's hand movements become both slower and smaller. Localization can also occur when the sensory stimulation is of something missing, absent, or ambiguous. An abscess in the body, sending the physical signal of a loss of tension, will localize hand movement. This is also the stimulation van Eyck contrived, in his parks, removing defined boundaries between street and playground so that children at play had to focus on that liminal zone to keep safe.

In cognitive studies, localizing is sometimes called "focal attention." Gregory Bateson and Leon Festinger suppose that human beings focus on the difficulties and contradictions they call "cognitive dissonances." Wittgenstein's obsession with the precise height of the ceiling in one room of his house derives from what he perceived as a cognitive dissonance in his rules of proportion. Localization can also occur when something works successfully. Once Frank Gehry could make titanium quilting work, he became more focused on the possibilities of the material. These complicated experiences of cognitive dissonance trace directly, as Festinger has argued, from animal behavior; the behavior consists in an animal's capacity to attend to "here" or "this." Parallel processing in the brain activates different neural circuits to establish the attention. In human beings, particularly in people practicing a craft, this animal thinking locates specifically where a material, a practice, or a problem matters.

The capacity to question is no less and no more than a matter of

investigating the locale. Neurologists who follow the cognitive dissonance model believe the brain does something like image in sequence
the fact that all doors in a mental room are locked. There is then no
longer doubt, but curiosity remains, the brain asking if different keys
have locked them and, if so, why. Questioning can also occur through
operational success, as in those moments of Linux programming when
problem solving prompts the programmer to ask new questions. This is
explained neurologically as a matter of a new circuit connection being
activated between the brain's different regions. The newly active pathway makes possible further parallel processing—but not instantly, not
all at once. "Questioning" means, physiologically, dwelling in an incipient state; the pondering brain is considering its circuit options.

This state makes neuronal sense of the experience of curiosity, an
experience that suspends resolution and decision, in order to probe.
The work process can be thus imagined as following a certain time
rhythm, in which action leads to suspension while results are ques-
tioned, after which action resumes in a new form. We have seen this
rhythm of action-rest/question-action to mark the development of
complex hand skills; merely mechanical activity, which does not develop technique, is simply movement.

The capacity to open up a problem draws on intuitive leaps, specifically on its powers to draw unlike domains close to one another and to
preserve tacit knowledge in the leap between them. Simply shifting
between domains of activity stimulates fresh thinking about problems.
"Open up" is intimately linked with "open to," in the sense of being open
to doing things differently, to shifting from one sphere of habit to
another. So elemental is this ability that its importance is often slighted.

The capacity to shift habits reaches deep into the animal kingdom.
Some biologists, following Richard Lewontin, believe that the capacity
to respond and problematize in different domains is the ethological key
to natural selection. However this may be, human beings are capable
both of switching habits and of comparing them. Factories draw on this

capability in switching workers from task to task; the logic here is to prevent boredom—the boredom that results from closed systems of routine. Release from boredom can occur only because the domain shift reengages us mentally. Studies of ability often dwell on the act of problem solving, but that act, we have seen, is intimately connected to problem finding. An elemental human capacity enables this connection, the capacity to switch, compare, and alter habit.

I've done my reader a disservice in reducing a vast territory of research to these three points; I don't mean to imply that the abilities human beings share to localize, question, and open up are themselves simple. I do mean to emphasize that we share these capacities, with other animals and with each other, and I want next to show why we share them in roughly equal measure.

Operational Intelligence
The Stanford-Binet Paradigm

Alfred Binet and Theodore Simon created the first intelligence tests in 1905. A decade later, Lewis Terman revised their work, creating the test still known as Stanford-Binet, now in its fifth revision. Over the course of a century the test has become quite sophisticated. It probes five basic mental domains: fluid reasoning, mostly in the use of language; basic knowledge, mostly of words and mathematical symbols; quantitative reasoning, mostly deductive; visual-spatial processing; and working memory.[14]

These domains seem to map out the raw materials of what any sort of skill will be composed. But they do not include the raw abilities out of which craftsmanship is formed. This is because the IQ tests remain true to Binet's three guiding principles: that intelligence can be measured by correct answers to questions, that the answers will separate groups of people into a bell-shaped curve, and that the tests test a person's biological potential rather than cultural formation.

The last has been the most persistently controversial: How can nature and nurture be divided? There's a real argument to be made that they should be. In the eighteenth century, Diderot and most other Enlightenment writers asserted that the two should be separated because ordinary maids, shoemakers, and cooks had more native intelligence than the upper classes allowed them to express. Binet had instead a contrary but still charitable purpose in studying raw intelligence; he wanted to find out what those who are slow and dull are actually capable of doing, in order to find them appropriate low-level work matched to weak ability. Terman's interest was both benign and malign; he wanted to discover exceptionally able individuals wherever they were to be found in the social order, but as a committed eugenicist, he wanted also to identity the exceptionally stupid and sterilize them. Neither Binet nor Terman was much concerned about the middle ground.

In the twentieth century the Stanford-Binet tests created a new stigma, based on group rather than individual scores. If racial or ethnic groups did relatively badly on the tests, the results were sometimes used to affirm the prejudice that, for instance, blacks on the whole were less intelligent than whites, "science" now invoked to affirm their supposed natural inferiority. To combat this, the tests themselves were faulted for cultural bias. The argument here was that whereas a middle-class white child might routinely come across the symbol π in school (a symbol tested in the basic knowledge section), the inner-city child might find it strange.[15]

This debate has become so familiar that the procedure first practiced by Binet has been neglected, but it is the statistical procedure that has continued to shape fundamentally our understanding of intelligence. Binet subscribed to the belief that the intelligence scores of people in groups would follow the curve of normal distribution, which means a few dullards at one end, most of us in the middle, a few Einsteins at the other, in a shape representing a bell. The specific shape of the bell curve was originally detected by Abraham de Moivre in 1734, refined by Carl Friedrich Gauss by 1809, and baptized as "normal" by Charles Sanders Peirce in 1875.

There are, however, many different ways a bell can swell. In tests of visual recognition, the curve looks more an inverted champagne flute than a gently sloping cloche. That means, most people share the same skills of recognizing that an image is connected to a word like "dog." In this particular ability, differences are not acute. In terms of numbers, if you start with a median intelligence of 100, and the standard deviation of $\delta = 15$, IQ scores of 115 are in the 84th percentile, scores of 130 are in the 97.9th percentile, 145 in the 99.99th percentile, 160 in the 99.997th percentile. Downward, the curve is similar. Thus the vast majority of human beings are just one standard deviation from the midpoint.

It's odd that neither Binet nor Terman was much interested in this densely populated middle ground. Just by setting the definition of "able" up one standard deviation, 84 percent of the population is eliminated. Or again, if we make a one-notch reckoning of inability, only 16 percent of the population can be considered so.

The words that are applied to this densely populated, flute-shape middle zone are often put-downs like "mediocre" or "nothing special." Yet these words are justified by a brutally simple statistical move. Does one standard deviation justify a difference in kind between mediocre and able, the mass and the elite? Individuals at the 85 IQ level can deal with many of the issues of the mass above them, only more *slowly*. This is particularly true of visual-spatial processing and working memory abilities. Going upward one standard deviation from 100 to 115, the one real cognitive break occurs in verbal symbolization. Even here, the issue is clouded, since the individuals who test at 100 may have the understanding of the symbol but confine it to tacit knowledge or express it in physical practice.

Finally, Binet and Terman arrived at the "normal" bell curve by adding all the aspects of intelligence they tested up into a single number. To do so assumes that all the dimensions of intelligence are interconnected. Modern testers involved the letter "g" to represent the glue between forms of intelligence. The psychologist Howard Gardner (who has appeared in another professional guise in the previous chapter as a student of good work) has strongly disputed "g." He believes that human beings possess a larger number of intelligent capacities than Stanford-Binet measures and that these capacities are distinct and independent from one another, which means you can't add them up into a single number.

Gardner's list includes more bodily senses than Stanford-Binet's: he adds touch, movement, and hearing to words, math symbols, and images as sites of intelligent thinking; he adds, more daringly, the ability to communicate with others as a form of intelligence, and even the capacity to explore and judge oneself objectively.[16] Gardner's technical critics riposte that his list is too big and sloppy. They defend adding up answers into one general number by saying that, within the Stanford-Binet frame, fluid reasoning, working memory, and visual-spatial processing indeed correlate—or, at least, the formulas for "g" compute.

Craft abilities pose an even more fundamental objection. They are unlikely to show up in intelligence tests, in part due to the basic paradigm of Stanford-Binet, in which questions are asked to which there are correct answers.

In principle, correct answers are the tester's version of "It works!" The equation $2 + 2 = 5$ does not work. There are correct answers to calculations. There is no equivalent correct answer for a verbal definition: here, for example are two verbal definitions for the word *incisive*:

Following Huntley's incisive analysis, the bond traders were immediately galvanized into a frenzy of selling.
Cheryl's incisive coverage of city hall affairs made her a formidable candidate for a Pulitzer Prize.

Putting aside all issues of cultural context, the test produces a conundrum of interpretation. On the test, the right answer on offer for a verbal equivalent in both is *acute,* whereas in the second case a better equivalent would be *exposed,* which is not on offer.[17] In the spirit of craftsmanship you want to dwell in this problem, making it more specific, puzzling over it—but time is running out. You have to answer as many questions as you can to raise your score, so you guess and go on. Intuitive leaps that open up a problem are impossible to test using multiple-choice questions. These leaps are an exercise of associating unlikely elements. There is no *correct* answer to the question "Are city streets like arteries and veins?"

Binet's method thus created a black hole for thinking that problematizes, penalized those who take the time required to reflect, and could not address the issue of the quality. A good total score on the tests may dictate abandoning just those problems that really are problems. Craft abilities are applied to depth of understanding, usually focused on a particular problem, whereas the IQ score represents a more superficial management of many problems.

As I've elsewhere argued, superficiality is put to particular use in modern society.[18] In business, testing regimes today aim to identify innate, potential ability that can be applied to the rapidly changing opportunities of the global economy. Doing one thing well, understanding it in depth, may be a recipe for a worker or a company to be left behind in these febrile shifts. Tests that measure a person's capacity to management of many problems at the expense of depth suit an economic regime that prizes quick study, superficial knowledge, all too often embodied by consultants who dart in and out of organizations. The craftsman's abilities to dig deep stands at the pole opposite from potential ability deployed in this fashion.

If no one could deny that abilities vary at the extremes, the shape of the IQ bell curve raises a question about the middle. Why the blind spot to its potential? The person with an IQ score of 100 is not much different in ability than the person with a score of 115, but the 115 is much more likely to attract notice. There's a devil's answer to this question: inflating small differences in degree into large differences in kind legitimates the system of privilege. Correspondingly, equating the median with the mediocre legitimates neglect—one reason why Britain directs proportionately more resources into elite education than into technical colleges and why in America it proves so hard to find charitable contributions to vocational schools. But these venal abuses are not how our account should end.

The capacity to work well is shared fairly equally among human beings; it appears first in play, is elaborated in the capacities to localize, question, and open up problems at work. The Enlightenment hoped that learning to do good work would make human beings more capable of self-governance. No lack of intelligence among ordinary human beings threatens that political project. The craftsman's heart may be a less solid rock. Rather than lack of mental resource, the craftsman is more likely to be threatened by emotional mismanagement of the drive to do good work; society can collude in that mismanagement or seek to rectify it. These are the reasons why I've argued in Part Three that motivation is a more important issue than talent in consummating craftsmanship.

Conclusion:
The Philosophical Workshop

Pragmatism
The Craft of Experience

This study has sought to rescue *Animal laborens* from the contempt with which Hannah Arendt treated him. The working human animal can be enriched by the skills and dignified by the spirit of craftsmanship. This view of the human condition is, in European culture, as old as the Homeric hymn to Hephaestus, it served Islam in the writings of Ibn Khaldun, and it guided Confucianism throughout several thousand years.[1] In our own time, craftsmanship finds a philosophical home within pragmatism.

For more than a century, this movement has dedicated itself to making philosophical sense of concrete experience. The pragmatist movement began in the late nineteenth century as an American reaction to the ills of idealism in Europe, embodied by G. W. F. Hegel, in the eyes of the first pragmatist, C. S. Peirce. Peirce sought instead to find the keys to human cognition in everyday, small acts; the spirit of scientific experiment in the seventeenth century animated him, as did Hume's empiricism in the eighteenth. From its origins, pragmatism addressed the quality of experience as well as sheer facts on the ground. Thus William James sought an alternative to the bitterness, irony, and tragic foreboding that seemed to him to infuse the writings of Friedrich

Nietzsche; in James's writings on religion, the philosopher attended to the small details of daily religious practices as well as to large questions of doctrine and found in these small details religion's reward.

Pragmatism occurred in two waves. The first spanned the late nineteenth century to the Second World War. There then was a lapse of two generations until our own time, in which the movement has re-vived and spread back to Europe. Its proponents now include Hans Joas in Germany, a school of young pragmatists in Denmark, and the Americans Richard Rorty, Richard Bernstein, and myself. Two world wars and the arc of the Soviet empire checked but did not extinguish the hope embodied in pragmatism; its animating impulse remains to engage with ordinary, plural, constructive human activities.[2]

The pragmatist in the first wave who addressed directly the condi-tion of *Animal laborens* was John Dewey, an educator unfairly blamed for the sins of touchy-feely progressive education, a student of biology who disputed the aggressive, competitive views of Social Darwinism, and above all, a socialist who set himself resolutely against doctrinaire Marxism. Dewey certainly would have subscribed to Hannah Arendt's critique of Marxism; the false hopes Marx held out to humanity can be measured, in Arendt's words, by "the abundance or scarcity of the goods to be fed into the life process."[3] Against this quantitative mea-sure, Dewey argued for a socialism based on improving the quality of people's experience at work rather than advocating, as did Arendt, a politics that transcends labor itself.

Many of craftsmanship's themes appear in Dewey's writings in a more abstracted form: the intimate relations between problem-solving and problem-finding, technique and expression, play and work. Dewey the socialist best assembled these connections in his book *Democracy and Education:* "Both work and play are equally free and intrinsically motivated, apart from false economic conditions which tend to make play into idle excitement for the well to do, and work into uncongenial labor for the poor. Work is psychologically simply an activity which consciously includes regard for consequences as part of itself; it becomes constrained labor when the consequences are outside of the activity, as an end to which activity is merely a means. Work which remains permeated with the play attitude is art."[4] Dewey was a socialist in just the way John Ruskin and William Morris were: all three urged workers to assess the quality of their work in terms of shared experiment, collective trial and error. Good craftsmanship implies socialism. The workings of a modern Japanese auto plant or a Linux chat room might have expanded their sympathy for collaboration of other sorts, but still, all three disputed the pursuit of quality simply as a means to profit.

Philosophically, pragmatism has argued that to work well people need freedom from means-ends relationships. Underlying this philosophical conviction is a concept that, I think, unifies all of pragmatism. This is *experience,* a fuzzier word in English than in German, which divides it in two, *Erlebnis* and *Erfahrung.* The first names an event or relationship that makes an emotional inner impress, the second an event, action, or relationship that turns one outward and requires skill rather than sensitivity. Pragmatist thought has insisted that these two meanings should not be divided. If you remain in the domain of Erfahrung alone, William James believed, you may be trapped by means-and-ends thinking and acting; you may succumb to the vice of instrumentalism. You need constantly the inner monitor of Erlebnis, of "how it feels."

But craftwork, as presented in this book, emphasizes the realm of Erfahrung. Craftwork focuses on objects in themselves and on impersonal practices; craftwork depends on curiosity, it tempers obsession; craftwork turns the craftsman outward. Within the philosophical workshop of pragmatism, I want to argue for this stress more largely: the value of experience understood as a craft.

The craft of experience traces, as an idea, back to Madame d'Épinay's writings in the eighteenth century on parenting. She argued against the self-sufficiency of instinctive love, and again, to nurture a child well, she maintained that the parent must restrain the impulse to command autocratically. Focusing on the child will turn the parent outward. In place of blind love or command, there need to be objective, rational, guiding standards of when to go sleep, what to eat, and where to play, or the child will be rudderless; implementing such standards requires skill that any parent develops only through practice. Outward-turned, skilled, hewing to objective standards, her view of parenting as a craft has indeed become the modern common sense of parenting. Its stress falls more on Erfahrung than on Erlebnis.

Taken just as a concept, what does the "craft of experience" imply? We would focus of form and procedure—that is, on techniques of experience. These could guide us even in encounters that happen only once by furnishing an envelope of tacit knowledge for our actions. We would want to shape the impress people and events have made on us so that these impressions are intelligible to others who do not know the same people we know or lived through the same events. As appeared in the discussion of expertise, we would try to make the particular knowledge we possess transparent in order that others can understand and respond to it. The idea of experience as a craft contests the sort of subjectivity that dwells in the sheer process of feeling. Of course this is a matter of weights; impressions are the raw materials of experience, but only that—raw materials.

The argument I've presented in this book is that the craft of making physical things provides insight into the techniques of experience that can shape our dealings with others. Both the difficulties and the possibilities of making things well apply to making human relationships. Material challenges like working with resistance or managing ambiguity are instructive in understanding the resistances people harbor to one another or the uncertain boundaries between people. I've stressed the positive, open role routine and practicing play in the work of crafting physical things; so too do people need to practice their relations with one another, learn the skills of anticipation and revision in order to improve these relations.

I recognize that the reader may balk at thinking of experience in terms of technique. But who we are arises directly from what our bodies can do. Social consequences are built into the structure and the functioning of the human body, as in the workings of the human hand. I argue no more and no less than the capacities our bodies have to shape physical things are the same capacities we draw on in social relations. And if debatable, this viewpoint is not uniquely mine. One hallmark of the pragmatist movement has been to suppose a continuum between the organic and the social. Whereas some sociobiologists have argued that genetics dictates behavior, pragmatists like Han Joas maintain that the body's own richness furnishes the materials for a wide variety of creative action. Craftsmanship shows the continuum between the organic and the social put in action.

An eagle-eyed reader will have noticed that the word *creativity* appears in this book as little as possible. This is because the word carries too much Romantic baggage—the mystery of inspiration, the claims of genius. I have sought to eliminate some of the mystery by showing how intuitive leaps happen, in the reflections people make on the actions of their own hands or in the use of tools. I have sought to draw craft and art together, because all techniques contain expressive implications. This is true of making a pot; it is also and equally true of raising a child.

I recognize also that the least developed side of my argument concerns politics—Arendt's domain, the domain of "statecraft." Modern pragmatism could be said to take on faith Jefferson's belief that learning to work well is the foundation of citizenship. Perhaps this Enlightenment faith remains compelling because it bridges the social and political realms, whereas Arendt, drawing on a long tradition of political thought stretching back to Machiavelli, believed that statecraft was a self-standing domain of expertise. The connection between work and citizenship may imply socialism, but not necessarily democracy; as appeared in the medieval guild, whose workshops served Ruskin,

Morris, and Dewey as models, hierarchy at work could morph seamlessly as hierarchy in the state. But there are craft reasons to credit pragmatism's faith in democracy; these lie in the capacities on which human beings draw to develop skills: the universality of play, the basic capabilities to specify, question, and open up. These are widely diffused among human beings rather than restricted to an elite.

Self-rule supposes the capacity of citizens to work collectively on objective problems, to suspect quick solutions; missing in Dewey's democratic faith is, however, an understanding of the disabling filter of mass media. High-concept news snippets or blogs filled with personal trivia do not develop communication of a more skilled sort. Still, pragmatism insists that the remedy to these ills must lie in the experience, on the ground, of citizen participation, participation that stresses the virtues of practice with its repetitions and slow revisions.[5] Arendt's reproach to democracy is that it demands too much of ordinary human beings; it might be better said of modern democracy that it demands too little. Its institutions and tools of communication do not draw on and develop the competences that most people can evince in work. Belief in those skills is the homage pragmatism pays to the craft of experience.

Culture
Pandora and Hephaestus

It is sometimes said that pragmatism makes a shrine out of experience, but craft experience cannot be blindly worshipped. From their origins in Western history, technical labors have aroused ambivalence, represented by the two deities Hephaestus and Pandora. The contrast in classical mythology between their personae helps make sense of the cultural value accorded to the craftsman.

Most of the eighteenth chapter of Homer's *Iliad* is devoted to the praises of Hephaestus, the builder of all the houses on Mount Olympus. Here we read that he is also a coppersmith, a jeweler, the inventor of chariots.[6] But Hephaestus is also lame—he has a clubfoot—and in ancient Greek culture physical deformity was a deep source of shame: *kalôs kagathos* (beautiful in mind and body) contrasted to *aischrôs*, the single word denoting both ugly and shameful.[7] This god is flawed.

There is something socially consequent about Hephaestus's clubfoot. The clubfoot symbolizes the craftsman's social value. Hephaestus makes jewelry from copper, an ordinary material; his chariots are fashioned from the bones of dead birds. Homer embraces Hephaestus in the midst of a story about heroes and heroic violence; the domestic virtues of home and hearth are beneath these heroes' contempt. The misshapen figure of Hephaestus is meant to suggest that material domestic civilization will never satisfy the desire for glory; that is his defect.

By contrast, Hesiod described Pandora as "the beautiful evil. . . . Wonder gripped the immortal gods and the mortal human beings when they saw the steep deception, entrancing for human beings." Pandora could, like Eve, be taken as the quintessential sexual temptress, but the fullness of the myth suggests another reading. The name *Pandora* itself means "all gifts"; the vessel containing her gifts is lodged within the home she shares with Epimetheus; when it is opened, only the most immaterial gift, that of hope, does not fly out to become a destructive force. The physical tools, the elixirs and medications within, do the damage; material goods compose the "beautiful evil."[8]

Pandora's "beautiful evil" seems to stand in stark contrast to Hannah Arendt's idea of the "banality of evil," which Arendt worked out in studying Adolf Eichmann and other engineers of the Nazi concentration camps. The banality of evil applies to the craftsman just trying to get the job done as well as possible. Further research on Eichmann and other Holocaust engineers has, however, leaned more to the presence of Pandora; these were destroyers animated both by hatred of Jews and by the seductions of Götterdämmerung, the beauty of destruction.[9]

Pandora's myth installed itself in Greek culture as a story in which only at the urging of others did she open the casket. The danger lay in their physical craving, their curiosity and desire for the things within. She satisfied their desire, but in opening the lid, she transformed the sweet perfumes into poisonous vapors, the gold swords cut their hands, and the soft cloths suffocated those who held them.

These mythological personae suggest the ambivalence about material culture that marked out our civilization from its origins. Western civilization has not chosen between these personae so much as fused them into ambivalence about man-made physical experience. Both Hephaestus and Pandora are artificers. Each of these artificers contains a contrary: a virtuous god who makes worthwhile everyday things yet whose person is ugly and inglorious; a goddess whose things are as beautiful, as desirable, as her body, and as malign. The fusion of these two personae was why Plato could celebrate the virtue of archaic, domesticating technologies yet assert the superior beauty of the immaterial soul; why early Christians could see virtue in acts of carpentering, sewing, or gardening yet scorn the love of material things themselves; why the Enlightenment at once embraced and feared the perfection of machines; why Wittgenstein could call a sickness his desire to realize a beautiful, perfect building. The man-made material object is not a neutral fact; it is a source of unease because it is man-made.

Such ambivalence about the man-made has shaped the fortunes of the craftsman. History has conducted something like a set of experiments in formulating the craftsman's images as drudge, slave, worthy Christian, avatar of Enlightenment, doomed relic of the preindustrial past. This story has a spine. The craftsman has been able to call to his or her aid a capacity and a dignity ingrained in the human body: signifying acts as simple human grip and prehension, as complex as the lessons of resistance and ambiguity that give to human tools and physical constructs an intelligible form. The unity of the craftsman's mind and body can be found in the expressive language that guides physical action. Physical acts of repetition and practice enable this *Animal laborens* to develop skill from within and to reconfigure the material world through a slow process of metamorphosis. The origin of all these powers is as simple, as elemental, as physical as playing games with toys.

The spine of the story recounted in these pages is thus, in a way, a familiar one: nature versus culture, the naturalness of what craftsmen do—no matter how skilled they become—set against Western culture's long-standing ambivalence about man-made things. Though no philosopher, Isaac Ware wanted to make sense of brick in this way. The contrast between honest brick and artificial stucco, though both are fabricated materials, became contrasting emblems of nature and culture, the first according with a skill developed under modest domestic circumstances, the second a material developed at the behest of social climbers, and yet seductive and beautiful to Ware himself.

One way out of this impasse might indeed be to ignore Hephaestus's clubfoot, as it were, and value him just for what he does; to get closer to this natural realm, in all its modesty, the archaic arcadia in which humankind first used tools and skills for the common good. This was John Ruskin's impulse, though his version of arcadia was located in the guilds of the medieval city. But a way of life that accords with the craftsman's natural capacities still does not account for Pandora. The craftsman's skills, if natural, are never innocent.

Ethics
Pride in One's Work

I've left for the very end of this book the subject that the reader may well think should have come first. Pride in one's work lies at the heart of craftsmanship as the reward for skill and commitment. Though brute pride figures as a sin in both Judaism and Christianity by putting self in place of God, pride in one's work might seem to remove this sin, since the work has an independent existence. In Benvenuto Cellini's *Autobiography*, obnoxious boasts about his sexual prowess are irrelevant to the gold work. The work transcends the maker.

Craftsmen take pride most in skills that mature. This is why simple imitation is not a sustaining satisfaction; the skill has to evolve. The slowness of craft time serves as a source of satisfaction; practice beds in, making the skill one's own. Slow craft time also enables the work of reflection and imagination—which the push for quick results cannot. Mature means long; one takes lasting ownership of the skill.

But pride in work also poses its own large ethical problem, exemplified, as we saw at the beginning of this study, by the creators of the atom bomb. They had taken pride in making something that, after the work was done, caused many of these makers great distress. The seductions of the work had, Pandora-fashion, led them to do harm. Those scientists who held to an absolute pride in the work itself, like Edward Teller, the organizer of the hydrogen bombs that followed on from the Los Alamos project, tended to deny Pandora. At the other end of the spectrum were the signers of the Russell-Einstein Manifesto of 1955, a document that launched the Pugwash Conferences movement for the control of nuclear weapons. The manifesto states in part, "The men who know most are the most gloomy."[10]

Pragmatism has no great solution to the ethical problem posed by pride in one's work, but it does have a partial corrective. This is to emphasize the connection between means and ends. In the course of fabrication the bomb maker might have asked, What is the minimum strength of the bomb we should make?—indeed a question asked by scientists like Joseph Rotblat, accused by many of his colleagues of being disruptive or even disloyal. Pragmatism wants to emphasize the value of asking ethical questions during the work process; it contests after-the-fact ethics, ethical enquiry beginning only after facts on the ground are fixed.

It is for this reason that I have emphasized, throughout this book, stages and sequences of the work process, indicating when the craftsman can pause in the work and reflect on what he or she is doing. These pauses need not diminish pride in the work; instead, because the person is judging while doing, the result can be more ethically satisfying. I recognize that this emphasis on staged reflection must be incomplete, because it's often not possible to reckon ethical or, indeed, material consequences. No one could have foreseen in the sixteenth century, for instance, that refining the metal composites used in knives would eventually produce less painful forms of surgery than that practiced with the barber's razor. Still, this effort to look forward is the ethical way to take pride in one's work. Understanding the inner sequence of development in practicing a craft, the phases of becoming a better craftsman, can counter Hannah Arendt's conviction that *Animal laborens* is blind. Ours would remain an innocent philosophical school, however, if pragmatism did not recognize that the denouement of this narrative is often marked by marked by bitterness and regret.

The clubfooted Hephaestus, proud of his work if not of himself, is the most dignified person we can become.

Notes

Prologue

1. Gaby Wood, *Living Dolls* (London: Faber and Faber, 2002), xix.

2. See Marina Warner, "The Making of Pandora," in Warner, *Monuments and Maidens: The Allegory of the Female Form* (New York: Vintage, 1996), 214–219.

3. This is testimony Oppenheimer gave to a government committee in 1954, reprinted in Jeremy Bernstein, *Oppenheimer: Portrait of an Enigma* (London: Duckworth, 2004), 121–122.

4. Two illuminating if depressing studies are Nicholas Stern, *The Economics of Climate Change: The Stern Review* (Cambridge: Cambridge University Press, 2007), and George Monbiot, *Heat: How to Stop the Planet from Burning* (London: Penguin, 2007).

5. Martin Rees, *Our Final Century? Will the Human Race Survive the Twenty-First Century?* (London: Random House, 2003).

6. Heidegger quoted in Daniel Bell, *Communitarianism and Its Critics* (Oxford: Clarendon Press, 1993), 89. See also Catherine Zuckert, "Martin Heidegger: His Philosophy and His Politics," *Political Theory,* February 1990, 71, and Peter Kempt, "Heidegger's Greatness and His Blindness," *Philosophy and Social Criticism,* April 1989, 121.

7. Martin Heidegger, "Building, Dwelling, Thinking," in Heidegger, *Poetry, Language, Thought,* trans. Albert Hofstadter (New York: Harper and Row, 1971), 149.

8. See Adam Sharr, *Heidegger's Hut* (Cambridge, Mass.: MIT Press, 2006).

9. Quoted by Amartya Sen in *The Argumentative Indian: Writings on Indian History, Culture and Identity* (London: Penguin, 2005), 5.

10. Quoted in Bernstein, *Oppenheimer,* 89.

11. David Cassidy, *J. Robert Oppenheimer and the American Century* (New York: Pi, 2005), 343.

12. Hannah Arendt, *The Human Condition* [1958], 2nd ed. (Chicago: University of Chicago Press, 1998), 176.

13. See ibid., 9, or again, 246.

14. Raymond Williams, "Culture," in Williams, *Keywords: A Vocabulary of Culture and Society* (London: Fontana, 1983), 87-93.

15. See Georg Simmel, "The Stranger," in *The Sociology of Georg Simmel*, trans. and ed. Kurt Wolff (New York: Free Press, 1964).

16. John Maynard Smith, *The Theory of Evolution* (Cambridge: Cambridge University Press, 1993), 311.

CHAPTER 1. The Troubled Craftsman

1. " 'Homeric Hymn to Hephaestus," in H. G. Evelyn-White, trans., *Hesiod, the Homeric Hymns, and Homerica* (Cambridge, Mass.: Harvard Loeb Classical Library, 1914), 447.

2. Indra Kagis McEwen, *Socrates' Ancestor: An Essay on Architectural Beginnings* (Cambridge, Mass.: MIT Press, 1997), 119. I am indebted to this brilliant essay for its rich store of definition and reference.

3. See ibid., 72-73, for a full list.

4. For a summary of the few literary descriptions of potters, see W. Miller, *Daedalus and Thespis: The Contributions of the Ancient Dramatic Poets to Our Knowledge of the Arts and Crafts of Greece*, 3 vols. in 5 (New York: Macmillan, 1929-1932), 3:690-693.

5. Aristotle *Metaphysics* 981a30-b2. The English translation is appears in Hugh Tredennick, ed., *The Metaphysics* (Cambridge, Mass.: Harvard Loeb Classical Library, 1933).

6. Again, my thanks to Indra Kagis McEwan for pointing this out.

7. See Richard Sennett, *Flesh and Stone: The Body and the City in Western Civilization* (New York: W. W. Norton, 1993), 42-43.

8. Plato *Symposium* 205b-c.

9. For a good general description, see Glyn Moody, *Rebel Code: Linus and the Open Source Revolution* (New York: Perseus, 2002).

10. The standards used by the Open Source Initiative can be found on http://opensource.org/docs/def_print.php.

11. See Eric S. Raymond, *The Cathedral and the Bazaar: Musings on Linux and Open Source by an Accidental Revolutionary* (Cambridge, Mass.: O'Reilly Linux, 1999).

12. Two views of the social problem involved are Eric Hippel and Georg von

Krogh, "Open Source Software and the 'Private Collective' Innovational Model," *Organization Science* 14 (2003), 209–233, and Sharma Srinarayan et al., "A Framework for Creating Hybrid-Open Source Software Communities," *Information Systems Journal* 12 (2002), 7–25.

13. See André Leroi-Gourhan, *Milieu et techniques,* vol. 2 (Paris: Albin-Michel, 1945), 606–624.

14. C. Wright Mills, *White Collar: The American Middle Classes* (New York: Oxford University Press, 1951), 220–223.

15. Karl Marx, *The Grundrisse,* trans. Martin Nicolaus (New York: Vintage, 1973), 301.

16. Ibid., 324.

17. Karl Marx, "Critique of the Gotha Program," in Karl Marx and Friedrich Engels, *Selected Works* (London: Lawrence and Wishart, 1968), 324.

18. Darren Thiel, "Builders: The Social Organisation of a Construction Site" (Ph.D. thesis, University of London, 2005).

19. Martin Fackler, "Japanese Fret That Quality Is in Decline," *New York Times,* Sept. 21, 2006, A1, C4.

20. Richard K. Lester and Michael J. Piore, *Innovation, the Missing Dimension* (Cambridge, Mass.: Harvard University Press, 2004), 98.

21. Ibid., 104.

22. The three books in this study are: Richard Sennett, *The Corrosion of Character: The Personal Consequences of Work in the New Capitalism* (New York: W. W. Norton, 1998); Sennett, *Respect in a World of Inequality* (New York: W. W. Norton, 2003); and Sennett, *The Culture of the New Capitalism* (New Haven and London: Yale University Press, 2006).

23. See Christopher Jencks, *Who Gets Ahead? The Determinants of Economic Success in America* (New York: Wiley, 1979); Gary Burtless and Christopher Jencks, "American Inequality and Its Consequences," discussion paper (Washington, D.C.: Brookings Institution, March 2003); and Alan Blinder, "Outsourcing: Bigger Than You Thought," *American Prospect,* November 2006, 44–46.

24. For this debate, see Robert D. Putnam, *Bowling Alone: The Collapse and Revival of American Community* (New York: Simon and Schuster, 2000), and Sennett, *Corrosion of Character.*

25. For a good general study, see Wayne Carlson, *A Critical History of Computer Graphics and Animation* (Ohio State University, 2003), available at http://accad.osu.edu/waynec/history/lessons.html.

26. Sherry Turkle, *Life on the Screen: Identity in the Age of the Internet* (New York: Simon and Schuster, 1995), 64, 281n20.

27. Quoted in Edward Robbins, *Why Architects Draw* (Cambridge, Mass.: MIT Press, 1994), 126.

28. Ibid.

29. Quoted in Sherry Turkle, "Seeing through Computers: Education in a Culture of Simulation (Advantages and Disadvantages of Computer Simulation)," *American Prospect,* March–April 1997, 81.

30. Elliot Felix, "Drawing Digitally," presentation at Urban Design Seminar, MIT, Cambridge, Mass., 4 October 2005.

31. Bent Flyvbjerg Nils Bruzelius, and Werner Rothengatter, *Megaprojects and Risk: An Anatomy of Ambition* (Cambridge: Cambridge University Press, 2003), 11–21. See also Peter Hall, *Great Planning Disasters* (Harmondsworth: Penguin, 1980).

32. For an excellent journalistic account of how piecework defines medical practice, see Atul Gawande, "Piecework," *New Yorker,* Apr. 4, 2005, 44–53.

33. The most concise statement of this view is Julian Legrand, *The Provision of Health Care: Is the Public Sector Ethically Superior to the Private Sector?* (London: LSE Books, 2001).

34. A good guide to views on practice appeared in the debate on the privatization of nursing at the 2006 conference of the Royal Council of Nursing. This material can be found on their Web site at http://www.rcn.org.uk/news/congress/2006/5.php.

35. The complete text of the speech can most easily be found online: http://bma.org.uk/ap.nsf/content/ARM2006JJohnson.

CHAPTER 2. The Workshop

1. Quoted, in English, in Peter Brown, *Augustine of Hippo: A Biography* (Berkeley: University of California Press, 1967), 143.

2. Augustine, *Sermons.* The Standard Edition authorized by the Vatican uses a common system of reference in all languages. This key passage occurs in 67,2.

3. See Richard Sennett, *Flesh and Stone: The Body and the City in Western Civilization* (New York: W. W. Norton, 1993), 152–153.

4. See Ernst Kantorowicz, *The King's Two Bodies: A Study in Mediaeval Political Theology* (Princeton, N.J.: Princeton University Press, 1981), 316ff.

5. Robert S. Lopez, *The Commercial Revolution of the Middle Ages, 950–1350* (Englewood Cliffs, N.J.: Prentice-Hall, 1971), 127.

6. Sennett, *Flesh and Stone,* 201.

7. Edward Lucie-Smith, *The Story of Craft* (New York: Van Nostrand, 1984), 115.

8. See J. F. Hayward, *Virtuoso Goldsmiths and the Triumph of Mannerism, 1540–1620* (New York: Rizzoli International, 1976).

9. Ibn Khaldun, *The Muqaddimah: An Introduction to History,* abridged ver-

sion, trans. Franz Rosenthal, ed. and abridged N. J. Dawood (Princeton, N.J.: Princeton University Press, 2004), 285–289.

10. Bronislaw Geremek, *Le salariat dans l'artisinat parisien aux XIIIe–XVe siècles: Étude sur la main d'oeuvre au moyen âge* (Paris: Mouton, 1968), 42.

11. Gervase Rosser, "Crafts, Guilds and the Negotiation of Work in the Medieval Town," *Past and Present* 154 (February 1997), 9.

12. See Hayward, *Virtuoso Goldsmiths.*

13. See Benjamin Woolley, *The Queen's Conjurer: The Science and Magic of Dr. John Dee, Adviser to Queen Elizabeth I* (New York: Holt, 2001), 251.

14. Keith Thomas, *Religion and the Decline of Magic* (London: Penguin, 1991), 321.

15. S. R. Epstein, "Guilds, Apprenticeship, and Technological Change," *Journal of Economic History* 58 (1998), 691.

16. See Phillippe Ariès, *Centuries of Childhood: A Social History of Family Life,* trans. Robert Baldick (New York: Alfred A. Knopf, 1962).

17. For an interesting discussion of this, see Rosser, "Crafts, Guilds, and Negotiation of Work," 16–17.

18. Ibid., 17.

19. See Rudolf and Margot Wittkower, *Born under Saturn; The Character and Conduct of Artists: A Documented History from Antiquity to the French Revolution* (London: Weidenfeld and Nicolson, 1963), 91–95,134–135; or again, Lucie-Smith, *Story of Craft,* 149.

20. See Wittkower and Wittkower, *Born under Saturn,* 139–142.

21. Benvenuto Cellini, *Autobiography,* trans. George Bull (London: Penguin, 1998), xix. The translator, like all scholars of Cellini, owes much to the textual labors of Paolo Rossi. Rossi struggled with establishing the text of this sonnet, and even in clear copy the Italian is not straightforward in sense. I have taken the liberty of inserting "only" before "one" in the lines I have quoted because this is what the boast seems meant to imply; remove my insertion, and it remains an astounding statement.

22. T. E. Heslop, "Hierarchies and Medieval Art," in Peter Dormer, ed., *The Culture of Craft* (Manchester: Manchester University Press, 1997), 59.

23. See John Hale, *The Civilization of Europe in the Renaissance* (New York: Atheneum, 1994), 279–281.

24. The following account is indebted to the Royal Commission on the Historical Monuments of England, which has reconstructed the sequence of building in "The Cathedral Church of the Blessed Virgin Mary, Salisbury" from 1220 to 1900. I thank Robert Scott for making this map available.

25. Augustine quoted in Stephen J. Greenblatt, *Renaissance Self-Fashioning: From More to Shakespeare* (Chicago: University of Chicago Press, 1981), 2.

26. Benvenuto Cellini, *Autobiography*, trans. George Bull (London: Penguin, 1998), xiv–xv.

27. See Elizabeth Wilson, *Mstislav Rostropovich: The Legend of Class 19* (London: Faber and Faber, 2007), chaps. 11, 12.

28. See Toby Faber, *Stradivarius* (London: MacMillan, 2004), 50–66. Though Faber is both accurate and evocative, the reader in search of a more technical account should consult what is still the greatest of all Stradivarius studies: William H. Hill, Arthur F. Hill, and Alfred Ebsworth, *Antonio Stradivari* [1902] (New York: Dover, 1963). Another biographical source is Charles Beare and Bruce Carlson, *Antonio Stradivari: The Cremona Exhibition of 1987* (London: J. and A. Beare, 1993).

29. See Faber, *Stradivarius*, 59.

30. Duane Rosengard and Carlo Chiesa, "Guarneri del Gesù: A Brief History," in Metropolitan Museum catalogue for the exhibition, *The Violin Masterpieces of Guarneri del Gesù* (London: Peter Biddulph, 1994), 15.

31. Almost every issue of the luthiers' professional journal, *The Strad,* is occupied with these problems. A particularly good guide to the varnishing issues in particular remains L. M. Condax, *Final Summary Report of the Violin Varnish Research Project* (Pittsburgh: n.p., 1970).

32. John Donne, *Complete Poetry of John Donne,* ed. John Hayward (London: Nonesuch, 1929), 365.

33. Robert K. Merton, *On the Shoulders of Giants* (New York: Free Press 1965).

34. Etienne de la Boétie, *The Politics of Obedience: The Discourse of Voluntary Servitude* [1552–53], trans. Harry Kurz (Auburn, Ala.: Mises Institute, 1975), 42.

CHAPTER 3. Machines

1. See Simon Schama, *The Embarrassment of Riches: An Interpretation of Dutch Culture in the Golden Age,* 2nd ed. (London: Fontana, 1988).

2. Jerry Brotton and Lisa Jardine, *Global Interests: Renaissance Art between East and West* (Ithaca, N.Y.: Cornell University Press, 2000).

3. John Hale, *The Civilization of Europe in the Renaissance* (New York: Atheneum, 1994), 266.

4. Werner Sombart, *Luxury and Capitalism* [1913], trans. W. R. Dittmar (Ann Arbor: University of Michigan Press, 1967), esp. 58–112.

5. See Geoffrey Scott, *The Architecture of Humanism: A Study in the History of Taste* (Princeton, N.J.: Architectural Press, 1980).

6. These replicants have speaking roles in Thomas Pynchon's novel *Mason and Dixon* (New York: Henry Holt, 1997). Gaby Wood provides more precise and

purely historical information: see Wood, *Living Dolls* (London: Faber and Faber, 2002), 21–24.

7. Wood, *Living Dolls*, 38.

8. Immanuel Kant, "Beantwortung der Frage: Was ist Aufklärung?" *Berlinische Monatsschrift* 4 (1984), 481. I am indebted to James Schmidt for this English translation, in Schmidt, *What Is Enlightenment? Eighteenth-Century Answers and Twentieth-Century Questions* (Berkeley: University of California Press, 1996), 58.

9. Moses Mendelssohn, "Über die Frage: 'Was heisst aufklären?'" *Berlinische Monatsschrift* 4 (1784), 193.

10. Mendelssohn's original reply was published in the *Berlinische Monatsscrift* 4 (1784), 193–200; the phrase comes from a letter to August v. Hennings in that same year, appearing in Moses Mendelssohn, *Gesammelte Schriften Jubiläumsausgabe*, vol. 13, *Briefwechsel III* (Stuttgart: Frommann, 1977) 234.

11. I am grateful to the late Karl Weintraub, of the University of Chicago, for drawing the connection between Mendelssohn and Diderot to my attention. Unfortunately, Weintraub did not live to complete his essay on their relations. His extant writings (he wrote little but always authoritatively) are best found in Karl Weintraub, *Visions of Culture* (Chicago: University of Chicago Press, 1969).

12. The original text is Denis Diderot and Jean d'Alembert, *Encyclopédie, ou Dictionnaire raisonné des sciences, des arts et des métiers, par une société de gens de lettres*, 28 vols. (Paris: various printers, 1751–1772). I'll be using in English translation the Dover edition (1959) of parts of this immense work, well if anonymously translated. To understand the complexities of the publishing enterprise, see Robert Darnton, *The Business of Enlightenment: A Publishing History of the Encyclopédie, 1775–1800* (Cambridge, Mass.: Belknap Press of Harvard University Press, 1979).

13. The best life in English remains, in my view, N. Furbank, *Diderot* (London: Secker and Warburg, 1992).

14. Philipp Blom, *Encyclopédie* (London: Fourth Estate, 2004), 43–44.

15. Adam Smith, *The Theory of Moral Sentiments* [1759] (Oxford: Oxford University Press, 1979), 9.

16. David Hume, *A Treatise of Human Nature*, ed. E. C. Mossner (London: Penguin, 1985), 627.

17. Jerrold Siegel, *The Idea of the Self: Thought and Experience in Western Europe since the Seventeenth Century* (Cambridge: Cambridge University Press, 2005), 352.

18. C. Wright Mills, *The Sociological Imagination* (Oxford: Oxford University Press, 1959), 223; Adriano Tilgher, *Work: What It Has Meant to Men through the Ages* (New York: Harcourt, Brace, 1930), 63.

19. See Albert O. Hirschmann, *The Passions and the Interests: Political Arguments for Capitalism before Its Triumph* (Princeton, N.J.: Princeton University Press, 1992).

20. Quoted in Furbank, *Diderot*, 40.

21. Ibid., as for the sentences quoted in the next paragraphs.

22. Sabine Melchior-Bonnet, *The Mirror: A History*, trans. Katharine H. Jewett (London: Routledge, 2002), 54.

23. The reader interested in teasing out this complicated history might look at three classics: Lawrence Stone, *Family, Sex, and Marriage in England, 1500–1800* (London: Penguin, 1990); Edward Shorter, *Making of the Modern Family* (London: Fontana, 1977); and Philippe Ariès, *Centuries of Childhood: A Social History of Family Life*, trans. Robert Baldick (London: Penguin, 1973).

24. See Francis Steegmuller, *A Woman, a Man, and Two Kingdoms: The Story of Madame D'Épinay and the Abbé Galiani* (New York: Alfred A. Knopf, 1991), and Ruth Plaut Weinreb, *Eagle in a Gauze Cage: Louise D'Epinay, Femme de Lettres* (New York: AMS Press, 1993).

25. Adam Smith, *The Wealth of Nations*, vol. 1 [1776] (London: Methuen, 1961), 302–3.

26. David Brody, *Steelworkers in America*, rev. ed. (Urbana, Ill.: University of Illinois Press, 1998), gives an excellent general picture of the steel industry in the nineteenth century.

27. See Richard Sennett, *The Corrosion of Character* (New York: W. W. Norton, 1998), 122–135.

28. The two volumes of Tim Hilton's biography are *John Ruskin, The Early Years* and *John Ruskin, The Later Years* (New Haven and London: Yale University Press, 1985, 2000).

29. For a review of this literature, see Richard Sennett, *The Culture of the New Capitalism* (New Haven and London: Yale University Press, 2006), chap. 3.

30. The concept of a "type-form" owes to Harvey Molotch, *Where Stuff Comes From: How Toasters, Toilets, Cars, Computers, and Many Others Things Come to Be as They Are* (New York: Routledge, 2003), 97, 103–105.

31. For information on the history of plate glass, see Richard Sennett, *The Conscience of the Eye: The Design and Social Life of Cities* (New York: Alfred A. Knopf, 1990), 106–114.

32. The reader might want to know that I've described both the Great Exposition and in particular Count Dunin's robot in more detail in a historical novel. See Richard Sennett, *Palais-Royal* (New York: Alfred A. Knopf, 1987), 228–237.

33. Quoted in Hilton, *Ruskin, The Early Years*, 202–203.

34. John Ruskin, *The Stones of Venice* [1851–1853] (New York: Da Capo, 2003), 35.

35. The following is summarized from John Ruskin, *The Seven Lamps of Architecture,* in the original 1849 "working-man's edition" (reprint, London: George Routledge and Sons, 1901).

36. For a full account of this phenomenon, see Richard Sennett, *The Fall of Public Man* (New York: Alfred A. Knopf, 1977), pt. 3.

37. Thorstein Veblen, *The Theory of the Leisure Class* [1899], in *The Portable Veblen,* ed. Max Lerner (New York: Viking, 1948), 192.

38. A useful compendium of Veblen's rather scattered ideas on conspicuous consumption is *Penguin Great Ideas: Conspicuous Consumption* (London: Penguin, 2005).

39. Mills, *Sociological Imagination,* 224.

CHAPTER 4. Material Consciousness

1. For the potter's wheel, see Joseph Noble, "Pottery Manufacture," in Carl Roebuck, ed., *The Muses at Work: Arts, Crafts, and Professions in Ancient Greece and Rome* (Cambridge, Mass.: MIT Press, 1969), 120–122.

2. Suzanne Staubach, *Clay: The History and Evolution of Humankind's Relationship with Earth's Most Primal Element* (New York: Berkley, 2005), 67.

3. John Boardman, *The History of Greek Vases* (London: Thames and Hudson, 2001), 40.

4. See E. R. Dodds, *The Greeks and the Irrational,* 2nd ed. (Berkeley: University of California Press, 2004), 135–144.

5. For an excellent summary, see Richard C. Vitzthum, *Materialism: An Affirmative History and Definition* (Amherst, N.Y.: Prometheus Books, 1995), 25–30.

6. Plato *Republic* 509d–513e.

7. Plato *Theaetitus* 181b–190a.

8. See Andrea Wilson Nightingale, *Spectacles of Truth in Classical Greek Philosophy: Theoria in Its Cultural Context* (Cambridge: Cambridge University Press, 2005).

9. M. F. Burnyeat, "Long Walk to Wisdom," *TLS,* Feb. 24, 2006, 9.

10. Harvey Molotch, *Where Stuff Comes From: How Toasters, Toilets, Cars, Computers, and Many Others Things Come to Be as They Are* (New York: Routledge, 2003), 113.

11. See Henry Petroski, *To Engineer Is Human: The Role of Failure in Successful Design* (London: MacMillan, 1985), esp. 75–84.

12. See Annette B. Weiner, "Why Cloth?" in Weiner and Jane Schneider, eds., *Cloth and Human Experience* (Washington, D.C.: Smithsonian Institution Press, 1989), 33.

13. For a simple statement, see Claude Lévi-Strauss, "The Culinary Triangle,"

New Society, Dec. 22, 1966, 937–940. A full explication of the culinary triangle appears in Lévi-Strauss, *Introduction to a Science of Mythology,* vol. 3, *The Origin of Table Manners,* trans. John and Doreen Weightman (New York: Harper and Row, 1978).

14. Michael Symons, *A History of Cooks and Cooking* (London: Prospect, 2001), 114, is wrong to believe that this famous formula represents status and prestige; for Lévi-Strauss the "thinking physiology" unifies all human sensation through symbols.

15. See James W. P. Campbell and Will Pryce, *Brick: A World History* (London: Thames and Hudson, 2003), 14–15.

16. Frank E. Brown, *Roman Architecture* (New York: G. Braziller, 1981).

17. See Joseph Rykwert, *The Idea of a Town: The Anthropology of Urban Form in Rome, Italy and the Ancient World* (Princeton, N.J.: Princeton University Press, 1976).

18. See James Packer, "Roman Imperial Building," in Roebuck, ed., *Muses at Work,* 42–43.

19. Keith Hopkins, *Conquerors and Slaves* (Cambridge: Cambridge University Press, 1987?).

20. Vitruvius, *On Architecture,* ed. Frank Granger (Cambridge, Mass.: Harvard Loeb Classical Library, 1931), 1.1.15–16.

21. Vitruvius, *The Ten Books of Architecture,* trans. Morris Vicky Morgan (New York: Dover, 1960) see 2.3.1–4, 2.8.16–20, 7.1.4–7.

22. For this observation, I am indebted to Campbell and Pryce, *Brick,* 44.

23. Alec Clifton-Taylor, *The Pattern of English Building* (London: Faber and Faber, 1972), 242.

24. See M. I. Finley, *Ancient Slavery and Modern Ideology* (London: Chatto and Windus, 1980).

25. Clifton-Taylor, *Pattern of English Building,* 232; the embodied language appeared in journals such as *Builder's Magazine,* cited in note 28, below.

26. See Jean André Rouquet, *The Present State of the Arts in England* [1756] (London: Cornmarket, 1979), 44ff.

27. See *Builder's Magazine,* a periodical published from 1774 to 1778; its descriptive language is analyzed in Martin Weil, "Interior Details in Eighteenth-Century Architectural Books," *Bulletin of the Association for Preservation Technology* 10, no. 4 (1978), 47–66.

28. Clifton-Taylor, *Pattern of English Building,* 369.

29. See Richard Sennett, *The Fall of Public Man* (New York: Alfred A. Knopf, 1977), pt. 2.

30. Alvar Aalto, quoted in Campbell and Pryce, *Brick,* 271.

31. William Carlos Williams, *Imaginations* (New York: New Directions, 1970), 110. See the excellent discussion of this declaration and its associations in Bill Brown, *A Sense of Things: The Object Matter of American Literature* (Chicago: University of Chicago Press, 2003), 1–4.

CHAPTER 5. The Hand

1. Or so he is quoted by Raymond Tallis, *The Hand: A Philosophical Inquiry in Human Being* (Edinburgh: Edinburgh University Press, 2003), 4.

2. Charles Bell, *The Hand, Its Mechanism and Vital Endowments, as Evincing Design* (London, 1833). This is the fourth of the so-called Bridgewater Treatises on "the power, wisdom and goodness of God as manifested in the creation."

3. Charles Darwin, *The Descent of Man* [1879], ed. James Moore and Adrian Desmond (London: Penguin, 2004), 71–75.

4. Frederick Wood Jones, *The Principles of Anatomy as Seen in the Hand* (Baltimore: Williams and Williams, 1942), 298–299.

5. Tallis, *Hand*, 24.

6. See John Napier, *Hands,* rev. ed., rev. Russell H. Tuttle (Princeton, N.J.: Princeton University Press, 1993), 55ff. An excellent popular summary of this change of views appears in Frank R. Wilson, *The Hand: How Its Use Shapes the Brain, Language, and Human Culture* (New York: Pantheon, 1998), 112–146.

7. Mary Marzke, "Evolutionary Development of the Human Thumb," in *Hand Clinics* 8, no. 1 (February 1992), 1–8. See also Marzke, "Precision Grips, Hand Morphology, and Tools," *American Journal of Physical Anthropology* 102 (1997), 91–110.

8. See K. Müller and V. Homberg, "Development of Speed of Repetitive Movements in Children . . . ," *Neuroscience Letters* 144 (1992), 57–60.

9. See Charles Sherrington, *The Integrative Action of the Nervous System* (New York: Scribner's Sons, 1906).

10. Wilson, *Hand,* 99.

11. A. P. Martinich, *Hobbes: A Biography* (Cambridge: Cambridge University Press, 1999).

12. Beryl Markham, *West with the Night,* new ed. (London: Virago, 1984).

13. See Tallis, *Hand,* chap. 11, esp. 329–331.

14. See Shinichi Suzuki, *Nurtured by Love: A New Approach to Talent Education* (Miami, Fla.: Warner, 1968).

15. D. W. Winnicott, *Playing and Reality* (London: Routledge, 1971); John Bowlby, *A Secure Base: Parent-Child Attachment and Healthy Human Development* (London: Routledge, 1988.

16. David Sudnow, *Ways of the Hand: A Rewritten Account,* 2nd ed. (Cambridge, Mass.: MIT Press, 2001).

17. Ibid., 84.

18. For an interesting discussion of this phenomenon, see Julie Lyonn Lieberman, "The Slide," *Strad* 116 (July 2005), 69.

19. See Michael C. Corballis, *The Lopsided Ape: Evolution of the Generative Mind* (New York: Oxford University Press, 1991).

20. Yves Guiard, "Asymmetric Division of Labor in Human Bimanual Action," *Journal of Motor Behavior* 19, no. 4 (1987), 488–502.

21. For this history, see Michael Symons, *A History of Cooks and Cooking* (London: Prospect, 2001), 144.

22. Norbert Elias, *The Civilizing Process,* rev. ed., trans. Edmund Jephcott (Oxford: Blackwell, 1994), 104. The reader should note that the revised edition incorporates some historical material unknown to the author in the original edition, *Über den Prozess der Zivilisation,* in 1939.

23. Cited in ibid., 78.

24. David Knechtges, "A Literary Feast: Food in Early Chinese Literature," *Journal of the American Oriental Society* 106 (1986), 49–63.

25. John Stevens, *Zen Bow, Zen Arrow: The Life and Teachings of Awa Kenzo* (London: Shambhala, 2007).

26. Elias, *Civilizing Process,* 105.

27. Ibid., 415.

28. For an account of how the Powell and Rumsfeld strategies conflicted in the war America began in Iraq in 2003, see Michael R. Gordon and Bernard E. Trainor, *Cobra II* (New York: Pantheon, 2006).

29. See, e.g., Neil Postman, *Amusing Ourselves to Death: Public Discourse in the Age of Show Business* (New York: Viking, 1985).

30. Daniel Levitin, *This Is Your Brain on Music* (New York: Dutton, 2006), 193.

31. Erin O'Connor, "Embodied Knowledge: The Experience of Meaning and the Struggle towards Proficiency in Glassblowing," *Ethnography* 6, no. 2 (2005), 183–204.

32. Ibid., 188–189.

33. Maurice Merleau-Ponty, *The Phenomenology of Perception* [1945] (New York: Humanities Press, 1962).

34. Michael Polanyi, *Personal Knowledge: Towards a Post-Critical Philosophy* (Chicago: University of Chicago Press, 1962), 55.

CHAPTER 6. Expressive Instructions

1. Frank R. Wilson, *The Hand: How Its Use Shapes the Brain, Language, and Human Culture* (New York: Pantheon, 1998), 204–207.

2. Sheila Hale, *The Man Who Lost His Language: A Case of Aphasia*, rev. ed. (London: Jessica Kingsley, 2007).

3. See D. Armstrong, W. Stokoe, and S. Wilcox, *Gesture and the Nature of Language* (Cambridge: Cambridge University Press, 1995).

4. See Oliver Sacks, *Seeing Voices: A Journey into the World of the Deaf* (Berkeley: University of California Press, 1989).

5. Richard Olney, *The French Menu Cookbook* (Boston: Godine, 1985), 206.

6. Julia Child and Simone Beck, *Mastering the Art of French Cooking*, vol. 2 (New York: Alfred A. Knopf, 1970), 362.

7. Elizabeth David, *French Provincial Cooking* (London: Penguin, 1960, rev. 1970), 402.

8. Max Black, "How Metaphors Work: A Reply to Donald Davidson," in Sheldon Sacks, ed., *On Metaphor* (Chicago: University of Chicago Press, 1979), 181–192; Donald Davidson, "What Metaphors Mean" in ibid., 29–45; Roman Jakobson, "Two Types of Language and Two Types of Disturbances," reprinted in Jakobson, *On Language*, ed. Linda R. Waugh and Monique Monville-Burston (Cambridge, Mass.: Harvard University Press, 1995).

CHAPTER 7. Arousing Tools

1. Reproduced in James Parakilas et al., *Piano Roles: Three Hundred Years of Life with the Piano* (New Haven and London: Yale University Press, 2002), fig. 8.

2. See the admirable book by David Freedberg, *The Eye of the Lynx: Galileo, His Friends, and the Beginnings of Modern Natural History* (Chicago: University of Chicago Press, 2003), 152–153.

3. Quoted, in this context, in Steven Shapin, *The Scientific Revolution* (Chicago: University of Chicago Press, 1998), 28. Shapin's book, along with that of Peter Dear, *Revolutionizing the Sciences: European Knowledge and Its Ambitions, 1500–1700* (Basingstoke: Palgrave, 2001), provides an excellent overview.

4. Cited in Shapin, *Scientific Revolution*, 147.

5. Herbert Butterfield, *The Origins of Modern Science*, rev. ed. (New York: Free Press, 1965), 106.

6. Andrea Carlino, *Books of the Body: Anatomical Ritual and Renaissance Learning*, trans. John Tedeschi and Anne Tedeschi (Chicago: University of Chicago Press, 1999), 1.

7. See the excellent explanation of Peter Dear, *Revolutionizing the Sciences: European Knowledge and Its Ambitions, 1500–1700* (Basingstoke: Palgrave, 2001), 39.

8. Roy Porter, *Flesh in the Age of Reason: The Modern Foundations of Body and Soul* (London: Penguin, 2003), 133.

9. Douglas Harper, *Working Knowledge: Skill and Community in a Small Shop* (Chicago: University of Chicago Press, 1987), 21.

10. Dear, *Revolutionizing the Sciences*, 138.

11. Francis Bacon, *Novum Organum*, trans. Peter Urbach and John Gibson (Chicago: Open Court, 2000), 225.

12. Richard Rorty, *Philosophy and the Mirror of Nature* (Princeton, N.J.: Princeton University Press, 1981).

13. See Robert Hooke, *Micrographia* [1665] (reprint, New York: Dover, 2003), 181.

14. Christopher Wren, letter to William Petty, ca. 1656–1658, quoted in Adrian Tinniswood, *His Invention so Fertile: A Life of Christopher Wren* (London: Pimlico, 2002), 36.

15. Ibid., 149.

16. Ibid., 154.

17. Ibid.

18. Jenny Uglow, *The Lunar Men: Five Friends Whose Curiosity Changed the World* (London: Faber and Faber, 2002), 11, 428.

19. This phrase from G. W. F. Hegel's *Philosophy of Fine Art* is translated by F. P. B. Osmaston and appears in Hazard Adams, ed., *Critical Theory since Plato*, rev. ed. (London: Heinle and Heinle, 1992), 538.

20. Edmund Burke, *A Philosophical Enquiry into the Origins of Our Ideas of the Sublime and Beautiful* (1757). I'll list the references in the Standard Edition and in the Boulton edition of 1958, which purged the text of impurities: 3.27 (Boulton, 124); 2.22 (Boulton, 86).

21. Quoted in Mary Shelley, *Frankenstein; or, The Modern Prometheus* [1818] (London: Penguin, 1992), xxii.

22. Ibid., 43.

23. The process is helpfully elucidated by Maurice Hindle, editor of the current Penguin edition of *Frankenstein*, at 267.

24. Ibid., 52.

25. Available at http://www.foresight.gov.uk/index.html.

26. Noel Sharkey quoted in James Randerson, "Forget Robot Rights, Experts Say, Use Them for Public Safety," *Guardian*, Apr. 24, 2007, 10.

27. There are many editions of Hobbes's *Leviathan*. I'll be using the text as carefully established by Richard Tuck in the series Cambridge Texts in the History of Political Thought. Because readers may own different versions, for reference purposes I'll provide the chapter and section divisions that are by now standard in

Hobbes scholarship, as well as page numbers in this edition. Thomas Hobbes, *Leviathan,* ed. Richard Tuck (Cambridge: Cambridge University Press, 1996), 2.5.15.

28. See Peter Dear, *Revolutionizing the Sciences* (Basingstoke: Palgrave, 2001), 61–62, from which the phrases by Bacon are cited. This text is an excellent introduction to changes in seventeenth-century science.

CHAPTER 8. Resistance and Ambiguity

1. William R. B. Acker, *Kyudo: The Japanese Art of Archery* (Boston: Tuttle, 1998).

2. Lewis Mumford, *Technics and Civilization* (New York: Harcourt Brace, 1934), 69–70.

3. David Freedberg, *The Eye of the Lynx: Galileo, His Friends, and the Beginnings of Modern Natural History* (Chicago: University of Chicago Press, 2003), 60.

4. The historian Rosalind Williams gives a brief account of this story in *Notes on the Underground: An Essay on Technology, Society, and the Imagination* (Cambridge, Mass.: MIT Press, 1992), 75–77.

5. The history of this work is also recounted in Steven Brindle, *Brunel: The Man Who Built the World* (London: Weidenfeld and Nicholson, 2005), 40–50, 64–66.

6. See Gustave Le Bon, *The Crowd: A Study of the Popular Mind* [1896] (New York: Dover, 2002).

7. Leon Festinger, *A Theory of Cognitive Dissonance* (Stanford, Calif.: Stanford University Press, 1957). Bateson prepared the way for this work in his theory of the "double bind"; see Gregory Bateson et al., "Toward a Theory of Schizophrenia," *Behavioral Science* 1 (1956), 251–264.

8. Henry Petroski, *To Engineer Is Human: The Role of Failure in Successful Design* (London: MacMillan, 1985), 216–217.

9. Coosje Van Bruggen, *Frank O. Gehry: Guggenheim Museum, Bilbao* (New York: Solomon R. Guggenheim Foundation, 1997), app. 2, statement by Frank Gehry, "Gehry on Titanium," 141, from which subsequent quotations are also taken.

10. John Dewey, *Art as Experience* (New York: Capricorn, 1934), 15.

11. For a fuller explanation, see Richard Sennett, *Flesh and Stone: The Body and the City in Western Civilization* (New York: W. W. Norton, 1993), 212–250.

12. See Liane Lefaivre, "Space, Place, and Play," in Liane Lefaivre and Ingeborg de Roode, eds., *Aldo van Eyck: The Playgrounds and the City* (Rotterdam: NAi in cooperation with Stedelijk Museum, Amsterdam, 2002), 25.

13. Illustrated in ibid., 6.

14. Illustrated in ibid., 20.

15. Illustrated in ibid., 19.

16. Aldo van Eyck, "Whatever Space and Time Mean, Place and Occasion Mean More," *Forum* 4 (1960–1961), 121.

CHAPTER 9. Quality-Driven Work

1. The most useful guide to his work is W. Edwards Deming, *The New Economics for Industry, Government, and Education*, 2nd ed. (Cambridge, Mass.: MIT Press, 2000).

2. Elton Mayo et al., *The Human Problems of an Industrial Civilization* (New York: Macmillan, 1933).

3. Tom Peters and Robert Waterman, *In Search of Excellence* (New York: HarperCollins, 1984).

4. See Pierre Bourdieu, *Distinction: A Social Critique of the Judgement of Taste*, trans. Robert Nice (London: Routledge and Kegan Paul, 1986).

5. Elliott A. Krause, *Death of the Guilds: Professions, States, and the Advance of Capitalism, 1930 to the Present* (New Haven and London: Yale University Press, 1996); Robert Perrucci and Joel E. Gerstl, *Profession without Community: Engineers in American Society* (New York: Random House, 1969).

6. See Kenneth Holyoke, "Symbolic Connectionism: Toward Third-generation Theories of Expertise," in K. Anders Ericsson and Jacqui Smith, eds., *Toward a General Theory of Expertise: Prospects and Limits* (Cambridge: Cambridge University Press, 1991), 303–335.

7. Vilma Patel and Guy Groen, "The Nature of Medical Expertise," in Ericsson and Smith, eds., *General Theory of Expertise*, 93–125.

8. Douglas Harper, *Working Knowledge: Skill and Community in a Small Shop* (Chicago: University of Chicago Press, 1987), 21.

9. A foundational piece of research here is William Kintch, "The Role of Knowledge in Discourse Comprehension: A Construction-Integration Model," *Psychological Review* 95 (1987), 163–182.

10. Howard Gardner, Mihaly Csikszentmihaly, and William Damon, *Good Work: When Excellence and Ethics Meet* (New York: Basic Books, 2002).

11. Matthew Gill, "Accountants' Truth: Argumentation, Performance and Ethics in the Construction of Knowledge by Accountants in the City of London" (Ph.D. thesis, University of London, 2006).

12. Richard Sennett, *The Corrosion of Character: The Personal Consequences of Work in the New Capitalism* (New York: W. W. Norton, 1998), 64–75.

13. See Miriam Adderholdt, *Perfectionism: What's Bad about Being Too Good* (Minneapolis: Free Spirit, 1999), and Thomas Hurka, *Perfectionism* (Oxford: Oxford University Press, 1993).

14. Otto F. Kernberg, *Borderline Conditions and Pathological Narcissicism* (New York: J. Aronson, 1975).

15. These labels have been the subject on an internal debate between Kernberg and the analyst Heinz Kohut. See Gildo Consolini, "Kernberg versus Kohut: A (Case) Study in Contrasts," *Clinical Social Work Journal* 27 (1999), 71–86.

16. Max Weber, *The Protestant Ethic and the Spirit of Capitalism.* The standard English translation is by Talcott Parsons (London: Allen and Unwin, 1976); the translation is more wooden than Weber's German. This passage, as translated by Martin Green, appears in Martin Green, *The Von Richthofen Sisters; The Triumphant and the Tragic Modes of Love: Else and Frieda von Richthofen, Otto Gross, Max Weber, and D. H. Lawrence, in the Years 1870–1970* (New York: Basic Books, 1974), 152.

17. Quoted in Paul Wijdeveld, *Ludwig Wittgenstein, Architect,* 2nd ed. (Amsterdam: Pepin, 2000), 173.

18. Quoted in ibid., 174.

19. Hermine Wittgenstein, "Familienerinnerungen," manuscript, quoted in ibid., 148.

20. Ibid.

21. Ludwig Wittgenstein, *Philosophical Investigations,* dual-language, 3rd ed. (Oxford: Blackwell, 2002), 208e–209e.

22. See Max Weber, "Science as a Vocation," in Weber, *From Max Weber: Essays in Sociology,* trans. Hans Gerth and C. Wright Mills (New York: Oxford University Press, 1958).

23. Trevor Blackwell and Jeremy Seabrook, "Len Greenham," in Blackwell and Seabrook, *Talking Work* (London: Faber and Faber, 1996), 25–30.

24. Ibid., 27.

25. See Simon Head, *The New Ruthless Economy: Work and Power in the Digital Age* (Oxford: Oxford University Press, 2005), chaps. 1, 9, 10.

CHAPTER 10. Ability

1. Friedrich Schiller, *On the Aesthetic Education of Man,* trans. Reginal Snell (Mineola, N.Y.: Dover, 2004). In the passage quoted from the fourteenth letter, I have taken the first phrase from page 75, the second from page 74.

2. This is a tantalizing subject that I am tempted, but forbid myself, to pursue. The two key texts are Freud's *Interpretation of Dreams,* and his writings on infantile sexuality in vol. 17 of *The Complete Works of Sigmund Freud,* trans. James Strachey.

3. See Johan Huizinga, *Homo Ludens* (London: Routledge, 1998).

4. Clifford Geertz, *The Interpretation of Cultures: Selected Essays* (London: Hutchinson, 1975).

5. See Erik Erikson, *Childhood and Society* (New York: Vintage, 1995). See also Erikson, *Toys and Reasons: Stages in the Ritualization of Experience* (New York: W. W. Norton, 1977).

6. Erikson, *Toys and Reasons*.

7. A foundational text in a large literature is Mihaly Csikszentmihalyi, *Beyond Boredom and Anxiety: Experiencing Flow in Work and Play* (New York: Jossey-Bass, 2000).

8. See Jerome Bruner and Helen Weinreich-Haste, *Making Sense: The Child's Construction of the World* (London: Methuen, 1987), and, as this book's basis, Jerome Bruner, *On Knowing* (Cambridge, Mass.: Harvard University Press, 1962).

9. The most accessible study I have read on this subject is Daniel Levitin, *This Is Your Brain on Music* (New York: Dutton, 2006), esp. 84–85. (The reader should not be put off by the unfortunate title; this is an excellent study.) More technical information appears throughout Isabelle Peretz and Robert J. Zatorre, eds., *The Cognitive Neuroscience of Music* (Oxford: Oxford University Press, 2003).

10. If I've understood right, this is the view of Gerald M. Edelman and Giulio Tononi in *A Universe of Consciousness: How Matter Becomes Imagination* (New York: Basic Books, 2000).

11. *See* Steven Pinker, *The Language Instinct* (New York: Morrow, 1994), and Pinker, *The Blank Slate: The Denial of Human Nature in Modern Intellectual Life* (New York: Viking, 2002).

12. Richard Lewontin, "After the Genome, What Then?" *New York Review of Books*, July 19, 2001.

13. Plato *Republic* 614b2–621b6.

14. See *Stanford-Binet Intelligence Scales*, 5th ed. (New York: Riverside, 2004).

15. The reader interesting in this infamous story might look at Richard J. Herrnstein and Charles Murray, *The Bell Curve: Intelligence and Class Structure in American Life* (New York: Free Press, 1994), and its critics: see Charles Lane, "The Tainted Sources of the Bell Curve," *New York Review of Books*, Dec. 1, 1994.

16. The best guide to his work remains an early book: Howard Gardner, *Frames of Mind: The Theory of Multiple Intelligences* (New York: Basic Books, 1983).

17. I have taken the liberty of drawing this example from another of my books, *The Culture of the New Capitalism* (New Haven and London: Yale University Press, 2006), 119.

18. See ibid., chap. 2.

Conclusion

1. See Ibn Khaldûn, *The Muqaddimah: An Introduction to History,* abridged ed., trans. Franz Rosenthal (Princeton, N.J.: Princeton University Press, 2004), 297–332; Confucius, *The Analects of Confucius,* trans. Arthur Waley (London: Allen and Unwin, 1938).

2. Pragmatism in its current state is illuminated by Hans Joas, *The Creativity of Action,* trans. Jeremy Gaines and Paul Keast (Chicago: University of Chicago Press, 1996); William Eggington and Mike Sandbothe, eds., *The Pragmatic Turn in Philosophy* (Albany: State University Press of New York, 2004); Richard Rorty, *Contingency, Irony, and Solidarity* (Cambridge: Cambridge University Press, 1989); and Richard Bernstein, "The Resurgence of Pragmatism," *Social Research* 59 (1992), 813–840.

3. Hannah Arendt, *The Human Condition* [1958], 2nd ed. (Chicago: University of Chicago Press, 1998), 108.

4. John Dewey, *Democracy and Education* [1916] (New York: Macmillan, 1969).241–242.

5. A criticism leveled at my own work, for instance, by Sheldon Wolin; see "The Rise of Private Man," *New York Review of Books,* Apr. 14, 1977.

6. Homer, *The Iliad,* trans. A. T. Murray (Cambridge, Mass.: Harvard-Loeb Classical Library, 1924). Houses: 1.603–4; chariots: 18.373–77; jewelry: 18.400–402.

7. See Kristina Berggren, "Homo Faber or Homo Symbolicus? The Fascination with Copper in the Sixth Millennium," *Transoxiana* 8 (June 2004).

8. Hesiod, *Theogony, Works and Days, Testimonia,* trans. Glenn W. Most (Cambridge, Mass.: Loeb Classical Library, Harvard University Press, 2006), 51.

9. See Hannah Arendt, *Eichmann in Jerusalem: A Report on the Banality of Evil* (New York: Harcourt, Brace, Jovanovich, 1963). The best revisionist history in English is David Cesarani, *Becoming Eichmann* (Cambridge: Da Capo, 2005).

10. The text of the Russell-Einstein manifesto can be found online at www.pugwash.org/about/manifesto.htm.

Index

Aalto, Alvar, Baker House, 143–144

Ability, 268–285; and the brain, 274, 276, 279; intelligence testing, 280–285; localization, 277–278; mental map of, 274–275; opening up, 279–280; questioning, 278–279; and rules, 269–274

Absolutism, 45–46, 49, 50–51, 52, 69, 79

Abundance, 82–83

Adam and Eve, curiosity of, 2

Adderholdt, Miriam, 252

Agency, 97

Alan of Lille, *Anticlaudianus*, 68

Alchemy, 62, 68, 127

Alhazen, 195–196

Altruism, 161

Amateurism, pride in, 115

Amati, Andrea, 75

Ambiguity, 231–235

American Federation of Labor (AFL), 107

Amsterdam, parks in, 232–235, 271

Animal laborens: Arendt on, 6–7, 266, 286, 296; and *Homo faber*, 6–7, 8

Anthropomorphosis, 135–144, 272

Aphasia and apraxia, 180, 192

Apple Computers, 242

Archery, Zen, 168, 214, 221

Architecture: blueprints in, 41–42, 133; brickwork in, 131, 132–134, 143–144; CAD used in, 39–45; disconnect between simulation and reality in, 42–43; drawing in, 44, 52; materiality in, 41; medieval, 108–109; naturalness vs. artifice in, 138–141; overdetermination in, 43; perfectionism in, 254–263; poured concrete in, 132; problem solving in, 222–226; relational understanding in, 43; Ruskin's *Seven Lamps* of, 113, 114–115, 117; scale in, 41, 85; stability in, 224; urban restoration, 202–203; voussoired arch, 131; walls, 227–229

Arendt, Hannah, 72, 290, 291; on *Animal laborens*, 6–7, 266, 286, 296; and atomic bomb, 4–5; on the banality of evil, 292–293; *The Human Condition* by, 1, 5; on natality, 5, 22, 60; and Pandora's casket, 1–3; as teacher, 6, 8; trust in public debate, 4–5, 7

Arete (standard of excellence), 24

Ariès, Philippe, 63

Aristophanes, 22–23

Aristotle, 23, 124, 125, 133

Art: vs. craft, 65–67, 73, 145; drawing, 70–71; as life voyage, 72; market for, 66; originality in, 66–67, 69–73, 104; subjective judgment of, 65–67, 71

Artifice vs. naturalness, 136, 138–140, 141

Artificial intelligence, 209

256 –